Little Talks With Jesus

Nancy Beck Irland

REVIEW AND HERALD® PUBLISHING ASSOCIATION
HAGERSTOWN, MD 21740

Copyright © 1985 by
Review and Herald® Publishing Association

This book was
Edited by Gerald Wheeler
Cover designed by Byron Steele
Photo by Meylan Thoresen

PRINTED IN U.S.A.

Library of Congress Cataloging in Publication Data

Irland, Nancy Beck, 1951-
   Little talks with Jesus.

   Summary: Presents a collection of anecdotes that
illustrate the meaning of various passages from the
Bible.
   1. Children—Religious life. [1. Christian life.
2. Seventh-day Adventists.] I. Title.
BV4571.2.I75 1985 248.4'8673202 85-14522
ISBN 0-8280-0279-7

ACKNOWLEDGMENTS

Special thanks to

My sons, Marc and David, who, by asking most of the questions tackled herein, forced me to find appropriate answers and then served as professional critics by judging the readings on their "child appeal."

Dr. and Mrs. Bill Hayton, Pam Booth, and members of my family, who shared their stories with me at one time or another without knowing they would be immortalized.

My parents, Elder and Mrs. E. C. Beck, who taught and showed me what love is by giving me a happy, secure childhood.

My husband, Gary, who endured more than a year and a half of lonely living, doing more than his share of diapers and dishes during that time. It's all over now . . . for a while.

Nancy Irland

Scripture quotations, unless otherwise credited, are from *The Living Bible,* copyright 1971 by Tyndale House Publishers, Wheaton, Ill. Used by permission.

Texts credited to K.J.V. are from the King James Version.

Texts credited to N.E.B. are from *The New English Bible.* © The Delegates of the Oxford University Press and the Syndics of the Cambridge University Press 1961, 1970. Reprinted by permission.

Texts credited to N.I.V. are from *The Holy Bible: New International Version.* Copyright © 1973, 1978, International Bible Society. Used by permission of Zondervan Bible Publishers.

Texts credited to R.S.V. are from the Revised Standard Version of the Bible, copyrighted 1946, 1952 © 1971, 1973.

With love to HOLLY,

in her second springtime.

CONTENTS

WHY THIS BOOK WAS WRITTEN

After a Vacation Bible School class several summers ago, some of us mothers of preschoolers stayed behind to visit. We began sharing our frustrations with keeping worship time interesting for our young children. Those of us who went over the Sabbath school lesson with them both morning and evening found that by the time we started into it for the sixth time (the third day of the week), our preschoolers were bored. Because of that, many of us had tried reading the junior devotional for worship but had discovered that no matter how well-written it was, the point was either not relevant to our youngsters or the readings had to be interpreted so much to the small fry that something was lost in the translation. There had to be *some* other source of lessons about God for our children besides the Sabbath school lesson.

Having recently run across some preschool devotionals by a non-SDA Christian writer, I said that I had read them for worship and that my children had really enjoyed them.

A new friend, who had just recently been baptized into the church, replied that she also had read the books to her children, but had noticed that not all of the conclusions the author drew were in keeping with the teachings of Adventism. She worried that she might not catch all of them and might teach her children wrong doctrines. "Besides," she added, "I think children remember lessons learned from stories better than from lectures, and I think his devotionals are more lecture than story."

Someone turned to me and said lightly, "You're a writer, Nancy—why don't you do something for our children?"

I thought it over for several months and finally decided to take up the challenge. I hope that what I have produced meets my friends' expectations.

It is often said that no one person ever writes a particular book, and that no one is ever completely orginal. That is true for this book.

During the time I considered this project, I pored over scores of other devotional books, gathering text and topic ideas, and then searching out stories from friends and neighbors to illustrate the point. On several occasions, someone would share a story with me, and the story would suggest a text and a lesson. Or sometimes, at get-togethers, friends would pass along questions their children had brought to them, and we explored possible satisfactory answers to such queries as: What does Jesus look like? How old is God? Why do bad things happen to good people? Why can't we see the angels? Will my puppy be in heaven? and many more.

My wish is that by hearing these readings throughout the year, our children (and their parents) will gain a good sense of self-worth and a personal understanding of and love for their special friend, Jesus.

GOD'S LOVE
IS LIKE FEATHERS

The Bible says, "He shall cover thee with his feathers."
Psalm 91:4, K.J.V.

WHEN I was a little girl I loved to go to Grandma's house. She had a special bedroom for my sister and me with a very special bed. The mattress and covers on this bed she called "feather ticks." Made of feathers, they were called "ticks," but they didn't scratch, and they didn't tickle; they just kept us cozy and warm.

Grandma had made them herself, using all the soft downy feathers she could find from the ducks on her farm.

The best thing about climbing into bed was that the feather tick, like a giant feather pillow, was soft and deep. When I got into bed, I sank way down into the feathers. They filled up all the spaces between my arms and under my neck and I felt safe and warm. Then Grandma would cover me with another feather tick so that I was really snug.

Even though the top covering was about as thick as the bottom one, it didn't smother me. I could easily push it off if I got too hot because it was so light.

Daddy used to tell me that the feather tick was like God's love. He said Jesus often spoke about birds and feathers when He wanted to explain how much God loves us. Jesus once said that He often wanted to call people to Him as a mother hen calls her chicks, and they scurry under her wings for protection, but the people wouldn't come. Jesus never *made* them come. He never forces us to do anything we don't want to do. He lets *us* decide whether or not we want Him to protect us.

When my daddy was a little boy and slept on a featherbed under a feather tick, he thought of God's love and how gentle and soft it is. It always made him feel safe and cozy to know that God loved him.

I feel the very same way!

PLAYING FOR
MISTER PADEREWSKI

The Bible says, "'For God loved the world so much that he gave his only Son so that anyone who believes in him shall not perish but have eternal life.'" John 3:16.

WILLIE had a dream: Someday he was going to be a famous concert pianist. Someday people would come from all over to hear him play the piano. But sometimes it seemed his dream would never come true as he sat at the piano and practiced his songs and finger exercises. Still, he tried to remember his dream whenever he got bored. Mother said that every musician was once a little child and had to practice.

One day Mother told Willie that a famous piano player named Mr. Paderewski was going to give a concert, and she was taking Willie to hear him. Can you imagine how excited he was? He had been to a concert hall only once before. The cushiony seats flipped up when no one was sitting in them, and the thick, red carpeting on the floor seemed deep enough for his shoes to sink into. There were tall curtains on the stage that fluttered and waved whenever anyone walked past. Everyone there was all dressed up.

Willie sat still through the first half of the program, imagining that he was the one playing the piano and everyone had come to hear him. Then the intermission came, when everyone stood up and walked around for a few minutes. Willie stood up too. Then he walked up onto the stage. He sat down carefully at the piano and got his fingers into the right position to play a song called "Chopsticks."

As soon as he started to play, some big men hurried out onto the stage. They frowned and pointed their fingers at him. Willie was afraid. He started to get up, when someone from behind placed warm hands on his shoulders.

When Willie looked up he gasped as he saw who was standing behind him: Mr. Paderewski himself!

"He's OK," Mr. Paderewski told the big men. Then he looked down at Willie. "Go ahead," he urged. "Play that song again. I'll help you!"

Willie started to play. And as he played, Mr. Paderewski

reached around Willie and played along with him. Now the boy's song sounded beautiful!

Did Willie have to play the piano really well before Mr. Paderewski would listen to him? No.

Do you think you have to be good before God will listen to you? No! He asks only that we believe in Jesus and love Him. That comes first. Then, when we love Jesus, He helps us to do good. Heaven is not a reward for being good. It will be the home of those who love and trust Jesus.

TODAY I FEEL STRONG

The Bible says, "By the meekness and gentleness of Christ, I appeal to you." 2 Corinthians 10:1, N.I.V.

ONCE, a long time ago, there was a Man who was very strong. He liked to build things. His arms were so strong that He could lift big, heavy pieces of wood easily and then take His saw and cut them quickly into the right lengths. His hammer made a loud noise in the workshop. Everyone knew when this Man was working because they could hear His saw or His hammer, or the hollow boom of wood being piled carefully in the corner for later use.

Some people who are so big and strong that their muscles look like baseballs are almost scary. It seems they could crush you with one handshake. But not this Man. While He was strong, He was also gentle. And He loved to be with children.

One day He was sitting outside in the sun, chatting with His friends and telling them stories. Some children came running up to play with Him.

"No! Go away, kids!" the Man's friends said, waving their arms in an effort to scare the children away.

The Man heard them talking to the children that way. He held open His arms. "Please don't do that," He said to His friends. "Let the children come to Me. Come, children!" He smiled at them.

And those strong arms that could lift heavy pieces of wood and hammer nails and saw through thick pieces of lumber reached out gently to the children. He touched their faces.

But He didn't hurt them. He lifted some of the children onto His lap. But He didn't squeeze them too tightly. Maybe He scratched their backs for a minute. But He didn't scratch too hard. That Man was Jesus. He is strong, but also gentle.

Maybe you are strong too. You like to jump high, and run fast, and throw balls hard. But you can also sit quietly and read books, or color and listen to music.

Strong is nice. But gentle is nice too. It's always nice to be gentle like Jesus.

BANDIT AND THE SUGAR CUBE

The Bible says, "It is possible to give away and become richer!" Proverbs 11:24.

CAN you remember the good feeling that you get when you share? I heard a story one time about a raccoon who shared something, even though he didn't plan to, and he was surprised by what happened. His name was Bandit.

Bandit grasped a white sugar cube tightly between his long, black fingers and hurried to his water dish. He had never seen a sugar cube before and didn't intend for any of the other raccoons to know about it.

As he ran past "Mitsy" she turned her back to him. Then he slipped behind "Frosty," and she darted off to get away from him. Nobody liked Bandit because he was so mean. He bit, shrieked at them, and pulled their tails. So nobody wanted to get near him. Nobody, that is, except "Bandito."

Bandito was new to the little raccoon family. She didn't know that Bandit was mean. Bent over his water dish, she lapped the milk that someone had poured into it just that morning.

When he saw her, Bandit shrieked as though to say, "Get out of here!" But Bandito just raised her head and looked at him, then went on lapping the milk.

Well, Bandit must have been in a hurry to eat his sugar cube, because he didn't waste time biting Bandito. He just dipped his sugar cube into the milk, as he did with all his food, and prepared to eat it himself. Can you guess what happened? What does sugar do when it goes into warm milk? It dissolves. The sugar cube just seemed to vanish in Bandit's hands.

Beginning to shriek, he threw his hands up into the air. He licked his fingers as though thinking that the sugar had somehow gone inside them. Then he felt around the bottom of the bowl. But his sugar cube had vanished; just disappeared!

Bandito kept on lapping the milk. It had seemed to become sweeter since Bandit had come over.

Finally Bandit raced to the place he had found the sugar cube. There was one more. Grabbing it, he hurried back to the milk. Cautiously he stared into the bowl, then lowered his second sugar cube into it. Again, the sugar cube vanished.

Bandit was really upset this time. But Bandito loved it. The milk was so sweet. She didn't think she had ever tasted anything this good before. And it had become sweeter since Bandit had come. She liked being with him.

From that time on, no matter what Bandit did to her, Bandito shared everything. She shared *her* favorite treats, and she shared her cozy nest, and she shared the pretty trinkets she found. Now Bandit had more things than he had ever had before, and all because he shared his sugar cubes.

Before too long, Bandit wasn't mean anymore. Do you know why? He had found a friend, by sharing.

ABOUT COMING BACK

The Bible says, " 'When everything [in heaven] is ready, then I will come and get you, so that you can always be with me where I am." John 14:3.

WHENEVER Mother left her at the baby-sitter's Beth always felt a little sad and a little scared. She watched at the window for as long as she could, until she couldn't see Mother's car anymore. Then she would start to play with the other children.

It often seemed a long time until Mother came to pick her up, but Mother always returned, just as she promised she would.

Do you ever have to stay with a baby-sitter? How do you feel when your parents go away? How do you feel when they come back to get you?

You can't follow them when they leave, or go find them, can you? After all, you don't know the way to get there. So you just wait patiently until they return to pick you up.

One night a little boy and his sister were looking at the stars. "I'll bet if we got a big enough spaceship, we could go up to heaven," he said to his sister.

"But we don't know which star is heaven," she replied. "What if we got lost?"

"We'll ask Daddy. He probably knows how to get to heaven!"

The children ran inside to ask their father how they could get to heaven.

Daddy smiled and put his arms around them. "Well," he said, "heaven isn't one of those stars that we can see up in the sky. Heaven is beyond the stars — farther than we can see. I don't have any way of getting there. I can't drive there, and I can't fly a spaceship there. I just have to wait until Jesus comes to pick me up. Just as you have to wait for me when you're at the baby-sitter's."

"But it's taking so long," the little boy said.

"Yes." Daddy nodded. "It seems to be taking Jesus a long time. But He will come back. He promised. And Jesus always keeps His promises."

When Jesus comes to take us to heaven, He won't need to bring a spaceship for us to travel in. We'll be changed so that we can breathe and fly in outer space without spaceships. Won't it be fun to go with Jesus and ask Him questions about the moon and the stars as we pass by them?

When we get to heaven after several days of flying, Jesus Himself will open the huge pearl gates of heaven. As we walk past Him, He will gently place a beautiful crown on your head, and He'll probably give you a big hug and a kiss and tell you how special you are to Him, and how happy you have made Him by choosing to be with Him in heaven.

Then you can take your angel's hand and walk with him to the beautiful home that Jesus is building now, just for you. And you will be happy and loved forever.

Heaven is a real city. Jesus is there now, getting ready to pick us up. He promised He would come back. And He will!

YOU CAN BE RICH

The Bible says, "If a man love me, he will keep my words: and my Father will love him." John 14:23, K.J.V.

ONCE upon a time there was a very rich man who was lonely. His wife had died, leaving him and his 6-year-old son Kenny alone. The little boy missed his mother terribly, as you would too, so the man hired a housekeeper to take care of the mansion and the little boy.

Miss Tyler, the housekeeper, had never been married. She had no children of her own, so she enjoyed caring for the little boy. Every morning when she arrived she laid out his clothes for him so he could get dressed while she made his breakfast. Together they would clean up the kitchen and the other rooms in the house, and then they would have time for playing together. There were lots of places to play. Sometimes they watched the big goldfish in the fishpond outside, or they walked under the tall trees in the garden and climbed into the secret hiding places that Kenny knew of behind the bushes.

One day when he was 12, Kenny became very sick. His father stayed home from work to be with him, even though Miss Tyler was there too, with the doctor. Kenny had a high fever and lay still in his big bed, the hair around his face wet with sweat. Nothing they did brought his fever down, and after several days Kenny died. His father was so sad about losing Kenny's mother and then his son that he couldn't eat, and he himself became sick. He died a few months later.

Nobody could find any instructions about what to do with the man's mansion and all his money. Usually when somebody dies, he leaves a special paper, called a will, that says who should get his belongings. But this man didn't leave a will. Since he had no relatives, either, the state government decided to sell all his things and use the money for roads and other projects.

Several days before the sale was to start, Miss Tyler talked to the man in charge and asked him if she could have the picture of Kenny that hung in the hall.

"I reckon you can," the man replied. "It's probably not worth anything to anybody else."

So Miss Tyler bought the picture for just a few cents and

took it home. She started taking the picture frame apart so she could clean it. As she lifted the picture from the back of the frame, a paper fell out. It was Kenny's father's will, with instructions that anyone who loved Kenny enough to want his picture should be the one who got the mansion and all of his money.

Miss Tyler hurried back to the man in charge of the sale. "Stop the sale!" she cried. "The house is not for sale. It is mine!"

If we love Jesus, the riches of heaven someday will be ours. God has promised them to everyone who loves His Son, Jesus.

GOD CAN DO ANYTHING

The Bible says, "For with God nothing shall be impossible." Luke 1:37, K.J.V.

ONE afternoon I was sewing doll clothes outside under one of the trees in my yard. Mother had cut out the pieces and shown me how to hold the needle carefully and push it in and out of the fabric just so. Slowly I stitched the little dress. Then, all of a sudden, the needle pulled free of the thread. The needle went flying out of my hand and landed somewhere in the grass.

"Oh!" I gasped. "I have to find my needle. I can't leave it out here. Someone might step on it!" Frantically I began pulling the grass apart to look down in the dirt for my needle. But I couldn't see it. Slowly I started looking in a circle around where I had been sitting—first close to where I was, and then farther away. But the needle was nowhere to be found.

For a moment I thought of running into the house to ask Mother for another needle, but I knew she would tell me to try to find the other one first.

"What shall I do now?" I wondered out loud. Then, all at once, I had an idea. Kneeling down right under that tree, I prayed about my missing needle.

"Dear Jesus," I whispered, barely moving my lips, "I know You're busy up there keeping the world going around and

20

everything, but I didn't mean to lose my needle. Could You help me find it, please? Thank You. Amen."

Slowly I opened my eyes and looked all around. And what do you suppose I saw beside my knee? The missing needle lying on top of the thick grass, twinkling in the sunlight.

I didn't get up off my knees. Without picking up the needle, I closed my eyes tightly again. "Thank You, Jesus. I knew You would do it! Amen!"

Jesus cares even about little girls and sewing needles, doesn't He? And He can even lift a needle out of the grass. God can do anything!

TODAY I DON'T FEEL LIKE OBEYING

The Bible says, "Honour thy father and thy mother." Exodus 20:12, K.J.V.

IT was almost time for Larry to go to bed, but he was playing with his sister Lynne.

Just then Mother called from the living room. "Larry and Lynne, pick up your toys now, please. It's almost time for bed."

"What did she say?" Larry asked.

His sister screwed up her face. " 'Pick up your toys, please. It's almost time for bed,' " she sang, making fun of what Mother had said.

"Lynne," Larry said quickly. "That's not the way to talk about Mother."

"But that's what she said," Lynne replied.

"Well, maybe it is, but you know it's not right to make fun of Mom and Dad like that. Remember our memory verse to honor them? Making fun of them is not honoring them!"

Lynne stopped smiling and began picking up her toys.

"Mother really does love us," Larry said. "Don't you think so?"

She nodded. "Yeah. And she never makes fun of me like that."

Your mother and daddy love you, too. Jesus gave them to

you because He loves you and He knows that children need somebody to keep them safe and teach them about their world.

Jesus asks us to honor and love our parents. But He never tells us to do something that He didn't do Himself. The Bible tells us that when Jesus was a little boy, He obeyed His parents. Imagine it! The same Jesus who came from heaven obeyed His mother. He was powerful enough to make the storm go away on the Sea of Galilee, but He still obeyed His mother. He could order the devils to go out of people, but He still obeyed His parents.

Jesus is our example. If He obeyed His parents, then it must be an important thing to do. Remember to listen to your parents, and don't make fun of them. Obey them. That's Jesus' way.

LET'S BE BEES!

The Bible says, Mary and Joseph took Jesus to the Temple to "be dedicated to the Lord." Luke 2:23.

LET'S imagine that you are a bee. Buzz your tiny wings. Nod your head. Wiggle your tiny feet. Oh, you're so pretty with your fuzzy black-and-yellow tummy. Up we go over the house and around to the garden. Do you see some pretty red flowers? Let's go inside them. It's kind of dark in here when we crawl in, isn't it? The light is sort of pinkish. Now stretch to get some of the sweet nectar to take home for some honey.

Out into the sunshine again. This time we'll go inside a blue flower, OK? The blue flower petals make a bluish light inside. The flower petals feel soft and springy as they nod under our feet. It seems like walking on a water bed to me. M-m-m! This nectar tastes good. It's very sweet, and will make good honey.

Out into the sunshine again. We'll visit a yellow flower, and a purple flower, and a white flower before we go home.

Now we're at the entrance to our beehive. Watch carefully as you step through the tiny door. Fold in your wings. There!

We're home. It's noisy in here. And hot air is blowing from somewhere. Where is it coming from? Oh, it's just the other worker bees buzzing around, telling where they found some good nectar today.

Shall we go into the nursery? It might be quieter in there. Look at that special baby bee in the center of the colony. That one will be the new queen bee. She gets the best honey to eat so she can grow up to be healthy and strong. The nurse bees clean and comb her. They all take good care of her because they have a special plan for her. When she grows up, she will serve the beehive in a very special way because of the special care and treatment she is getting today.

Let's give her some of our sweet nectar, shall we? Now we'll store the rest in the pantry. Then why don't we fly home and be people again? Out into the sunshine again, and soon we're home.

Would you like to be a queen bee and have everyone take special care of you? You are, if you have been dedicated.

Dedicate means to ask God to bless you. When parents dedicate their children to God in a special service at church, they are promising God to take special care of their child and help him or her to grow up to love God. Your parents feed you the best food they can, keep you clean and healthy and happy, and teach you about God. They are helping to prepare you for your special work of serving God and living in heaven. Ask your parents about your dedication. If you have not been dedicated, maybe you can be at the next service. You are very, very special.

RONDI THE ELEPHANT

The Bible says, "Teach a child to choose the right path, and when he is older he will remain upon it." Proverbs 22:6.

WHEN I was a little girl in India I heard a story about a baby elephant we'll call Rondi. A man from a village in India found him in the jungle one day. He could see from how skinny Rondi was that he hadn't had much to eat lately. The man looked for the elephant's mother but couldn't see any signs of her having been around in a long time. So he put a rope around Rondi's neck and gently led him home to his village.

The man gave the animal tender banana trees to eat and bathed him every day in the river, scrubbing his back with a coconut fiber brush. The elephant would spray water into the air with his trunk and get both his master and himself all wet. But the man just laughed. He knew Rondi was playing.

Rondi grew and grew until he was quite a big elephant. He learned to love the man who had cared for him and was always gentle with him. Never did he eat the trees or bushes close to the man's house, but he learned to wander off into the jungle to find food.

One day Rondi didn't come home. He had gone off into the jungle the previous evening. His master wondered where the animal had gone. He was a bit worried, although he knew that Rondi probably had found a family of elephants to live with. And though he missed him, he knew it was best that Rondi live with elephants instead of people. But still he wondered if he would ever see Rondi again and if the elephant would remember him.

One day the man was working by the river, tying some logs together to make a raft. He was so busy that he didn't see or hear the leopard that was slowly sneaking up on him.

All of a sudden the man heard an elephant trumpeting.

"Awurra!" It was a loud, shrill noise like a trumpet. The man looked up to see a huge elephant running through the jungle toward the river. Then he saw the leopard leap out of the tree and race away in the opposite direction. Afraid, the man jumped into the water to get away from the charging elephant. But when the big animal got to the river, he stopped and stood very still, swaying his trunk and blowing into the dust. Then, as the man watched, the elephant sucked up some water into his trunk, blew it into the air, and held out his trunk toward the man. The elephant was Rondi!

Happily the man walked toward him with his hand outstretched. Rondi swayed his trunk and placed it in the man's hand like a kiss. Then he turned and walked away. He had remembered his friend and had saved him.

Someday you will be a grown-up man or woman. Probably you will be a kind, honest grown-up who loves Jesus. Do you know how I know? Because you are learning about God now. The Bible says that the things we learn while we are children will determine what kind of grown-ups we are. When you grow up you will remember your friend Jesus, just as Rondi remembered his friend.

WHO WAS SMARTER?

The Bible says, "A fool's fun is being bad; a wise man's fun is being wise!" Proverbs 10:23.

"HEY, there's Mrs. Green's cat," Charlie whispered as he and Kevin passed his neighbor's yard. "Watch this!"

Picking up a stick, Charlie threw it at the cat. It hit the animal on the tail.

"Yeoww!" the cat cried as it raced around the house.

Charlie giggled. "Oh, wow! I love to do that! That old cat gets so scared!"

"Pretty soon that cat's not going to like you," Kevin replied. "You might make it mean by hurting it."

"So what?" Charlie shrugged. "It's not my cat!"

Kevin kicked a stone on the sidewalk. He was thinking about Charlie. Just about everything the boy thought to be fun was something mean. One day he knocked over the tray of flowers that Mr. Siebert was planting. Another time, because he thought it would be fun to see the garbage spill out, he poked holes in somebody's garbage bags that had been put out to be picked up by the garbage men. He got in trouble for that one, though, and couldn't play outside for a whole week. Kevin couldn't see how *that* could be any fun. It scared Kevin to be with Charlie when he did mean things. Kevin feared that people would think *he* did mean things, too, and would be angry with *him*.

One day Charlie and Kevin were at the park. They liked the swings the best. They pumped themselves as high as they could go. Pretty soon they were tired out and decided to go home.

"Let's wind the swings around the top pole so nobody else can use them after we're gone," Charlie suggested with a grin. He tried to throw his swing around the top bar so it would be too short to swing on.

"Oh, don't do that," Kevin said. "We wouldn't have liked it if somebody had done that before we got here."

"But nobody will know we did it," Charlie said. "I wish I could see their faces when they find the swings like this!"

"I'm not doing it," Kevin told him. "I'm going home."

"Aw, come on!" Charlie urged.

"No, I'm going home," Kevin repeated. "I don't think it's fun to do mean things. Why don't you come home with me, and we'll play in my treehouse. I'll show you what's fun."

Charlie sighed and dropped the swing. "OK, I guess," he said. "I might get in trouble, anyway."

Which boy was the smartest? Was it Charlie? Or Kevin? The Bible says that foolish people have fun being bad. Charlie wasn't very smart, was he? But Kevin was. I'm sure you are smart too. You like to have fun in a good way. And that makes everybody happy.

WHAT GROWN-UPS SHOULD BE LIKE

The Bible says, "Whosoever therefore shall humble himself as this little child, the same is greatest in the kingdom." Matthew 18:4, K.J.V.

IT was Sabbath. Kim walked around the table that Mother had set so beautifully and carefully counted all the plates.

"One, two, three, four, five. Who is the extra plate for, Mother?"

"A special visitor," Mother said with a wink.

"Anyone I know?" Karen asked.

Mother nodded. "You'll see. Dinner will be ready in just a few minutes. Why don't you go wash your hands?"

When everyone was seated around the table, Karen asked about the extra plate again. Nobody was sitting there.

"Where's our guest, Mother?" Karen asked.

"He's here," Mother answered, smiling.

"Oh, I know who it is. It's Jesus!" Karen said.

"You're right! When I was a little girl, my mother had a plaque on the wall that said, 'Christ is the head of this house, the unseen guest at every meal, the silent listener to every conversation.' I used to like to set a place for Jesus, especially on Sabbath, because that is His special day."

"I'd like to hug Him after we pray," Scottie said. "I love You, Jesus," he said to the empty place. "I can almost see Him sitting there!"

"I can hardly wait to get to heaven and really eat with Jesus," Karen said. "I'll bet the grapes in heaven are as big as melons. And heaven's peaches are probably about as big as watermelons!"

"Maybe we could use the bananas as walking sticks!" Scottie suggested. "And can you imagine a piece of corn as long as my arm?"

"We won't be able to see the yellow lines down the middle of the streets of gold," Karen added.

"We won't need yellow lines down the middle," Daddy told her. "We'll probably just walk on those streets. I don't think we'll need cars in heaven."

"Yeah, we can just fly wherever we want to, as the angels do! Oh, it's going to be fun!" Karen exclaimed.

What do you think heaven is like? Do you picture clouds, or green grass and blue lakes and streams? What do you think God looks like? I picture Him smiling. One lady I know always thinks God's eyes are like her father's. They are always warm and smiling.

Sometimes children find it easier to believe in God than grown-ups do.

Children are good at believing. I think that's why Jesus said grown-ups should be like little children. Tell your mother and daddy what you think heaven is like, and how you picture Jesus. They would like to know.

ABOUT FEELINGS

The Bible says, "Even in laughter the heart may ache, and joy may end in grief." Proverbs 14:13, N.I.V.

IF you could choose between feeling excited, lonely, or sleepy, which would you choose? What is your favorite feeling? What is your least favorite feeling?

I don't like to feel afraid. When people are angry with me, I feel afraid. Or when I'm driving on slippery roads, I feel afraid. Elevators scare some children. Staying with a baby-sitter frightens others. Even grown-ups don't like being apart from people they love. But it helps to know that Mother or Father will always come back and pick you up from the baby-sitter after a while. Then you don't feel afraid anymore, do you? You feel happy!

Feelings sometimes come and go quickly. Often when we're happy we wish we could stay that way forever. When we're full, we wish we'd never get hungry again.

A friend of mine works in a chocolate candy factory. When she went to work there, her boss told her she could eat all the candy she wanted to while she was at the factory, but she couldn't take any of it home.

My friend was really excited about that. She ate candy all day long the first few days. Then she ate it only in the mornings. After a while, she took only one or two pieces each day. By the time she had worked there a whole month, she didn't eat any candy at all. Just thinking about it made her sick. She had had too much.

Probably being happy all the time wouldn't make us sick—it would be good for us. But because of Satan it can never be that way on this earth. We will feel sad, or frightened, or angry sometimes. Everyone occasionally has such feelings. And everyone's moods come and go. If a friend is angry with you, those feelings will usually go away, and he'll be your friend again. And if you think you have felt sad more often than not, remember that feeling happy is going to feel especially good when it does come.

You would get bored if you ate the same food all the time. And you would get bored if you felt only one way all the time. Don't be afraid of your feelings. Tell the person who is reading this book to you about how you feel. There's something

magical about talking about feelings; it helps sad feelings to
go away if we share them with someone. And it helps happy
feelings last longer if somebody else knows.

THE HOOT OWL

**The Bible says, "The ravens brought him bread and meat
each morning and evening." 1 Kings 17:6.**

ONE time I read a story about a boy we'll call Luis. As I
remember the story, Luis lived close to the woods, and sometimes he liked to go into the forest during the day, to play.
There were many trees to climb, and lots of nice bushes to
hide under. Usually Luis found his way back home all right.

But one day he didn't. He had gone farther into the woods
than ever before, and now he was lost. All day long Luis
played among the trees. Toward evening, when the sun started
to go down, he became hungry. He found some berries to eat.
They weren't as good as Mother's food at home, but they
helped. After eating a few berries, he curled up in a hollow
tree to go to sleep. Luis was cold and hungry and scared.

Meanwhile, back at home, his mother and father were
worried about him. They called their friends together.

"Luis went into the woods to play this morning, and he
hasn't come back home yet," they said. "Will you go with us to
look for him? It's getting very cold out there."

"Of course we'll come!" the friends said. "We'll get our
flashlights, and we'll meet you back here right away."

Before long everyone had returned with flashlights and
blankets, and some people even brought first-aid kits in case
the boy was hurt.

They started into the forest.

"Luis! Luis!" they called as they parted the bushes with
their hands and shone their flashlights all around.

By now it was really dark. There's one bird that stays awake
at night to hunt. Do you know what it is? An owl! And that's
the kind of bird that perched on top of the tree that Luis was
hiding in that night. But the boy didn't know it. The bird

ruffled its feathers and settled into the branch. "Who-oo! Who-oo!" it cried.

Suddenly Luis woke up. Somebody's calling me! he thought. They want to know who I am. So he called out his name. "Luis! Luis!"

Again the owl hooted. "Who-oo? Who-oo?"

The boy shouted a little bit louder. "Luis! Luis!"

Again the owl hooted. "Who-oo? Who-oo?"

This time Luis climbed out of the tree. Standing beside it, he looked up into the branches. "I'm Luis!" he screamed as loud as he could.

A short distance away his mother and father stopped searching and stood still.

"I hear him! Luis! Where are you?" they called.

"Over here! Over here!" the boy shouted back. He was happy to be found. Just as a bird had helped Elijah, a bird had helped Luis, too.

TODAY I FEEL POLITE

The Bible says, "Let your speech be alway with grace, seasoned with salt." Colossians 4:6, K.J.V.

"COULD I taste some of *your* food, Grandma?" Angela asked one evening when she was visiting her grandma in the hospital. She wondered what hospital food tasted like. It looked so pretty on Grandma's tray, with everything in its own little dish.

Grandma laughed. "Oh, I don't think you'd like my food, honey," she said.

"I might," Angela pleaded. "Couldn't I try it? Please?"

"Well, OK," Grandma said. "But you'd better take just a little bite, because I'm not sure you'll like it!"

Angela took the spoon that Grandma held out to her. She dipped it into the mound of mashed potatoes and gravy. It smelled good. Angela looked quickly at her grandmother before she ate it.

"Go ahead." Grandma nodded. "Try it."

Quickly, Angela put the spoon in her mouth. Then she made a face. She swallowed hard.

"What's the matter?" Grandma asked with a soft chuckle. "Don't you like mashed potatoes?"

"Not these!" Angela said. "You can have 'em, Grandma. They're awful! They need salt. Where's the shaker?"

"I don't have one," Grandma said. "The doctor says I mustn't eat any salt for a while on account of my heart. I had a hard time getting used to salt-free food at first, but I don't mind it now, though I still prefer a little salt on my vegetables."

How do you like your food? Does your mother put a little salt in it for you? Even cookies have a little bit of salt in them. We don't want to eat too much salt, but a little bit makes our food taste much better.

Jesus said that we must season our words with salt. He didn't mean we should put salt in our mouths before we talk, but that we should always talk kindly. Some of the salt we can put into our words are polite things like "please" and "thank you" and "you're welcome." Sometimes people call them "magic words" because people do things for you faster if you use them. And they make people smile. Which sentence sounds best to you? "Give me that toy!" or "May I have that toy, please?" If people say "please" when they ask you things, you like those people, don't you? And that's just the way they feel about you when you talk that way. Try putting some salt into your speaking today. Use the magic words!

JESUS' DAY

The Bible says, "Remember the sabbath day, to keep it holy." Exodus 20:8, K.J.V.

THE sun shone in Marsha's window early one special morning. She opened her eyes slowly and tried to rub the sleepiness away. There was something different about this day, she thought. What was it?

"Good morning, birthday girl!" Mother peeked her head around the corner. "It's your birthday today!"

"Oh, yeah! I knew something special was happening today," Marsha said. "Today's my birthday. Am I 5 now?"

"You most certainly are, honey. Five years ago today you were a little tiny baby in my arms. It was so exciting!"

"I can hardly wait for my party," Marsha said as she sat up on the edge of her bed. "Oh, it's going to be such fun!"

"The birthday girl gets to choose what we have for breakfast," Mother said. "What will it be?"

Marsha didn't have to think very long. "Pancakes and eggs!" she said. "Oh, I do hope everyone remembers to come to my party this afternoon."

Mother nodded. "Everyone's coming," she said.

At last it was time for the party. Everyone did show up, as her mother had said, and Marsha was delighted. She felt good that her friends had remembered her special day. It showed her that they cared. Today was her birthday. And she had invited her friends to do special things with her instead of playing the usual games they did on other days. They all dressed up and had a wonderful time together.

I like special days. Jesus has given us an invitation to spend a special day with Him every week. Do you know what day of the week it is? The seventh day—Sabbath. Sabbath is a special day when the whole family can be together and take more time to learn about Jesus than they do on other days of the week. Some people like to go on bike rides and pick wildflowers to make a bouquet. Others have a special box of Sabbath toys with coloring books about nature, and maybe some Bible story felts with which they can tell stories, or a Noah's ark set, or other things they play with only on Sabbath.

What are some ways you can make Sabbath special? Do you know when Sabbath begins? Some people like to light a Sabbath candle at supper on Friday night, when Sabbath begins. Sabbath lasts from when the sun goes down Friday until sunset on Saturday. We set the table nicely with a tablecloth and special dishes, and we all hold hands around the table while we pray. Jesus is happy to see us praising Him and going to church on Sabbath. Sabbath is His special day, just as your birthday is your special day. Let's keep Sabbath special for Jesus.

YOU ARE A PRESENT

The Bible says, "Children are a gift from God; they are his reward." Psalm 127:3.

EDDIE was the littlest boy in his family. Except for a baby sister, he was the youngest child his parents had. They didn't have just two or three children like most people these days. His parents had eleven children! Eddie's oldest sister was old enough to get married and be a mommy herself when he was born.

You might think that with so many children, Eddie's parents didn't have time for everybody. But they did.

One day Eddie's uncle came to visit. Now, his uncle and aunty didn't have any children of their own, even though they wanted some. God hadn't given them the gift of children. But they had what they thought was a great idea. "You know, my brother Peter and his wife have so many children that they probably wouldn't mind letting us adopt one of the younger ones," Eddie's uncle had said to his wife one day. "I'd like to have a boy. How about if we ask Peter if we can adopt Eddie? Since we don't have any children, we would have lots of time and money to spend on him. I'll bet Peter would be happy to know that his son would be so well taken care of. Let's go ask him for Eddie."

So the uncle and his wife went to Eddie's home. They visited for quite a while and chatted about other things. Then they began to talk softly.

Now, what do you do when people start to talk softly and quietly when you're around? You try to listen to the secret, don't you? That's just what Eddie did. Standing quite still in the other room, he put his head as near the door as he could without being seen. Then he heard his uncle ask about adopting him.

Oh, no! he thought. Ma and Pa can't just give me away! I don't want to go live with my uncle and aunt. I want to stay with my own family! As Eddie sucked his breath in hard to keep from crying he strained to hear what his father was saying.

His father laughed—sort of a soft chuckle—and he leaned back in his chair. "Oh, we can't give up Eddie! Oh, no! None of my children is available for adoption! We love every one!"

Eddie smiled. He was glad that no matter whether he had ten sisters and brothers or just one, he was special to his father.

Eddie grew up and became my daddy.

You are special to your parents, too. When you go to school or to a friend's house for a little while, your parents miss you. No one else is exactly like you. Nobody can take your place. And nobody wants to get rid of you. You are special.

WHAT IS YOUR NAME?

The Bible says, "If you must choose, take a good name rather than great riches; for to be held in loving esteem is better than silver and gold." Proverbs 22:1.

WHAT do you think of when I say "ice"? How about "cactus"? Or "onion"? "Puppy"? "Jesus"?

All of those words are names. Whenever anybody mentions ice to me, I think of being very cold. "Cactus" reminds me of something prickly that I would want to stay away from. Onions make me cry, puppies are warm and wiggly, and Jesus is my best friend. I think of smiling when I hear His name.

Frankie read a story once about a little boy who saved a neighbor girl from drowning in his pool.

"I would like to do something so my name could be in the newspaper, too," he said.

It feels good to see our name written down or to hear someone call us by name. Newspapers print the names of people who do kind things for others. But newspapers also publish the names of those who do bad things like stealing or killing. I don't think they are very proud to see their names in the newspaper. I know I wouldn't be very proud if I were one of them!

What do you imagine people think of when they hear your name? Do they think of nice things? Like how you almost always say "please" and "thank you"? Or how thoughtful you are to help your mother with the cleaning or with the grocery bags? Do they remember how kind you are to smaller children?

Many years ago there was a boy named "Abe." His father

didn't have much money, and because of that, Abe couldn't go to school very much of the time. He had to help his father support the family. But whatever Abe did, he always did his very best. People liked to have him work for them, because he was honest and did the best he could.

When Abe grew up he studied and became a lawyer. Abraham Lincoln finally became one of the best-loved Presidents of America. Even today, whenever we speak of honest people, we sometimes say they are as "honest as Abe."

Wouldn't it be nice to have people smile when they hear your name and think good things about you? I'm sure they do! Gold is worth a lot of money. And so is silver. But the Bible says that having a good name is more precious and makes you happier than having a lot of money.

As you grow up you'll be sure to keep your name good, won't you, so people will think only good things when they hear it.

SAMSON'S VISITOR

The Bible says, "My God hath sent his angel, and hath shut the lions' mouths, that they have not hurt me." Daniel 6:22, K.J.V.

SAMSON could not wait until he was 9 years old. His father had said that once he was a big boy of 9, he could go up into the hills of India to gather wood with the men.

At last it was Samson's birthday. On that day, his mother packed a lunch of rice and curry for both him and his father, wrapping it securely in a banana leaf and tying it tightly with string. How excited Samson was! He strode up the mountain trail proudly with his own walking stick and kept up with the men pretty well. At last they reached the top of the mountain, and Samson helped collect wood for a while. But then he became tired of just gathering wood and started chasing butterflies. He could hear the *chop, chop, chop* of the men's machetes in the distance. Finally, he became hungry and started back to where his father was.

Samson listened for the machetes. All was silent. He looked

around him, trying to remember from which direction he had come, but all the plants and underbrush in the jungle looked the same. The boy could not find the trail back.

"Father!" he called. "Father!" But all he heard was the echo of his own voice. Father must be eating his lunch, Samson thought. That's why I can't hear the machetes. I'll start walking toward the hilltop, and soon I should hear the men.

But Samson did not find his father. Night came, and he grew sleepy. He found a cozy nook beneath a tree and pulled his knees against his chest to keep warm.

Meanwhile, Samson's father and the other men missed the boy when it was time to eat. They called his name, but heard nothing. Then the men began searching up and down the mountain. "Samson! Samson!" they shouted. The boy still didn't answer them.

Samson's father went back down to the village that night, for dangerous tigers lived in the mountains. He prayed that Samson would be safe.

Early the next morning Samson's father and uncle started back up the trail to find Samson. The air was very quiet. "Samson! Samson!" they called, beating the bushes to scare away the wild animals.

At last they heard a faint sound.

"Father! Father! Over here!"

Samson's father ran toward his voice. "Samson! You're OK!" his father said, throwing his arms around him. "But how did you sleep? It's cold and dangerous up here at night!"

His son smiled. "I was OK," he said. "A big doggy came and lay down next to me and kept me warm."

Samson's father looked in the dirt around the boy. He saw from the paw prints in the dirt that it was a tiger—not a dog—that had kept the boy warm.

Just as in Bible times, God can keep animals from hurting us.

TODAY I FEEL USELESS

The Bible says, " 'Beware that you don't look down upon a single one of these little children.' " Matthew 18:10.

THE door was locked, and Richard's family didn't have their keys. By accident, they had locked them inside the house.

"Do you have your keys?" Daddy asked Mother as he turned the handle and pushed on the door.

She shook her head. "No, my purse is inside too. What are we going to do now?"

They were supposed to be leaving for summer vacation.

Daddy started around the house. "Maybe I can find a window that's open," he said. He tugged at all of them. Then he tried the back door too, but it was locked securely.

Finally, Daddy went to a tiny little window in the kitchen that was above the sink. He remembered that he had locked all the other windows, but since that one was so tiny, he had forgotten it.

Daddy pushed on the window and at last it opened. But it was such a small one, that he certainly couldn't fit through it. "I know!" he said. "I'll send Richard through the window. Then he can run to the living room and open the front door for us."

Richard wasn't sure. "I don't know if I'll fit," he said.

"Well, we'll try carefully," Daddy told him. He lifted his son up. Slowly, carefully, Richard squeezed his shoulders through the window. Then he turned sideways and slipped his legs through. Now he was sitting on the sink.

"Hooray. He's in!" Mother said as she clapped her hands. "Now go to the front door and open it for us."

Jumping down from the sink, Richard ran to the door.

"We surely are glad we have a little boy at our house," Mother said as she gave him a hug. "There are some things that you can do that grown-ups can't!"

Richard smiled. He was glad someone needed his help.

You, too, are important to your family. Not just for the things you can do for them, but because you belong to them. Your mother, daddy, sisters, and brothers need to know that you love them. How you feel about them is important to them because they love you. Why not tell them how special they are to you? Tell them why you like to be with them.

JUST HOW IT'S SUPPOSED TO BE

The Bible says, "Christ has given each of us special abilities —whatever he wants us to have out of his rich storehouse of gifts." Ephesians 4:7.

DADDY'S noisy tractor plowed deeply into the ground. Joel watched quietly as he held his hands over his ears to protect them from the noise. He could imagine what their garden was going to look like once things started to grow. Daddy had said Joel could plant pumpkins this year. Then Mother could make fresh pumpkin pie.

When the garden was ready, Daddy parked the tractor and jumped down. "Do you have your seeds?" he asked his son. "We can plant now."

Joel held up a big pumpkin seed between his fingers. "Yup. I'm ready," he said with a grin. The seeds weren't pumpkins; they were seeds. But that's just what they were supposed to be.

In a few weeks Joel spotted two little leaves that had pushed their way up out of the ground. They weren't pumpkins— they were leaves. But that's just what they were supposed to be.

The pumpkin plant grew more and more leaves, and more and more stems, until it covered a large patch of the garden. Still it wasn't a pumpkin; it was a plant. But that's just what it was supposed to be.

One day Joel discovered large, yellow flowers among the leaves. While they were pretty, they weren't pumpkins. They were just flowers. But that's just what they were supposed to be.

At last the day came when little green pumpkins appeared along the stems of the plant. They were the size of a small ball at first, but Joel was excited. "Pumpkins! I've got pumpkins!"

he yelled as he ran to the house to get Daddy. The pumpkins weren't ready to pick, yet. They were small and green. But that's just how they were supposed to be.

Every day Joel checked on his pumpkins. They grew fast. Some were bigger than the others, and some started turning orange before the others. But that was OK. That's just what they were supposed to do.

Finally, toward the end of summer, when the nights began getting real cold, the plant started dying and Joel could easily see the bright-orange pumpkins.

"We can pick the pumpkins now," Daddy said. "Maybe Mother will fix some pumpkin pie for supper!"

Some of the pumpkins were large and round and some were kind of flat where they had lain on the dirt. Others were small enough so Joel could carry them all by himself. They were all different. But that's how they were supposed to be.

Joel saved some pumpkins for himself. The others he sold. Some of the people chose big pumpkins to carve. Others bought the little ones for pies. Everyone chose a pumpkin he could use. All the pumpkins were different, but each one was special. And that's just how it's supposed to be.

WHAT'S INSIDE?

The Bible says, "But the Lord said to Samuel, 'Don't judge by a man's face or height. . . . I don't make decisions the way you do! Men judge by outward appearance, but I look at a man's thoughts and intentions.' " 1 Samuel 16:7.

"ARE there really red people in the world?" Treena asked her mother one day. "And yellow ones?" She looked down at her arms. They were sort of a peachy color. Amy, her best friend in Sabbath school, had dark-brown arms. But she had never seen a yellow person or a red one—except when the person was sunburned. They sang a song in Sabbath school about all the children of the world: "Red and yellow, black and white, all are precious in His sight."

Mother smiled. "Well, there really aren't people who are red like your red crayon," she said, "or yellow, exactly. But sometimes we say that American Indians are 'red Indians' because their skin is sort of that color, like brown and red. And sometimes people from Japan and countries like that have skin that looks more yellow than pink. But they're not a bright yellow."

"Is their blood yellow?" Treena wondered.

"I used to think so when I was little," Mother said. "And then I heard a story about two little boys who lived long ago when the white men and Indians were fighting for land. This little boy—I'll call him Jim—had an Indian friend we'll call Harry. Even though their parents were fighting, Jim and Harry were good friends. They would meet in a secret place whenever they could and play together.

"One day Harry told Jim about a special thing the grown-up Indians did. Sometimes they would have a friend who was so dear to them that they wanted to be blood brothers. They both made a cut in one of their fingers and then put their fingers together so their blood could mix for a few minutes. Then they considered themselves blood brothers, just as though they had been born into the same family.

"Jim decided he would like to be a blood brother with Harry. So Harry found a sharp thorn and poked his finger until it started bleeding. Quickly Jim did the same thing.

"Jim looked at the blood on his finger. It was the same color as Harry's. Even though their skin on the outside was different, their blood was the same color! Carefully Jim pressed his finger against Harry's. He and Harry smiled at each other. It didn't matter what they looked like on the outside, they were the same inside."

"So yellow people and black people and white people all have the same color of blood?" Treena asked.

Mother nodded. "God gave us different faces and colors for variety. He doesn't care what color your skin is. Good people come in all colors. We are all the same inside, where God sees. God likes your skin color. He likes Amy's skin color. It's just right for each of you. It doesn't matter what you look like on the outside. God loves you just as much as He loves anyone else."

TODAY I FEEL
AFRAID OF STORMS

The Bible says, "[God] sends lightning with the rain." Psalm 135:7, N.I.V.

TODD was sure that his daddy was the strongest person in the world. Why, whenever Mommy had a problem with opening a jar of something, she would call Daddy, and he could always get the lid off! Daddy carried in huge armfuls of wood for the fireplace—all at one time. And he could swing the heavy ax to split wood into smaller pieces. Todd was just sure that no one else's daddy was quite as strong as his.

It made him proud to tell his friends how strong his daddy was. He was proud to be his daddy's little boy.

One day clouds rolled over Todd's neighborhood. The sky was dark gray, and as Todd watched out the window, he saw a bright flash of lightning in the sky. Then thunder that sounded like a hundred bass drums rolled loudly through the air. Todd was scared.

"Daddy!" he called, running downstairs to the living room. "Daddy, I don't like that thunder and lightning!" he said, climbing up quickly onto his father's lap.

"What are you afraid is going to happen?" Daddy asked.

"I don't know," Todd answered. "I'm just afraid of it."

"Let me tell you something about thunder and lightning," Daddy said. "Did you know that God makes it? Whenever I hear thunder and see the lightning, I think of how big and strong God is. And I am not afraid, because I am His child and I know that He wants to do only what is good for me. God loves us very much."

"But what *is* thunder and lightning?" Todd wanted to know.

"Thunder and lightning are just the electricity in the air that we can see during a storm," Daddy told him. "As long as we're in our house, away from the windows, we're safe."

Todd smiled. Now he wasn't afraid. "I have the strongest daddy in the world, and the strongest God," he said proudly. "I'm not afraid of the storm anymore."

PETER'S GUN

The Bible says, "Thou shalt not kill." Exodus 20:13, K.J.V.

PETER received a brand-new BB gun for his eighth birthday. Excited, he couldn't wait to show it to Dominic, his next-door neighbor and best friend.

"Now, remember that it's just for target shooting," Daddy reminded Peter as he ran out the door. "Don't ever aim your gun at people or animals."

"I know," Peter replied. And he was gone.

"Hey, that's a really neat gun," Dominic said as he stroked the brown, wooden sides. "Can I try it?"

"Sure!" Peter said. "But I promised my dad it wouldn't be used to shoot people or animals — just tin cans."

All morning Peter and Dominic played together. They were becoming pretty good at hitting the cans lined up in front of the wall. Then Dominic had to go home.

For a while longer Peter shot at the cans by himself. Then he became bored with just cans. He heard a crow's familiar "Caw! Caw!" a short distance away in the grass.

I probably couldn't hit that bird if I wanted to, Peter thought to himself as he cocked the gun. I'm not that good at shooting this thing, yet.

"You really shouldn't aim the gun at that bird," a voice inside his head seemed to say. "You promised . . . "

"But I doubt I could hit it," Peter argued with himself. "I'll just take one shot at it."

Peter lay down in the grass, aimed, and fired. The bird let out a startled "Caw!" Then all was quiet.

I must have hurt him! Peter thought as he scrambled up and ran over to the bird. It lay very still. Peter saw a spot of blood on the bird's wing, and all of a sudden he knew what he had done.

"I killed it!" he said, his heart pounding in his chest. "I killed a little bird . . . and I promised I wouldn't even try . . . "

Now Peter understood why Daddy had said not to point the gun at people or animals. Daddy didn't want him to feel this way.

Tears stung Peter's eyes as he dug a grave for the bird. He had a terrible feeling in his tummy and didn't feel like eating at lunch. All afternoon he had a terrible, gloomy feeling. Finally that evening he told his father what had happened.

"We are always unhappy when we break one of God's commandments," Daddy said. "God gave them to us because He loves us. He knows what is best for us."

"I'm never even going to *pretend* I'm killing anything again!" Peter said. He didn't enjoy his BB gun very much after that. And pretty soon he didn't play with any kind of gun at all.

TODAY I FEEL AFRAID TO PRAY

The Bible says, "How I thank God for you, Timothy. I pray for you every day." 2 Timothy 1:3.

THE telephone at Grandma's house was ringing as she hurried to answer.

"Hello," she said.

"Hi, Grandma! It's Shannon! How are you?"

Grandma smiled a big smile. "Hi, honey! I'm so glad you called!"

"We've been trying to call you all day, but you didn't answer," Shannon said. "How come you didn't pick up the phone? I wanted to talk to you!"

"Well," Grandma explained, "Grandpa and I were out shopping today. We just got in. If we had been home, you can be sure we would have answered!"

Have you ever tried to call someone and received no answer? Or maybe the line was busy? That's frustrating, isn't it?

Sometimes grown-ups say that praying is like talking to Grandma on the telephone. Although Grandma is far, far away, we can still speak to her and she can hear us. But sometimes Grandma isn't home. Then we can't talk to her. Sometimes she is speaking to somebody else, and her line is busy. Then we can't reach her, either. We have to wait. And if you don't remember her telephone number in the first place, you can't call her at all, can you?

That's where praying is not like calling up Grandma on the

phone. God is always there when we need to talk to Him. He is never busy with someone else so that we have to wait. God hears us every time we pray, any time of the day. And we don't have to know special numbers or words to speak to Him.

Derek was afraid to pray. In family worship when Daddy asked him to pray he always said No.

"I don't know what to say," he told his daddy. He thought he had to have something really serious to tell God about. And he thought he had to use big words and a deep voice.

One day Daddy said, "If Grandma were here today, what would you tell her about?"

"I'd tell her about the baby rabbits that Shawn has," Derek replied.

"Well, why not tell God about them?"

"Because He sees them all the time. He already knows about them!"

"But He likes to know how you enjoyed them," Daddy said. "Just thank Him for making them so furry. Or thank Him that they belong to your friend Shawn so you can see them often."

Praying is really easy. It's like talking to anyone else. No, it's better than that. Praying is like talking to a friend who always understands and who never laughs at what you have to say. God is always there, listening, waiting to hear from you. Why not share your day with Him?

TODAY I FEEL LIKE BEING A MISSIONARY

The Bible says, "God has forgiven you because you belong to Christ." Ephesians 4:32.

WHEN I was a little girl I lived in Ceylon, a tiny island next to India. My mother and daddy were missionaries.

Many of the people in Ceylon worshiped someone they called "Buddha." Many of the statues of him were made of wood or stone and often covered with gold. People would light candles in front of the idols of Buddha, and bring fruits and vegetables as an offering to them. Sometimes, at a special gathering once a year, the people would hurt themselves badly to try to make the idols do something kind for them, or forgive them for something they had done wrong.

One day my parents went to one of these gatherings to see just what the people did to make their gods listen to them. As soon as they walked through the gates of the meeting grounds, Mother and Daddy had to step over people rolling over and over on the hot sand in the street. Some of the men didn't have shirts on. The sand must have hurt their bare backs and arms; but they had made a promise to their god that if he did something nice for them—such as make their mother well, or give them a baby, or forgive them for doing something wrong—they would roll in the sand every year to say Thank you.

One man had small, curved needles stuck through the skin on his arms and back. Some people were walking on shoes with nails poking into their feet. Others danced with heavy wooden boxes on their shoulders until they fell down exhausted. Men and women, and even children, ran through a long bed of coals that glowed red with fire. They hurt themselves in many ways just so their gods would forgive them!

Of course, we know who made those people think they had to do that, don't we? The devil doesn't want those people to know that all they have to do is pray to Jesus and believe in Him, and their sins will all be forgiven. The Bible says that God has forgiven us, because we belong to Jesus. But those people don't know that. That's why we send missionaries to tell them, so they can love Jesus and stop hurting themselves. When you give your offerings in Sabbath school, you are being a missionary too.

WHAT DOES JESUS LOOK LIKE?

The Bible says, "You love [Jesus] even though you have never seen him." 1 Peter 1:8.

"MOMMY, what does Jesus look like?" Betty asked. She had a picture hanging in her room of Jesus and the children, but the picture in her Bible was a bit different from that one. "Does anybody know what Jesus really looks like?" she wanted to know.

"No one really knows what Jesus looked like," Mother replied, "because there were no cameras when Jesus lived on this earth. And no one painted His picture while He was here. The pictures we have are just the way some painters thought He may have looked."

"You mean all the pictures we see are just make-believe?" Betty asked.

"That's right," Mother answered. "But does it really matter what Jesus looked like? Can you still love Him, even if you don't know exactly how He looks?"

"Oh, sure!" Betty answered. "I guess it's kind of like Stephanie and the baby her mother is having. They love that baby, even though they haven't seen it yet and don't know what it looks like."

"That's right!" Mother said. "We love a baby even before we know if it is a boy or a girl, and certainly before we know what it looks like. We love babies because they're special to us."

"You know what I think Jesus looks like?" Betty said with a smile.

"No. Why don't you tell me?" Mother replied.

"Well, you always say that 'pretty is as pretty does,' and 'handsome is as handsome does,' so I think Jesus is very, very handsome because He does so many kind things," Betty explained.

"You're right," Mother agreed. "And when we read our Bibles and learn of all the wonderful promises Jesus has made, and when we look around and see the beautiful things in nature He has given us, we know that He *is* a very loving person."

"It really doesn't matter what Jesus really looks like," Betty commented softly. "You know why?"

Mother shook her head.

"Because I love Him for who He is and not for what He looks like."

And that's how Jesus loves us, too.

THE MAN WITH A BLACK MUSTACHE

**The Bible says, "He saved others; himself he cannot save."
Matthew 27:42, K.J.V.**

IT was wintertime. On an airport runway in Washington, D.C., a jet airplane loaded with people waited in line to take off. Because there was so much snow and ice on the runway, the jets ahead of this one had to check to make sure they had no ice on their wings before they took off. They had special chemicals they used to remove the ice.

Finally it was the waiting jet's turn. Its wings had been checked a little while before and the ice melted. But no one had looked at the wings just before takeoff. It was too bad no one had, because once the pilot started up into the air, he realized that his wings had too much ice on them. The ice made the airplane too heavy, and it couldn't get up high enough into the air.

The jet crashed into a bridge and then into the river below. The people who could, tried to swim away from the sinking airplane. But the water was icy. It took their breath away and made their legs stiff so they couldn't swim very well. Finally they just hung on to the large chunks of ice in the water while someone called the rescue helicopters to pull them out of the water.

At last a helicopter came. The men in it lowered a life preserver down to the people struggling in the river. One man with a mustache caught the life preserver. But he didn't keep it for himself. He handed it over to a lady in the water next to him. She grabbed onto it, and the helicopter lifted her out of the water and carried her away to safety.

The helicopter returned and lowered the life preserver again.

Again the man with the mustache passed it over to another person. That woman was saved, too.

Again and again the helicopter came back to take more and more people to safety, and each time the man with the mustache handed the life preserver to somebody else. Finally, on the last trip, the helicopter returned to pick up the man with the mustache. But he couldn't be found. He had waited in the water so long, and it was so cold, that he had finally sunk into the water. He had saved everybody else, but by saving them, he had died.

Jesus died to save us from Satan. And because He died, one day we can be in heaven with Him. When I get to heaven I want to throw my arms around Jesus and say, "Thank You, Jesus, for saving me!" Don't you?

FINISH UP

The Bible says, "Finishing is better than starting!" Ecclesiastes 7:8.

YOUNG Abe chewed slowly on a blade of grass as he stared across the fence at Mr. Harding's cornfield. There was lots and lots of corn there, and Mr. Harding didn't have any boys to help him. Abe sure needed a job. His father sold firewood for money, but just the day before, he had hurt his arm and wouldn't be able to work for a while. While Abe knew *he* couldn't chop firewood and deliver it as his father could, he did know how to hoe a garden pretty well. He had helped his father a lot in their own garden. And Mr. Harding's corn patch certainly could use a good hoeing to get all those weeds chopped down.

The boy sighed, then, his mind made up, he jumped over the fence and headed for Mr. Harding's door where he knocked smartly. When it opened, a tall, gray-haired man stood looking down at him. "What do you want, boy?" the man asked gruffly.

Straightening his shoulders, Abe swallowed hard. "Please, sir, I would like a job hoeing your corn," he said.

"Can you do a good job?"

"Oh, yes! I always do my best, sir!" Abe answered with a smile. "Father tells me I'm a real—"

"I don't care what your father thinks," the old man interrupted gruffly. "Tell you what. You start on that first row over there, and when you finish that, I'll know whether you do a good job or not!"

"Thank you!" Abe said as he hurried over to the corn patch.

It was hard work. Tangled weeds and vines grew among the stalks of corn, and it took a long time to chop them out and stir the ground. Although the sun was hot on his back, Abe still worked on. Even when Mr. Harding called to say that it was quitting time, Abe replied, "I'm almost finished, sir, and I'd like to complete this job before I go home!"

He had just one more row to hoe, and he couldn't see leaving that for another day.

When Abe finished and went back to Mr. Harding's cabin, the man was smiling. "You got the job, son," he said. "I never saw a boy before who would keep working till the job was done. You can work on my farm all summer until the crops are in!"

Many years later Abraham Lincoln became President of the United States. He was successful because he knew that finishing something was more important than starting. And how good we feel when we have finished a job well!

(Adapted from *When They Were Children* by Helena Welch).

TODAY I FEEL FORGIVING

The Bible says, "For thou, Lord, art good, and ready to forgive." Psalm 86:5, K.J.V.

RUDY held a little cardboard tepee he had made for his mother to see. "How do you like it?" he asked with a grin. He had carefully glued the sides together to make it just right.

"Hey, that looks like a real Indian tepee," Mother said. She held it in her hand and looked it all over. "It's just the right size for your little people, isn't it?"

"Yeah! Could you take care of it for me while I go and get them?"

Mother nodded. "I'll put it right here on the table for you. I've got to go start some laundry."

Rudy hurried back with his people. He laid out a village on the floor and put his people inside. They did fit nicely, and he wished he could be one of them. It looked so cozy in there.

After a little while Rudy's dog, Togo, wandered into the kitchen and dropped a ball at Rudy's feet. She wanted to play.

"OK, girl," Rudy said. "But we have to play with balls outside. Come on!"

Yelping delightedly, the dog hurried after Rudy. They both enjoyed playing ball, and it seemed no time at all before Mother was calling Rudy in for lunch. Togo was hungry, too. She raced through the door ahead of him. And she was still in such a playful mood that when she saw his Indian village all spread out on the floor, she growled playfully and bit into one of the tepees Rudy had made.

"Togo! Stop that!" he yelled. But the dog just barked and bit into the tepee again, tossing it into the air with a flick of her head. She pawed on it and chewed on it so much that she soon destroyed it.

"Togo! You ruined my tepee! Bad dog!" Rudy cried. When he talked like that to her, Togo knew she was in trouble. She didn't feel so playful anymore. Putting her head down and her tail between her legs, she slumped to the floor.

Sadly, Rudy picked up the scattered pieces and showed them to Mother. "Look what Togo did. She ruined my tepee."

Mother glanced at the dog, who watched carefully from the floor. Togo's eyes looked sad. She seemed to realize she had done something bad. As Mother watched, the dog got up, walked over to Rudy, and licked his fingers as if to say she was sorry. Then she whined softly.

Rudy bit his lip as he thought about his tepee. Then suddenly he put his arms around the animal's neck and hugged her. "OK, Togo, I forgive you. You didn't know what you were doing, I guess."

Mother nodded. "That makes Jesus very proud of you to see you show your love by forgiving. Now you know how Jesus feels when He forgives you for mistakes that you make. He's eager to forgive."

Togo licked Rudy's face. She was glad to be friends again.

TODAY I FEEL FORGETFUL

The Bible says, " 'Yet God does not forget a single one of them.' " Luke 12:6.

HAVE you ever forgotten something?

Robbie was going to his grandma's house. He was extra excited because he had something special to tell her.

Grandma's house was pretty far from Robbie's house, so it took all morning to get there. As he and his parents drove along he thought of all the things he wanted to share with Grandma. He would tell her about his loose tooth and the new shoes he got last week and the memory verses he had learned.

"I hope I can remember all those things," he said to himself as he stared quietly out the window of the car.

At last they reached Grandma's house.

"Grandma! Grandma!" Robbie shouted as he jumped out of the car. "You wanna see my loose tooth?" He opened his mouth wide and wiggled the tooth. "Touch it!" he said. "You can wiggle it, too."

Grandma put her finger on the tooth. It moved all right.

"You *are* a big boy, Robbie." she said. Then she looked at his mother and daddy. "Come in, come in. I've got a warm lunch all ready for you."

Robbie went for a walk with his daddy in the afternoon and picked up some pine cones. As he walked he tried to remember the things he wanted to tell Grandma. He had showed her the tooth, and he had told her about the memory verses he had learned. But he couldn't remember what else he wanted to share with her. What was it?

All too soon Robbie had to go to bed. He and his parents would leave early the next morning.

Before breakfast, Robbie finally remembered what the other thing was. He showed Grandma his new shoes. But they were all muddy now.

"Why don't we put them here by the door, and you can put them on when you leave?" Grandma suggested. "Come and eat now. I have some waffles ready."

Robbie looked at the waffles. Then he put his hand to his mouth.

"But, Grandma," he cried, "I can't eat waffles. I have a loose tooth!"

"Oh!" she exclaimed as she gave him a hug. "I forgot about that tooth! Of course you can't eat waffles. I'll make you some oatmeal instead."

Sometimes we forget things. Sometimes mommies and daddies, and even grandmas and grandpas, forget things that are really important to us. But there's someone who never forgets. That someone is Jesus. He never forgets a single one of us, or anything that we tell Him, because we are so special to Him and He is such a very special person, too.

WHEN BAD THINGS HAPPEN TO GOOD PEOPLE

The Bible says, "The good man does not escape all troubles— he has them too. But the Lord helps him in each and every one." Psalm 34:19.

ERIN stumbled through the back door.

"What happened?" Mother asked when she heard her crying in the kitchen.

"I fell off my bike!" Erin wailed. "I thought my angel was going to take care of me . . . and I tried riding without holding onto the handlebars . . . and he let me fall down!"

"Oh, honey. Your angel didn't do it," Mother said gently. "You were doing something careless."

"But I thought my angel would keep me safe!" the girl sobbed.

Mother put her arms around her daughter until she stopped crying. Then she explained, "Bad things happen to both good *and* bad people. Bad things happened to Jesus, and He was the best person who ever lived."

"But how come the Bible says angels will take care of us?" Erin insisted.

"Our angels sometimes do perform miracles and don't let us get hurt at all," Mother said, "even when we do foolish things."

"How come they help us sometimes, and other times they don't?" the girl persisted.

Mother shook her head. "We can't understand it all right now," she said. "But when we get to heaven, God will explain it to us. Getting hurt and feeling sad are things that happen because of sin. This is Satan's world, and we're just living in it for a while. He hates us and doesn't want us to go to heaven because *he* can't go. Satan does whatever he can to make us angry at God. Sometimes, when we're happy, he tries to make us forget about Jesus because we're having so much fun. Other times, he wants us to hurt so badly that we think God doesn't love us any more and isn't taking care of us. The devil wants to keep us out of heaven. You see, Satan can't go there. He used to be a very special angel who stood beside God's throne. He was called "Lucifer," and he had a lot of very important jobs to do as choir director and messenger for God. But when God and Jesus made Adam and Eve, Satan got angry because They didn't ask him to help. So he told all the angels that God was unfair. Some of them believed him, and they tried to make war in heaven. Because of that they had to leave.

"They chose to come to this earth that God and Jesus had created, and Satan started telling Adam and Eve that God was unfair."

"Really?"

Mother nodded.

"Satan is still trying to do that. He wants us to think that we shouldn't get hurt at all because we love God. He wants *us* to get angry at God so *we* won't go to heaven. But God doesn't hurt us—Satan does.

"Our angels keep Satan from doing more to us than we can bear. When the devil tries to hurt us more than we can stand, our angels step between Satan and us and tell him to stop it. That's when they keep us safe, even though we may not know about it." Mother finished cleaning Erin's cut and put a bandage on it as she continued.

"And every time Satan does hurt you, your angel helps you to feel better and reminds you that God loves you. He helps the pain go away. God can make something good come from everything bad that Satan does."

The girl looked down at her newly bandaged knee. "It doesn't hurt so bad," she said happily. "I guess my angel knew I could bear to scrape my knee. But he's helping it to feel better. My angel *is* taking care of me after all!"

THE LONELY BABY SEA LION

The Bible says, "Follow my advice, my son; always keep it in mind and stick to it." Proverbs 7:1.

A BABY sea lion lay all alone on a cold beach in Washington State, hollering and squealing. Somehow he had gotten separated from his mother. He was hungry and tired from his long journey, but no mother seal was nearby to take care of him. The only people on the beach were two early-morning joggers hurrying along the sand. When they heard the little sea lion crying and saw he was alone, they went over to help.

"I'll stay with the little fellow to make sure he doesn't go back into the water," the man said to his wife, "and you go call the zoo. They'll know how best to take care of him."

Before long the zoo people came with a special truck to take the baby sea lion to the zoo nursery. There, specially trained animal doctors and nurses took good care of the baby animal and gave him lots of attention. He was happy in his new home.

One day a Mr. Amundsen heard about him. Mr. Amundsen had other seals that did shows for people, and he wanted this baby sea lion to join his family. He was kind to his animals, and the zoo people knew that folks enjoyed his shows. So when the baby was well they gave him to Mr. Amundsen to train.

Pretty soon the baby seal had learned to balance a ball on the tip of his nose. He could raise one front flipper up in the air and wave with it, and he could toss a ball through a hoop. Whatever Mr. Amundsen showed the sea lion to do, he would do. Pretty soon the baby sea lion was good at doing lots of things. Always he received a whole fish as his reward when he did the trick right. The animal enjoyed doing what his trainer asked. He remembered what he was supposed to do when Mr. Amundsen blew his whistle, and it made them both happy.

Sea lions learn tricks, and so can dogs. But not every animal is smart enough. Only the smart ones do what their trainers ask them to do, over and over, until they get it right.

Your parents are *your* trainers. That's why they have worship with you and read good stories to you. And that's why they sometimes say No when you want to do things that aren't good for you. God gave your parents to you to help you be happy. They don't give you fish as a reward for doing right, do they? Sometimes they hug you and smile, and sometimes they give you a treat. But the best reward for doing things right is a good feeling inside. Try it and see!

THE MYSTERY OF THE TREES

The Bible says, "Be careful—watch out for attacks from Satan, your great enemy." 1 Peter 5:8.

THE story is told of a man who had a new house. It had just dirt around it, so the man had to plant all his own trees and bushes if he wanted a pretty yard.

Now, trees and bushes are expensive, and the man didn't have a lot of money, so you can imagine how happy and excited he was to find a tree farmer who sold him some evergreens for $5 each. They were small trees, but the man felt sure they would grow. The bottom of each tree was wrapped in a gunnysack.

"Make sure you don't take the sack off the roots," the tree farmer said. "Just dig your hole and put the tree in the ground with the gunnysack tied around the roots—don't take off the sack!"

The man followed the instructions exactly. Every day he watered his new trees and dreamed of the day they would be strong and tall and beautiful.

But one day he noticed that the tips of his trees were turning brown.

"You're watering your trees too much," his neighbors told him. "Don't water them every day. Then they'll be fine."

So the man stopped watering them as much. But that didn't work. The trees kept turning browner and browner. Soon every tree was brown and dried up. They looked awful. The man was really disappointed. After all, he had done all that the tree farmer had told him. "I guess I'll have to dig them up," he said sadly as he went to the shed for his shovel. As he did so he thought about all the money he had wasted.

The man dug up the first tree and untied the gunny sack

to check the tree's roots. When the sack fell away, the man saw that the tree had been sawed off at the trunk and nailed to some wood to make it stand up.

Hurrying to the next tree, he dug it up. It didn't have any roots, either. Every single tree had been cut off and fastened to a piece of wood. The farmer had sold the man some cut Christmas trees that nobody had bought. Of course they wouldn't grow without roots!

Sometimes Satan does that to us. He wraps up the bad things and makes them look OK so we will like them. But all they bring us is unhappiness.

Sometimes it's hard to know what is good and what is bad. God knew it would be hard for you to know, and that's why He gave you such good parents. They can help you to know what's good and what's bad. Ask them.

JESUS FIRST

The Bible says, "Thou shalt have no other gods before me."
Exodus 20:3, K.J.V.

DOTTIE had a brand-new little puppy that was all her own.

"What are you going to name him?" Mother asked, stroking his soft, brown fur. He nipped Mother's finger playfully and rolled over so she would rub his tummy.

"I think I'll name him ... Butterball," Dottie said. "He's so fat and round like a ball."

"That's a good name!" Mother replied with a smile.

Butterball was a good little puppy most of the time. But he was extremely curious. If Dottie ever left the gate open, Butterball would dash out to explore the sidewalk.

"I'm afraid one of these days, your puppy is going to get lost" Father told Dottie one evening. "You must be careful not to leave that gate open again."

She tried to remember. But one day Butterball ran out and down the street before she could stop him. She couldn't find him anywhere.

"Now what are we going to do?" Dottie cried. "Nobody will

love Butterball as I do. Oh, I wish he had obeyed me and stayed in the yard!"

"Why don't we go around and ask the people who live on our street if they have seen your puppy?" Mother suggested. "They might already be taking care of him until we come."

So Mother and Dottie went to every house on the street. Finally, at the house on the corner, they saw Butterball tied to a pole with a chain.

"Butterball! There you are!" Dottie said, racing toward the yard. The puppy yipped and tried to reach Dottie, but the chain held him back. "Oh, Butterball! I'm so happy we found you at last!"

She petted Butterball while Mother went to the house to talk to the people who lived in it.

"I knew he was too nice a puppy to be a stray," the man said. "And he seemed to be looking for somebody every time someone passed by on the sidewalk."

Dottie took Butterball home.

He stayed close to her from that time on. Finally he had learned that Dottie and her family loved him the best, and he was happiest if he stayed close to them.

God loves you more than you love your pets. He says, "Please don't go away from Me and pray to anyone else. Please don't watch so much TV or get so busy playing that you don't have time to talk with Me."

Jesus likes to have us with Him every day. He likes to be with you when you have worship, as you are doing now. Right now you're making Jesus very happy.

TODAY I FEEL KIND

The Bible says, " 'And if . . . you give even a cup of cold water to a little child, you will surely be rewarded.' " Matthew 10:42.

DO you have a baby sister or brother at home? We do. Her name is Holly, and she loves to stand on my lap while I pull her hands up high, past her ears, and over her head. She's so-oo big!

You are bigger than she is, though. Why, you can walk and talk, and feed yourself, and play outside. You were once a baby, but now you're a big boy or a big girl, aren't you?

It's fun to grow up. The more you grow, the more things you can do for others. And the more things you do for others, the happier you become.

My son Marc has a kitten he calls Frisky. When he found her, she was just a tiny little thing all alone in the street. She was wet and cold and hungry. But Marc picked her up, tucked her snugly under his coat, and carried her all the way home.

"Can we keep her, Mommy?" he asked, stroking her wet fur tenderly and looking into her eyes. He knew that his mother liked kitties too, and we didn't have any pet at the time.

I said the kitten could stay.

"Oh, goody!" he cried. "Let's give her some warm milk, then." Marc knew that if you feed a hungry animal, it becomes your friend.

Little Frisky lapped the warm milk hungrily until soon her little sides stuck out like a blown-up balloon. Then she washed her face with her paws and curled up on a towel in Marc's lap.

He smiled. "She likes me!" he said as he gently stroked her fur.

Frisky loved Marc because he was kind. It feels good to be liked, doesn't it? Maybe you are big enough to reach the faucet and get a drink for a smaller child. Or perhaps you are big enough to push a smaller child on the swings. Big people like you don't need to talk loudly or punch other kids or take their things. Big people like you can be kind to smaller kids. The Bible says you will be rewarded. Do you know how? You'll have lots of friends. But better than that, you'll feel good inside!

TODAY I FEEL ASHAMED

The Bible says, "[God] will throw [our sins] into the depths of the ocean!" Micah 7:19.

SOME men were making a new sidewalk in front of Carrie's house. A big cement-mixer truck backed up to the curb and poured wet, gray cement out of a chute into the special place where the sidewalk would be. Then the men took special tools that looked like garden tools, and pushed and patted on the cement to get it just right and smooth everywhere.

To Carrie, the cement looked like gray mud. I wonder what it feels like? she thought. I wonder if I could just poke one finger into it and see how cold it is? But the men kept watching her, and she was a bit afraid of what they might do if they saw her touching it.

Finally, the men finished the sidewalk. "Now don't you put your hands or feet into this, OK?" they said sternly, putting up wooden barricades to keep people away.

Carrie shook her head. But after the men left, she stood looking at the shiny, wet cement for a long time. I'll bet if I just poked my finger in the edge, no one would notice, she thought.

Slowly she bent down, leaned under one of the wooden barricades, and pushed her finger into the cement. Oh, it was delightful! So cool and grainy—almost like wet sand at the beach.

She stuck another finger into the cement. Then another, and another, until finally it covered almost her whole hand. But suddenly she realized what she had done. Quickly pulling her hand out, she noticed with alarm that she had left a deep hole in the cement. She scraped it off her fingers and tried to fill in the hole, but the more she patted the cement, the more lumpy it became. It was obvious that someone had been playing in it. What would the men do to her now?

Racing to her backyard, she rinsed off her hand so Mother wouldn't know. But mothers have a way of finding things out, don't they? Her mother guessed what had happened.

"What are the men going to do to me?" Carrie cried.

"Probably nothing," Mother said. "But every time you walk on that sidewalk, you'll see the holes that you put in it. And you'll remember that you ruined it, won't you?"

Carrie nodded. "I guess I lied to those men," she said. "I promised I wouldn't play in the sidewalk, but then I did, anyway. Will Jesus forgive me? Or will He always remember what I did too?"

Mother smiled. "When Jesus forgives, He forgets that we ever did wrong. The Bible says it's as if He throws our sins into the deepest parts of the ocean where no one can see them. Then He forgets we ever sinned."

"I'm glad God doesn't remember everything," Carrie said. And I am, too.

WHY YOU ARE SPECIAL

The Bible says, "[Jesus] created everything there is." John 1:3.

IT was almost Mary's birthday, and she was getting excited. Mother had said she could choose a new doll for her birthday present this year. Carefully she looked through Mother's toy catalogs to choose just the doll she wanted. Should it be a doll that cried? she wondered. Or one that had movable arms and legs? Or maybe a soft cloth doll that was cuddly, like a real baby. Mary couldn't decide.

At last she circled three dolls she especially liked. She would let Mother pick one from those three.

The days passed. At last it was Mary's birthday, and she received her gift. Eagerly she ripped the paper off the box, opened it, and looked inside. There lay the most beautiful doll she had ever seen! It had curly, blonde hair with a pink ribbon in it, and long, dark eyelashes. And when Mary lifted her new doll out of the box, it was soft and cuddly—just like a real baby.

Carefully Mary studied the doll's face. When she held it up, it opened its eyes. Well, it opened *one* eye! The other eye stayed closed. Mary lifted it open with her finger and it seemed OK. Then why didn't it open by itself?

"My doll!" Mary cried, holding it out toward Mother. "She's broken already!"

Even Mother couldn't make the doll's eye stay open. "I guess we'll have to take it back," she said. "I can't fix it."

Mary was so disappointed!

Too bad that doll wasn't as well made as the things Jesus made. The Bible says that Jesus created everything there is. That doesn't mean He made dolls and toys, but He *did* create people and give them good minds to use in making dolls and toys for children.

Jesus made children. He made you. And unlike Mary's doll, your eye will usually get better if it ever gets hurt. The things Jesus made are much more special and wonderful than anything people can make.

Jesus made the sun and the moon and the stars. People can't make those! And Jesus made all the cows and tigers, puppies and kittens. The Bible says that in the beginning nothing was made without Jesus. And just as Mary was sad when she found that her doll was broken, Jesus, too, is sad when you get hurt or "broken." Because Jesus made you. And that makes you very special to Him.

TODAY I FEEL LIKE LAUGHING

The Bible says, "There is a time to laugh." Ecclesiastes 3:1-4.

DO you know when to laugh? Sometimes it's hard to learn the right times to laugh and the right times to be serious.

Hannah loved to tease. In the summertime her mother got out the wading pool, and Hannah invited her neighborhood friends over to play in it with her. Sometimes they would splash one another. They would laugh and giggle and pour water over each other's heads. And sometimes they would sit down hard in the water on purpose to make a big splash.

One day Hannah's neighbor Laura brought a friend with her. Laura's friend Amy was afraid of the water. She stood on the grass in her swimsuit and watched the other children playing.

"Come on in!" Hannah called. "It's not cold!"

But Amy shook her head. She just wanted to watch.

Laura and Hannah played together in the pool. When the water splashed out onto Amy's legs, she laughed. But she still didn't want to get into the pool.

After a while, when Amy had grown tired of just watching Hannah and Laura play, she went over to play on the swings.

"Hey, Laura!" Hannah whispered. "Let's play a trick on Amy!"

"What do you want to do?" Laura asked.

"Let's dump her into the pool! You could take her legs and I'll take her arms, and we'll carry her over here and dump her in. That would be funny!" Hannah laughed.

"I don't know," Laura said slowly. "It might make her cry."

"But it's just playing," Hannah replied.

"It's playing to us, but it wouldn't be playing to Amy. It would be scary to her!" Laura explained. "I don't think we should do it!"

Laura knew when to laugh. If something we do makes somebody else scared or hurt, then it isn't funny. We don't laugh at somebody who is sad or embarrassed. That isn't kind.

But if what we do makes that other person laugh, then we can laugh too.

God likes to hear you laugh. But always be sure that when you laugh it is the right time!

TODAY I FEEL LUCKY

The Bible says, "Always be thankful." Colossians 3:15.

ELISE was going to spend all summer at her grandpa's farm. Excitedly she imagined herself walking around barefoot in soft dirt with her jeans rolled up.

"Sorry," her daddy said when she told him about her plans. "Grandpa said he just put up a new barn, and there might be nails and other construction leftovers around that you might step on. You'll have to wear shoes. I don't want you stepping on one of those nails."

"But, Daddy," Elise pleaded.

"No," Daddy said firmly. "Keeping you from getting hurt is more important than going barefoot."

"Well, may I wear sandals?"

"No, we want something with a good, heavy sole. Those nails can poke up through sandals in a minute."

Elise made a sour face and went outside to sit on the porch while she thought about it. She was sure her summer was ruined.

The next day Elise and her father went shopping for shoes.

"I want something with a good, heavy sole," Daddy said.

The salesman shook his head. "I'm sorry," he said. "All I have for girls are sandals and pumps and tennis shoes. If you really want a heavy sole, I could see if we have some boys' shoes that would fit her."

Daddy agreed, and the salesman went back into the storeroom to look. When he came out a few minutes later, he carried some dark-brown shoes with brown shoelaces. They looked heavy. And they felt heavy. But Daddy said they were just the thing for the farm, and he bought them.

The first few days at the farm, Elise's feet ached in her new brown shoes. They were much heavier than her sandals, and felt hot. But Grandma said she would get used to them, and even though Elise couldn't believe it, the shoes did begin to feel comfortable after a few days. But Elise still thought they were ugly, and said so from time to time.

One day Grandpa took Elise to town with him. They hadn't walked very far down the street when Elise heard a strange rumbling sound behind her. She turned to look, and saw something she would never forget. Coming toward her was a man on a little cart with special rubber-tipped sticks to push himself along. The man had no legs. As he rolled past, he smiled and called a cheery hello.

Grandpa bent down to whisper in Elise's ear, "I cried because I had no shoes until I saw a man who had no feet."

"What happened to his feet, Grandpa?"

"He was in a car accident that crushed both of his legs."

Elise looked down at her ugly brown shoes. She wiggled her toes inside of them. They weren't pretty at all. But somehow she didn't mind them anymore.

There will always be people you think are lucky because they have things you don't have. But remember: You have things that somebody else would like to have too. Try to remember your blessings. And "always be thankful."

(Adapted from a story in *Guide* magazine.)

SAYING "I LOVE YOU"

The Bible says, "Loving God means doing what he tells us to do." 1 John 5:3.

DADDY always said something as soon as he got in the car. What do you suppose it was?

"Fasten your seat belts!"

Nona sighed. "Oh, Daddy. Why do you always say that? I hate this old seat belt. It's so tight, and I can't move when it's on. Do I have to wear it?"

"Yes, you do. Because I love you."

"You mean you hate me. You just want me to be uncomfortable," Nona grumbled as she struggled with the seat belt.

"What does it mean when I give you a present?" Daddy asked.

"It means you love me," Nona said, puzzled.

"What does it mean when I put on my coat?"

"It means you're going outside."

"And what does it mean when I get a glass out of the cupboard?"

Nona laughed. "I guess it means you're thirsty and you're going to get a drink," she said.

"Do I have to tell you I'm thirsty and I'm going to get a drink?" Daddy asked, looking at her reflection in the rearview mirror.

"No, I just know."

"Well, what would it mean if I put my arms around you?"

"It would mean that you love me, I guess," Nona said.

"That's right!" Daddy smiled. "When we're driving I can't drive and keep my arms around you, so I ask you to put on your seat belt. That's sort of like loving arms holding you in and keeping you safe. Children who don't wear seat belts get hurt more often than children who do, and I don't want you to get hurt."

"So when you tell me to put on my seat belt, you are saying you love me?" Nona asked.

"That's right! Even though you may not think you need a seat belt, it is for your protection. A seat belt says 'I love you.' "

God has given us some rules called the Ten Commandments that say He loves us too. Even though we think we don't need them, they are for our happiness and protection.

The Ten Commandments are the rules God has for happiness. They tell us to worship God, to go to church on Sabbath, to obey our parents, and not to kill or steal or tell bad stories about other people. They remind us not to "covet," or want to take other people's things away from them. As you get older you will learn more about the Ten Commandments and you will understand them better. But whenever you hear about them, remember that when God asks you to obey them He is saying, "I love you."

THE SWANS THAT RING FOR DINNER

The Bible says, "Only a fool despises his father's advice; a wise son considers each suggestion." Proverbs 15:5.

MICHAEL Dawson lives in a palace in England. But he's not a king or a prince. His father is a gardener at the Bishop's Palace at Wells.

All around the palace is a water-filled moat, like a small river, which was supposed to keep enemies out of the castle in the olden days. Now there is no danger of enemies attacking, but the moat still circles the palace. It is the home of several different kinds of ducks and mute swans.

Michael's job at the palace is to feed the swans every morning and afternoon. But he does not have to worry about ever forgetting to feed them. They ring a bell for their food!

Over one hundred years ago the daughter of one of the bishops taught a swan to pull the rope attached to a bell whenever he was hungry. Only after it rang the bell did she feed it. The swan was very smart, and taught the trick to its children. Ever since then, only the swans that live in that moat know how to ring the bell. And only the swans that ring the bell get fed.

What do you suppose would happen if one of the little baby swans decided that he wasn't going to bother ringing the bell? He wouldn't get fed, would he? He would show himself not to be very smart. And I think his mother would be very sad to see him hungry.

God gives every animal and insect the knowledge it needs, called instinct, to survive when it is young. When you were first born, you didn't know how to talk, and you didn't know what people were saying to you. You couldn't hold a spoon and feed yourself, and you couldn't even turn yourself over or sit up. But you could do one thing very well—one thing that kept you alive. You knew how to suck. Sucking was the way you got your milk so you could grow. And then as you got bigger, you saw your parents and other people doing exciting things like holding a spoon or fork, and *you* learned how to eat that way, too. Pretty soon *you* learned how to talk, and how to walk, and how to do many other things your parents showed you.

Now see how smart you are! You can look at books by yourself, you can help get yourself dressed, you can feed yourself and can understand many words. Yes, you are very smart! Do you know how you got that way? By listening to your parents and doing what they said to do. When you do that, you make them very happy. Keep on listening and learning and doing what they tell you. That is very smart!

TODAY I FEEL SELFISH

The Bible says, "The earth is the Lord's, and the fulness thereof." Psalm 24:1, K.J.V.

"THIS hammer is mine, and you can't have it!" Bradley shouted to his brother Ron as they played outside one summer day. They were pretending to work on their playhouse with their daddy's tools.

"But I need the hammer!" Ron insisted, grabbing for it and trying to jerk it free. Bradley held on tightly. He reached to pull his brother's hair. Just then their mother walked outside to see what all the commotion was about.

"Boys!" she called loudly.

"What?" Bradley replied, looking down at his feet. He knew he had done wrong.

"What are you boys fighting about?"

"Bradley says the hammer is his, but I want to use it. And besides, it isn't his, it's Daddy's!" Ron explained, talking so fast he had to stop for a big breath at the end.

"Whose did you say it was?" Mother asked slowly.

"Bradley says it's his, but it's really Daddy's!" Ron repeated.

"Oh," she said, nodding. "Come here a minute, boys. I want to talk to you."

Bradley dropped the hammer and walked slowly to Mother, following his brother.

"Sit down." Mother patted the soft grass beside her. "You know, God gives us many things: food to eat, clothes to wear, a house to live in, and a job for Daddy. God keeps Daddy healthy so he can go to his job every day. Also, God gives us wood and metal to make cars and TVs and toys. But all things really belong to God."

Ron understood what Mother was trying to say. "I know," he nodded. "We say these things are ours, just as Bradley thought the hammer was his, but they're really God's. And God could take away these things, couldn't He, just as Daddy could take away his hammer."

"He could, but He would rather give us things than take things away. God wants us to take care of the things that He gives us, and He wants us to share with other people," Mother replied.

"OK," Bradley said slowly. "Ron, you can use Daddy's hammer for a while, and then I'll use it again."

It feels good to share. Try it!

IF EVERYTHING WERE FREE

The Bible says, "Say there! Is anyone thirsty? Come and drink—even if you have no money!...It's all free!" Isaiah 55:1.

HAVE you ever wished you could have anything you wanted? One time I had a dream like that. In my dream I walked down a busy city street and went into a clothing store. In it were some beautiful clothes: Dresses in all sorts of colors and styles with matching shoes and hats, pretty slacks and blouses—anything you could have dreamed of to wear. Of course, this was just a dream, so everything I liked fit me and looked nice on me. The store manager wrapped the things I had chosen and said, "These are free today. Go ahead and choose anything else you want, too. All the clothes are free!"

What would you have done? Of course! I went back and selected some more things to wear. When I went out of the store I had boxes and boxes of new clothes.

Then I went in the big grocery store next door. As I passed by the long rows of delicious fruit, the manager smiled and held up two apples.

"Here! These are for you! They're free today. All the food is free."

Well! Naturally I filled up several grocery carts of food. I chose some beans and some rice, some fresh vegetables and frozen vegetables, and some milk and cheese. And then I pointed to the ice cream. Was that free, too?

The store manager nodded. "Help yourself," he said. "Take all you want."

I reached for the freezer door, but for some reason, I couldn't make myself open it. Somehow I couldn't believe that the ice cream was free! I tried again to get some ice cream, but I couldn't make myself take any.

Then I stood at the checkout stand. As I looked at the people around me, I saw that they all had ice cream in their grocery carts. Mine was the only cart that didn't have any ice cream in it. Why do you suppose that was?

Right! Because I wouldn't reach in and take any!

God gives His love to us freely, just as those store managers gave their clothes and their food. He offers to love us and forgive us our sins and take us to heaven if we will just take the offer. Just reach out and say, "Thank You, Jesus, for loving and forgiving me. I accept Your gift of heaven. I believe that what You say in the Bible is true."

God's love is free. We don't have to be good all the time for God to love us. He doesn't love us because *we're* good, but because *He's* good. God loves us always, and He always will.

GOLD STARS AND REWARDS

The Bible says, "Behold, I come quickly; and my reward is with me." Revelation 22:12, K.J.V.

SCRUFFY was a little lost dog in the animal shelter in Los Angeles, California. Nobody knew where he came from, or whom he belonged to, or if he had ever had a home. He was lost and hungry and cold when he was found. Now he had to find a new home in two weeks or leave permanently. You can be sure that Scruffy did a lot of tail wagging and finger licking to try to get somebody to notice him. But he wasn't a puppy anymore, and most people didn't want a full-grown terrier—they wanted a puppy.

One day when the two weeks were just about over, a man named Carl Miller came into the animal shelter to find a dog. He had a squeak toy with him as a present for whichever dog he chose. Luckily for Scruffy, he showed his delight in the toy, and barked and whined and tried to lick it through the bars of his cage.

"That's the dog I want," Mr. Miller said. And so, with lots of squirmy wiggles and wet, happy kisses, Scruffy went to Mr. Miller's house to live.

Then the work started. Because Mr. Miller had chosen him to be an animal actor for movies and commercials, Scruffy had to learn a lot of tricks.

Scruffy learned to play the piano—not as you or your mother play the piano—but he could play pretty well for a dog. He learned to turn lamps on and off and to pick up papers from the floor and put them in the waste can. But his best trick was for a movie. For it, Scruffy learned to chase one of the actors out the door of his house and down the sidewalk, do a backflip through the gate, and slam the gate shut with his hind feet. I don't think even I could do that. But Scruffy did. And after each trick, he got to play with a little squeak toy. That was his reward.

Scruffy's love for squeak toys came in handy one time when they were making a commercial for dog food. Perhaps you've seen it. It shows Scruffy curled up, sleeping on a rug, when a tiny horse and covered wagon come scurrying across the floor in front of his nose, and he gets up and chases it to the kitchen cupboard.

When the commercial was made, Scruffy really wasn't chasing a horse and wagon. Those who made it put two movies together to make it look like that. What Scruffy really was after was a squeak toy. Mr. Miller sat in the kitchen cupboard, squeaking the toy, and when Scruffy heard it, he dashed into the kitchen to find it. After they filmed the commercial, Scruffy received his reward of playing with the toy.

Rewards are nice. They give us a reason for doing things. When Mommy and Daddy go to work, their reward is getting money to share with you. Sometimes rewards are gold stars or stickers. Other times rewards are just a feeling inside that we have done something good.

HOW TO LOVE BULLIES

The Bible says, " 'Love one another as I have loved you.' " John 15:12, R.S.V.

HAS your mother ever said, "Now, that's the second time I've told you!"?

Roger's mother asked him to put on his shoes. He mumbled, "Uh huh," and kept on playing with his cars. In a few minutes she said it again.

"I asked you to put on your shoes, Roger! Please do it!"

The boy looked up from his playing. "Oh, I forgot," he said.

"Well, you'd better hurry, because I have to leave for an appointment in ten minutes," Mother told him, looking at her watch.

Then Roger hurried!

Why do you suppose his mother asked him twice to put on his shoes?

Because it was very important.

Jesus told His disciples and us something very important, too. He asked us to love one another. In fact, He said it two times close together, and in between He said, " 'You are my friends if you do what I command you.' "

One day my little boy asked me, "Mommy, but how can I love the robbers?"

Do you think *you* can?

We certainly don't love what the robbers do, do we? Nobody likes to have somebody else take his things. Jesus doesn't like what the robbers do, either. But He still loves them, and if the robbers ask Jesus to forgive them and they stop stealing and love Jesus instead, the Bible says that they can go to heaven.

But how do we love the robbers while they are stealing things?

We love robbers differently from the way we love people in our family. Our mothers and fathers we love because they love us—we like to be with them. But we don't want to be with robbers, do we? At least not while they're acting that way. But we can pray for them and ask Jesus to help them see that they are doing wrong, so they will stop stealing and start loving Jesus. Then they can go to heaven and be happy, too. When we want other people to be happy, we are loving them. That's not so hard after all, is it?

LETTERS FROM JESUS

The Bible says, "Thy word is very pure." Psalm 119:140, K.J.V.

THE mailbox one morning had a special letter with Danny's own name written on it. It was from his grandma and grandpa.

Eagerly he tore open the envelope to see what Grandma and Grandpa had to say. It made him feel proud to read his name at the top.

"Shall we throw the envelope away?" Mother asked as she took the letter from him to read it.

"Oh, no," Danny replied. "I want to keep it. *It* has my name on it, too!"

"OK, when I am finished, you can return it to its envelope and put it somewhere in a safe place," Mother said.

Slowly she read the letter. His grandparents said they missed Danny and his family, and they were planning a trip to visit them. Grandma was making some special things Danny liked to eat, and she was getting everything ready for the trip. Then she told her grandson about a funny little trick her dog did.

"And it says 'Love, Grandma and Grandpa,' " Mother said as she folded the letter carefully.

Her son smiled proudly. "It's my very own letter, isn't it?" he asked.

"Yes, it surely is."

"And Grandma and Grandpa are coming here to see me!"

"That's right. And they're coming to see your brother Andrew, and Daddy and me too," she added.

"Well, this is a very special letter. I'm going to put it in the treasure box I have on my dresser so Andrew doesn't grab it and wrinkle it all up. I want to keep it nice and clean!" Danny said. And that's just what he did.

You and I may not have a letter from Grandpa and Grandma, but do you know who has given us an even more special letter?

Jesus has! The Bible is a special book of letters from Jesus that tells us how much He loves us. Those letters say that Jesus is coming on a special trip to see us and take us to heaven. And since they mean so much to us, we are careful not to put other books on top of the Bible. And we don't sit on it or just throw it around carelessly either. The Bible is a very special book. I'm sure you take very good care of yours, don't you?

LITTLE BOY JESUS

The Bible says, "Then [Jesus] returned to Nazareth with [His parents] and was obedient to them." Luke 2:51.

"OH, Mom, do I have to?" Ernie grumbled, slouching down in his chair as far as he could. He had just come in from playing outside, and his mother had asked him to hang up his coat and put away his boots.

Mother nodded. "Yes, I want you to hang up your coat," she said. "It takes all of us to keep our house looking nice."

"I wish I were a grown-up," he mumbled as he slowly got up from the chair and trudged over to pick up his coat.

"Why do you say that?" Mother asked with a smile.

"Because then I could do things when I wanted to and not just because somebody told me to do them."

"Well, grown-ups have to do things because they are told to, also," Mother said. "Daddy has a boss who tells him things that should be done, and he has to do them."

"He does?"

"Yes, he does."

"Well, I'll bet the President doesn't have to do what other people want him to do... or a king!" Ernie was sure there was *somebody* who could do whatever he wanted to do whenever he wanted to.

"No, I'm afraid even the President has to do what other people want him to do," Mother said. "He has to go to his office and make decisions even if he doesn't feel like it and would rather stay at home. And kings have to do some things even though they don't feel like it just then. And do you know"—Mother paused a moment as she thought—"that even Jesus, who made our world, was obedient to His parents? The Bible tells us that He was loved by God and man, so I'm sure that means He obeyed willingly and was not grumpy about it. I can imagine that when Mary asked Jesus to get her some water from the well, He said, 'Sure, Mom!' and hurried off to get it. Or when His father needed somebody to hold a piece of wood for him while he sawed, Jesus helped him. He probably helped Mary sweep the house, too, and cleared the dishes after meals. Jesus didn't *have* to obey, but He *chose* to. He is our example."

"Then when I obey you I am being like Jesus?" Ernie asked. He shut the closet door where his coat hung neatly inside.

His mother nodded. "You are loved by God and us, too," she said as she reached out her arms to hug him. "Very, very much!"

GOD MADE ME WONDERFUL

The Bible says, "I am ... wonderfully made." Psalm 139:14, N.I.V.

DANNY stood very still while he studied the cut on his finger. Just a few days before, it had been bleeding and sore. Then it got all puffy and red. And now, it looked as if there was some dirt in it. Around the black piece of dirt, Danny could see some yellow stuff. His finger ached so much he decided to tell his mother about it. She would know what to do.

Mother held Danny's finger carefully as she looked at the cut. There seemed to be an infection, all right.

"What can we do?" he wanted to know.

"It's not bad enough to see a doctor about, so we'll try nature's method," Mother said. "Nature's method is God's method. He made you and everything in nature, so we'll use what He has given us to make your cut better."

The boy watched as his mother set out two bowls of water. One bowl she filled with tap water and added some ice to make it real cold. Into the other bowl she poured hot water—just as hot as her hand could stand.

"Now, we'll soak your finger in this water. Ten minutes in the hot water and ten minutes in the cold. Back and forth, OK?"

Danny nodded. The hot water felt good to his cut. It made his hand all red and warm. Then it was time for the icy-cold water. That caused his hand to tingle. But he kept it in there, just the same.

After a while, Danny noticed that the yellow stuff was coming out of the cut in his finger. "Look, Mommy!" he said in an excited voice. "The infection is going away!"

"Yes! That yellow stuff is made of dead germs and of cells that your body used to fight the infection. Now we are helping your body get rid of all that garbage," Mother explained.

"Boy! And we didn't even need a doctor this time!" he said.

"God was our doctor," Mother explained, "He made us and He knows how to make us well. As soon as you got that cut, your body began killing the germs and closing your skin

74

back together. You didn't need to think about doing it — God just took care of it."

In a few days, Danny's cut had healed. He didn't even have a scar. That's how wonderful God made our bodies!

I LIKE TO BE DEPENDABLE

The Bible says, " 'Let your good deeds glow for all to see, so that they will praise your heavenly Father.' " Matthew 5:16.

ERICA'S teacher, Mrs. Grant, had a special surprise for her class. Since she had to go outside to get it ready, she asked the class to remain in their seats, reading, until she returned.

All the students opened their books to their lesson and started reading quietly. They wondered what the surprise was. But they had to wait.

Before too long, though, one of the boys got tired of waiting. He stood up to look out the window.

"What's she doing?" somebody whispered. "Can you see anything?"

The boy shook his head. "I can't see her," he said softly.

Pretty soon somebody came to stand quietly beside him. Then more and more children left their desks and crowded around the window. But Mrs. Grant wasn't where they could see her.

"I'm going outside," the first boy said, as he pushed his way through the others and started for the door.

"Me too!"

"Me too!" everyone shouted eagerly. Everyone, that is, except Erica.

She stayed at her desk, reading, as Mrs. Grant had asked. How do you suppose Erica felt? She felt left out! Erica wondered what everyone was doing outside together. Everyone else except her knew what the surprise was.

"If Mrs. Grant didn't send them back in, then it must be OK to go outside," a little voice suggested softly.

"No, Teacher told us to stay in our seats and do our lesson," another voice seemed to say.

"But the others are not doing *their* lesson," the first voice insisted. "Why should you?"

"Because Mrs. Grant said so! And I obey!" Erica said flatly as she bent her head to her work.

In a few minutes Mrs. Grant and the other students came back into the room. "Why, Erica!" the teacher exclaimed. "Have you been in here all the time by yourself?"

The girl nodded slowly.

"Well, class," Mrs. Grant said, smiling broadly at Erica. "You have all seen the surprise, our little white bunny. Now Erica gets her chance to hold him. And because she was the only student who obeyed, I am going to let her take our bunny home overnight and take care of him for us. I know I can trust Erica to take good care of him, because she obeys."

Erica smiled happily. She felt good and special inside. We always feel good when we obey and keep our promises.

TODAY I FEEL LIKE REMEMBERING

The Bible says, "Remember now thy Creator in the days of thy youth." Ecclesiastes 12:1, K.J.V.

CLOSE your eyes and picture a park. Can you see a slide? What color is it? Does it have a hump in it, or does it curl round and round? Are there swings? Can you imagine some children on those swings? Picture them laughing, swinging way up high.

Now open your eyes. Even though you weren't really there, you saw that park, didn't you? You were using your imagination—you made a picture in your mind.

God has given you a good mind. Can you remember your memory verse? What you ate for supper last night? Or your phone number?

Chad worried about fires.

"If there was a fire, Mommy, how would we get the firemen to come?"

"We would call the emergency number, and they would send the fire trucks to our house."

"But what if I couldn't remember our address?" Chad questioned. His address was quite long.

"You could tell them our phone number, and they would know where to come," Mother explained. "Let's practice it today."

All day long Chad sang the numbers to himself. By that evening he knew his phone number very well. He had remembered it by saying it over and over in his mind and out loud. That is how we remember our memory verses, too.

Have you ever lost something and needed it later? You have to think about what you did with it. Remembering is like walking backward through our minds. We remember what we just did, and then what we did before that, and before that, until finally we think of what we did with the lost object.

Sometimes we can't remember where we put things.

One day Jessie's grandpa was searching for his glasses. He looked on the end tables and on the dining table. On the refrigerator and on his desk. He even checked outside on the patio, but still couldn't find them.

"Have you seen my glasses, Jessie?" Grandpa asked.

She looked at him and started giggling. "I know where your glasses are, Grandpa," she said.

"Where?"

"They're on top of your head!"

Sometimes we need other people to help us remember things. Reading the Bible and talking about Bible stories help us remember how much God loves us. I like to remember that, don't you?

BETSY ASKED

The Bible says, "A little child shall lead them all." Isaiah 11:6.

BETSY couldn't understand it. Every Sabbath morning her mother would get her washed and dressed in her best dress, her shiny black shoes, and white socks with lace around the top, and send her off to church in the bus that picked people up in her neighborhood. She enjoyed Sabbath school. But she wished her mother and father would come, too.

I'm sure they would enjoy the program for grown-ups, she thought. And I would like to see *them* all dressed up on Sabbath. Then it would be an extra-special day.

How could she get her parents to go with her to Sabbath school? Betsy thought and thought. I know! she decided one morning. I'll just be extra nice and helpful around the house, and then Mom and Daddy will want to be with me lots and lots—even on Sabbath morning!"

So the whole next week Betsy swept the kitchen every morning and made up her bed as best she could. She carefully remembered to feed the cat, tried hard not to get into any arguments, and tried to be the most perfect little girl she could be. When Sabbath morning came, Betsy got up before her mother did. Quickly she took her bath and combed her hair, and even put on her dress without being asked. Mother was surprised to see Betsy all ready when she went into her room. But Mother didn't go to church with her.

That morning in Sabbath school, Betsy's memory verse was "Ask, and it shall be given you" (Matt. 7:7). "That's a promise from God," she said quietly to herself. And all at once she knew how she could get her mother and father to go to church with her. She decided to ask God.

Every day that week Betsy prayed that her mother and father would go to church with her the next Sabbath. Even her Sabbath school teacher called and invited her parents to attend a special Sabbath school the next week.

Sabbath came. But only Betsy was ready when the church bus pulled up. So she went alone.

All the next week Betsy prayed. But on Sabbath morning, again, she was the only one ready for Sabbath school when the bus pulled up.

"I'm not going," she said, a determined look in her eye.

"But Betsy—" her mother began.

"I'm not going," the girl repeated softly, "unless you and Daddy go with me."

Mother looked at Daddy for a long moment. Then she and Daddy went upstairs, got dressed, and they all drove together to church for the first time that Betsy could remember.

Maybe you would like someone to go to church with you. Tell God about it, and then ask that person. Sometimes people will go to church if a child asks them, even though they say No to everyone else. Why don't you try it?

TODAY I FEEL UNFRIENDLY

The Bible says, "Be kind to each other." Ephesians 4:32.

SALLY stared at her brother for a long moment. She didn't like what he had just said.

It was Wednesday, and she and Mother had just returned from the grocery store after doing some shopping.

"Who shall we invite for Sabbath dinner?" Mother had asked as she put the groceries away.

Sally wanted to invite her best friend, Julie, and her family again, but Mother said No. "We were just at their house a few weeks ago," she said.

"I know, but we had a good time!" Sally insisted.

Just then, Gary, her brother, walked into the kitchen. "What are you all planning?" he asked, peering into a sack.

"I was just asking Sally whom we should invite for Sabbath dinner," Mother explained. "Do you have any suggestions?"

He scratched his ear. "Yeah. I do have a suggestion," he said slowly. "Last week there were some new Sabbath school members in my class—a boy and his sister. They had just moved into town, and they looked awfully lonely. I'd sort of like to invite them."

His sister made a face. "But we don't know them!" she said. "We want to invite someone we know so we can have fun!"

Mother turned to look at her. "I think Gary has a good idea," she said. "Why don't we invite the newcomers this time? Who knows, they might even become our best friends!"

"I guess so." Sally sighed as she walked slowly out of the room.

All that week she thought about Sabbath and the horrid time she was sure they were going to have with those strangers.

Sabbath finally came, and what a surprise Sally had! It turned out to be the best Sabbath she had had in a long time. She learned that the family had just moved to their state from Texas. The girl, Linda, had all kinds of exciting stories to tell about their grandfather's ranch there, and about things she used to do. And she taught Sally some new songs she had sung at her old Sabbath school in Texas.

By the time Linda and her family left, she and Sally had become good friends.

"I'm glad we invited them over," Sally said at worship that evening. "Just think what a good friend I would have missed making if we hadn't been kind!"

BRUISES AND FORGIVENESS

The Bible says, "Oh, thank the Lord, for he's so good! His lovingkindness is forever." Psalm 118:1.

MR. Dawson had the biggest, juiciest apples on the trees in his yard. When they were ripe, he picked them and sold them to people who passed by. But he sold only the ones that he picked. Some of the apples fell to the ground. They were still good for applesauce or apple pie, but they had brown bruises on them and didn't look pretty.

"I wonder if Mr. Dawson would let us gather some of the fallen apples," Mother said to Scottie one day. "Why don't we ask him if we can have some of the bruised ones?"

"Why, yes," Mr. Dawson said, "you may have the bruised ones that have fallen down. I'll even let you have them for free. But please be sure you don't damage the trees with your wheelbarrow. And don't let the children climb the trees. I don't want them to get hurt."

Mother and Scottie gathered the apples all morning long. But Scottie grew tired of bending over and picking up apples. He wanted to do something that was fun.

Slowly he walked to an apple tree far from where Mother was working. It was a tall tree and had lots of inviting branches.

"I could climb that tree and not get hurt," he said to himself. "Mr. Dawson just doesn't know what a good tree climber I am."

Carefully he climbed the lowest branch. Then he grabbed the one above his head and pulled his legs up to it. Oh, how high up he was! He must be as tall as Daddy now. Next he stepped out on one of the limbs. With a crack, the branch snapped.

"Help!" Scottie yelled as he fell through the air.

Mother came running as fast as she could. When she saw Scottie sitting on the ground, she hugged him. "Oh, I'm so glad you're not badly hurt," she said. "But you disobeyed Mr.

Dawson. Now we have to tell him that you broke a branch on one of his trees."

Mr. Dawson looked serious as Scottie told him what happened. Scottie's heart pounded in his chest as he talked. He was scared.

"Well, son, I'm afraid I can't let you come back and pick up any more apples. I give them only to people who obey my rules," he said.

Aren't you glad that God isn't like Mr. Dawson? Sometimes we do something wrong. Sometimes we tell a lie, or hurt somebody, or take something that isn't ours. We must always ask forgiveness of that person if we do that. And we must ask forgiveness of God, too.

Sometimes people don't forgive us for what we have done that is wrong. But I'm glad that God and Jesus always forgive! They love us all the time. We can never do anything to make God stop loving us.

HOW TO KEEP THE DEVIL AWAY

The Bible says, "Resist the devil and he will flee from you." James 4:7.

"MOMMY, where does the devil live?" Jason asked his mother one morning at breakfast.

"Where do you think he lives?" she replied.

"Well, Bobby says that he lives in a deep, dark cave somewhere. But Bobby doesn't know where it is. If we go into a cave, will we see the devil?"

Mother shook her head. "No, the devil doesn't live in caves. He lives in people's houses."

"He does?" Jason's eyes grew big and round. "Well, does he live in our house?"

"No, sir!" Mother said confidently. "The devil doesn't live here with us. Do you know why?"

Jason shook his head.

"Because we have worship every day here, and the devil

knows we choose Jesus and not him. The Bible says that if we resist the devil, or tell him to go away, and if he can see that we really do love Jesus, he will run away from us! Our guardian angels protect us from the devil. That reminds me of a story I once heard about some missionaries," Mother said. "They were telling the jungle people about Jesus and how much He loves them, and the witch doctor got mad. He didn't want the people to love Jesus. So he decided he would kill the missionaries and get rid of them.

"One night the witch doctor and his helpers crept through the jungle toward the missionaries' house. They surrounded the house and began chanting a song together. Of course, the missionary heard them. But he wasn't afraid. He gathered his family together, and they all knelt down in their kitchen and prayed for Jesus and His angels to protect them. Before they got up from their knees, the chanting had stopped. It was very quiet outside except for the sound of running feet. The witch doctor and his friends were racing away, going back into the jungle.

"The next day one of the men who had been with the witch doctor that night came to see the missionary.

" 'We tried to kill you last night!' the man said. 'We began chanting to our devil gods. All at once we saw that your house was protected by tall, shining men standing side by side. They looked very strong, but also very good. They scared the witch doctor, and when he ran, we ran! Tell me,' the man said, 'who were those men?' "

"The missionary smiled. 'Why, those were angels sent from my God up in heaven,' he said. 'And they will protect you, too, if you will let them.' "

The Bible says that everyone has a special angel. And when the devil and his angels see you with your angel, or see you praying, the devil runs away. Now, isn't that good to know?

HOW TO SHOW
THAT I LOVE JESUS

The Bible says, "Even a child is known by his actions." Proverbs 20:11, N.I.V.

ESTHER was just about the only little girl in her neighborhood. Most of her neighbors' children were grown and gone away. But even though she didn't have many children to play with, she wasn't really lonely. Mrs. Wilcox lived next door and spent most of every day in her flower garden. She enjoyed having the girl come over to help pull weeds and water the flowers, and sometimes she let Esther pick a pretty bouquet to take home to her mother.

One day Mrs. Wilcox stood talking to her other neighbor, Mrs. Bradbury.

"There's something special about Esther," Mrs. Wilcox said fondly. "A lot of other little girls I know wouldn't care to help an old lady in her flower garden. But that Esther—she likes to talk to me and she pulls weeds so carefully. She's polite, too. And so helpful!"

Mrs. Bradbury nodded. "She sounds special, all right," she agreed. "Why don't you find out what the secret is?"

"Perhaps I will!" Mrs. Wilcox said.

The next day when Esther came over to help, Mrs. Wilcox told her what she had said to Mrs. Bradbury. "And we were wondering what it is that makes you so careful about your work."

"Oh, I didn't know I was so different!" Esther laughed. "Mother just says that we should do things like Jesus did, and when I work, I pretend that He's right there working beside me. And I do the very best I can."

"Well, I'm sure Jesus *is* beside you, dear," Mrs. Wilcox said. "It's easy to see that you love Jesus. Your mother has probably told you, too, that the Bible says, 'Even a child is known by his actions.'"

"Yes, she has," Esther answered. "Mother said that means that even though I'm just a little girl, people are watching me to see if I really love Jesus or not."

"It shows," Mrs. Wilcox said with a smile as she patted Esther's head. "I can tell you really love Jesus!"

FINISHING THE WEEK

The Bible says, "I was glad when they said unto me, Let us go into the house of the Lord." Psalm 122:1, K.J.V.

CERTAIN things go together. A car wouldn't be any good if it didn't have wheels. And spaghetti wouldn't be much good without sauce, would it? And the week isn't finished until we go to church on Sabbath.

One Sabbath morning Lester woke up with a sore throat. He could hardly speak. When he did, his voice came out raspy and low. It made him cough when he talked.

Mother felt his head. "I'm afraid we'll have to stay home from church today," she said. "You're too sick to go, honey. But Daddy and Janis will go and pick up your Sabbath school papers for you."

Lester nodded. Then he climbed back into bed.

When Daddy and Janis had gone to church, Mother and Lester had their own Sabbath school at home. Mother sang songs while he put up felts on one of the pillows off the couch. Then she read him some stories. But after a while, Lester was tired again and just wanted to sleep.

He went to sleep again after dinner and slept until supper. Then he sat up in a chair while Mother read some more stories. Finally Lester went to bed early, even though he had slept almost all day.

The next day Lester felt much better. But the next week seemed very long!

"I miss my friends," Lester said one afternoon. "I really don't like missing Sabbath school and church. I like to see all my friends and to hear everybody singing together in church."

It was a happy Lester who got to go to church the next Sabbath.

In some countries people are not allowed to go to church. They meet secretly in each other's houses to sing songs and learn about Jesus. Those people would feel lucky to be able to go to church without being afraid of what might happen.

Jesus made the Sabbath for us. It is a special day for families to worship Him. Jesus went to church every Sabbath, and we do too. Enjoy the Sabbath. It is the most special day of all the week.

SOMETIMES I FEEL SAD

The Bible says, "Then [God] turned my sorrow into joy!" Psalm 30:11.

DOWN the sidewalk and over the cracks, Grandpa pushed baby Sara's stroller.

"Hold on!" he would call as they hurried through the spray from a neighbor's sprinkler on the lawn. Sara would laugh and chuckle, as babies like to do.

"You are lucky," Grandpa's friends would tell him as they watched. "She really loves to be with you!"

Sara didn't stay a baby long—babies rarely do. Pretty soon she was a big 5-year-old, and didn't ride in strollers anymore. But now Grandpa was sick. He couldn't have pushed her anymore, anyway. Grandpa had to go places in a wheelchair. But Sara was old enough to push his wheelchair. "Hold on!" she would call as they hurried through the water from a neighbor's sprinkler on the lawn. Grandpa would chuckle and cover his head with his hands.

"You are lucky," his friends would call from their porches. "We don't have anyone to take us for walks. Sara really loves to be with you!"

One day Grandpa wasn't home when Sara came over to take him for a walk. Grandma said they had taken Grandpa to the hospital during the night and he was very, very sick. He was probably going to die.

Sara felt scared. She felt a little bit angry. Why did Grandpa have to die? He couldn't do that to her! He couldn't die! She liked being with him. How could he just die and leave her?

The next day Grandpa did die. Sara wondered if Grandpa would miss her now. She really missed him! Mother said Grandpa didn't have any feelings anymore. He didn't breathe or eat, as he used to. And mother explained it was like the time Sara fell asleep on the couch and woke up the next morning in her own bed. She didn't know she was being moved, and she didn't feel a thing. It would be like that for Grandpa. He was in his hospital bed one day, and the next thing he would know, he would wake up looking at the beautiful face of Jesus. Grandpa didn't hurt anymore.

Sara cried at the funeral. She thought she could never stop crying, and would feel sad for the rest of her life.

Have you ever been sad? Lots of things can make us sad. Jesus knows how it feels to be sad. When His friend Lazarus died, Jesus cried. When we lose our favorite toy, or when it breaks and we have to throw it away, we are sad. But after a while we find something else to play with. When a friend moves away and we have to say Goodbye, we feel sad and lonely. But after a while we make new friends. Saying Goodbye is always hard to do. But after a while the sadness goes away. We might always wish we had that toy or that person with us, but we won't feel like crying forever. After we are sad for a while, we can feel happy again.

PICKLES

The Bible says, " 'For a man's heart determines his speech.' " Matthew 12:34.

"MOMMY, what are pickles made of?" my son David asked me one day. He was picking the pickles out of his sandwich and studying them very carefully.

"Pickles are little cucumbers," I told him.

"Oh. Like the kind we grew in our garden?"

"That very kind!" I nodded. "They just pick when they're small and put them into salty, sour water. After they sit in that special water for many months they become dill pickles."

"But Daddy likes sweet pickles. How come those are sweet? Are they a different kind of cucumber?" David continued.

What do you think? Do you know why some pickles are sour and some are sweet? It really isn't much of a secret: It all depends on what kind of water they soak in.

When people want to make dill pickles, they just put the little cucumbers in salty water with some seasonings. After a while the cucumbers soak up enough of the water so they taste like it.

When people want to make sweet pickles, they put the cucumbers in sweet water with some special seasonings. Any cucumber can become a sweet pickle or a sour pickle—it all depends on what kind of water you place it in.

Children and grown-ups are somewhat like cucumbers. We

can become sweet or sour by how we live. If we read mean books and stories or view mean television programs, we become mean ourselves. That's what our minds think about all the time, so that's how we act.

But if we read good books and listen to kind stories and good music, we will become like the sweet pickles; we will be happy and sweet.

Are there any things you look at or listen to that you think might turn you into a sour person? What do you watch or listen to that makes you sweet and good?

It is important to ask yourself when you're reading a book or listening to music or watching TV what kind of a person it will turn you into. The Bible says that whatever we put into our minds through our eyes and ears will make us act good or bad. Let's try to be sweet pickles instead of sour ones today.

THE PARROT'S SURPRISE

The Bible says, "How forcible are right words!" Job 6:25, K.J.V.

WHEN Daddy came home from work one afternoon, he had an interesting brown box in the back of his car. It was about three feet high and two feet wide, and when he carried it into the house, he set it down carefully. Robbie heard a scratching sound inside.

"What's inside the box?" he asked eagerly, jumping up and down.

"Yeah. What's in there?" his sister Darcy chimed in.

"Just a minute and I'll show you," Daddy said. He laid his coat on a chair and slowly lifted off the top of the box. There inside was a beautiful green parrot in a shiny gold cage.

"He'll learn to say what we say," Daddy said.

"Polly want a cracker?" Darcy asked. But the bird just cocked his head and stared at her with his black, beady eyes.

Every morning at worship, Daddy always asked, "Which day do we go to church, Robbie?"

"On Sabbath," the boy replied. "The seventh day is the Sabbath."

Polly the parrot listened quietly from her perch. She didn't say any words for several weeks. Each day, when the milkman came, he said Hello to Polly, but she just cocked her head and squawked. It was the same with the mailman.

But one day—nobody knows why—when the milkman said Good morning to Polly, she ruffled her feathers, stretched her neck, and squawked, "The Sabbath! The Sabbath! The seventh day is the Sabbath! The Sabbath! The Sabbath! The Sabbath!"

"Strange bird," the milkman said, scratching his head. And he went on his way.

The same thing happened to the mailman. "Hello, Polly!" he said.

Ruffling her feathers, she squawked, "The Sabbath! The Sabbath! The seventh day is the Sabbath! The Sabbath! The Sabbath! The Sabbath!"

The mailman shook his head in disbelief.

Every day that week Polly said the same thing when anybody said Hello to her.

Finally the milkman started reading his Bible to see if Polly knew what she was talking about. The mailman asked his preacher. And they both discovered that the seventh day really *is* the Sabbath, and that it was the day on which Jesus went to church. Pretty soon both the milkman and his family and the mailman and his family began going to church on Sabbath with Robbie and Darcy's family. And all because of a parrot.

We never know who's listening to what we say, do we? And we never know what effect our words are going to have on others. Let's be careful to say only good, helpful words today.

FEET ARE BEAUTIFUL

The Bible says, "How beautiful . . . are the feet of those who bring good news." Isaiah 52:7, N.I.V.

LOOK at your feet. Can you wiggle your toes? Can you point them up? And down? And in toward each other? Or move them round and round? Feet are wonderful things, aren't they? Why, if we didn't have feet, we couldn't pump our swing, or run and jump, or kick a ball, or any of those fun things. With feet we can tiptoe up behind someone and say "Boo!" Or we can run quickly to the door to welcome Mommy or Daddy with a big hug and a kiss.

One day I sat in my living room folding clothes while my two boys played outside. All at once I heard someone running as fast as he could up the driveway. Before I could get to the door, it had opened and there stood David, breathing real hard. His face was red, and the hair around his ears was wet with sweat.

"What's wrong?" I asked quickly.

"Marc's hurt," he said. "He needs you—fast!"

Well, how do you suppose my feet went then? They ran! Around the corner to the place where Marc had fallen from his bike and scraped his knee really badly. I helped him up, and then our feet walked slowly home.

You can tell a lot about how someone is feeling by watching the way he walks.

How do you walk when you are sad? You move quite slowly, don't you? And when you are afraid? Have you ever gone up to the big platform at church to sing for the grown-ups? How did you walk? When I was a little girl, I felt shy up there in front of everybody. Sometimes I would be so shy that I would stumble, and then I'd giggle. My shoulders would curl up around my ears, and I would look down at my shoes. Have you ever done that?

Feet can run quickly to get help, and they can tiptoe softly in church. Our feet can take us away from things we should not do or places we should not go. They can keep us out of danger.

But do you know one of the nicest things our feet can do? They can run up to people so we can put our arms around them, hug them real tightly, and say, "I love you!" That's good news! The Bible says that feet that bring good news are beautiful. Make your feet beautiful today.

SOMETIMES I THINK
I'M A BAD PERSON

The Bible says, "When I want to do good, I don't; and when I try not to do wrong, I do it anyway." Romans 7:19.

" '...AND Bobby never told another lie again,' " Mother read, closing the book. "OK, now, it's time for bed."

Philip moved slowly in his chair. "Mommy," he said hesitantly. "Did Bobby really never tell another lie again in his whole life?" he asked.

"I don't know," Mother said. "The story says so, doesn't it?"

"Yeah. But how come I can't stop doing things that are wrong, like Bobby did? I don't want to tell lies either, but sometimes they just come out! Is something wrong with me? Sometimes I think I'm just a bad person."

"No," Mother said with a smile. "There's not a thing wrong with you, and you are not a bad person. Just the fact that you aren't proud of lying shows that you are a good person. My guess is that the Bobby in this story may have told another lie again sometime in his life, but the storyteller just didn't know about it. Or maybe telling lies was easy for him to stop doing, but he did other things that were wrong over and over again. That doesn't make them right to do, but God understands how we are."

"I always say I'm sorry, and I usually tell the person the truth after a while," Philip continued, "so does God forgive me each time?"

"I'm sure He does," Mother assured him with a hug. "The Bible says that Paul, the man who preached for God and was specially called by God, had the same problem you and all of us have. Paul didn't want to do bad things, but he found himself doing them anyway—just as we do.

"You don't want to fight with your brother, but sometimes you reach out and punch him anyway, don't you?"

Philip nodded.

"But each time you apologize for lying, and each time you want to punch your brother but don't, makes it easier to stop doing it. And you'll find, as you get older, that you'll feel like punching your brother less and less if you start working on it now."

"I wish I could make God proud of me, as He was of King David," Philip said.

"God *is* proud of you, honey," said Mother. "And did you know that even King David had a hard time doing right things *all* the time? But God loved him. And He loves you, no matter what you do. We don't try to do kind things to make Jesus love us—He already does that! We want to be kind and honest because we want to be like Jesus."

The boy nodded. "Sometimes it seems like nobody else does bad things as much as I do, and I'm the only one who can't stop," he said.

"No," Mother assured him. "You're not the only one. Even mommies and daddies and grown-ups make mistakes and do things they know they shouldn't. Jesus is the only person in the world who has never done wrong. He can help us be kind and honest more often than we are unkind. Just ask for His help. He knows how you feel."

TODAY I FEEL LIKE DOING RIGHT

The Bible says, "Cling tightly to your faith in Christ and always keep your conscience clear, doing what you know is right." 1 Timothy 1:19.

IT was a rainy afternoon. Mother had said Leanne could play at Cindy's house for one hour. Leanne thought it would be fun to play dolls, so she took her dolls for a walk to Cindy's house next door. She knocked on the door and was invited inside to play.

"I brought my dolls," Leanne told her friend as she stepped inside and slipped off her raincoat. "Let's play house."

"Well, I was going to watch some cartoons," Cindy said. "I don't feel like playing dolls right now."

"Oh, please," Leanne pleaded. "I don't want to watch some old cartoons! I want to play dolls."

"Well, you play dolls then, but I'm watching cartoons!" Cindy turned on the TV and flopped into the nearest chair.

Leanne hesitated. Her parents didn't want her to watch cartoons because they said the programs had so much hurting and meanness in them. Mother had watched one with her once and showed her how unreal the cartoons are. It had shown somebody falling off a cliff. And instead of getting killed or hurt really bad, that person just made a hole in the dirt by falling and then climbed back out. Her mother explained that when children watch such things, they may start thinking that nobody is really going to get hurt if they punch him or knock him down, or push him in front of a moving car. They might really do those things sometime and actually hurt somebody.

So Leanne knew that she shouldn't watch cartoons, because she didn't want to put bad things into her mind. But she didn't want Cindy to laugh at her, either. And she didn't want to just go home again. Of course, she thought, Mother would never know that she had watched cartoons if she didn't tell her.

So Leanne sat down. "I guess I'll watch a little," she said. But she didn't feel right inside. She knew she was doing something her parents didn't want her to do. Suddenly *she* didn't want to do it, either. For her, it was wrong. Leanne stood up. "I'm going home, Cindy," she said. "I don't really enjoy cartoons."

"Well, 'bye then," Cindy said. The girl didn't even go to the door with her.

Leanne ran home as quickly as she could.

"Back already!" Mother said, surprised, as Leanne hurried inside.

"Yeah. Cindy's just watching cartoons, and I didn't want to stay. I don't want to waste my time on them."

"I'm proud of you, honey," Mother said as she gave her a hug.

"I'm kind of happy, too," Leanne said with a big smile. "I know I did the right thing."

Next time your friends do something you know is wrong, what will you do?

ABOUT SMILING

The Bible says, "[God] confused them by giving them many languages." Genesis 11:9.

IF I said, "Ich liebe dich," would you know what I mean? How about if I said, "Magay nama Nancy"? Do you know what "Abierto" means? You probably don't know any of those. They are words from three languages. The first one says, "I love you," in German. The next one says, "My name is Nancy," in a language called "Sinhalese" that they speak in Sri Lanka. And the last one says, "Open," in Spanish. Who made the languages? How can you be friends with someone who doesn't understand what you say?

John was a new member of Sandy's Sabbath school. A little Vietnamese boy, he had a ready smile and thick, black hair. He had just come to America a short time before, so he didn't know English very well, but he could certainly smile.

One day in Sabbath school, the teacher asked John to say their prayer for them. She said he could pray in his own language.

John's prayer sounded like nonsense sounds to Sandy. She wondered if God knew what he was saying.

"Does God understand other languages?" she asked her mother at dinner that day.

"Yes, He knows every language," Mother said.

"But how?"

"Well, long ago after the Flood, Noah's grandchildren began to worry that God would send another flood. They didn't believe His promise of never flooding the whole earth again. So someone had the idea to build a tower up to heaven so they could just climb up it and get into heaven if another flood came.

"God was sad. He didn't want them wasting their time building that tower, since no one can build a tower to heaven, so He did the best thing to stop their work. He just confused their language.

"One day, perhaps, someone asked for a *rinata*. His friend didn't know what it was, so what he brought was the wrong thing. Pretty soon nobody was able to work on the tower anymore. You can't work if no one brings you what you need! All the people who could understand one another went to one

93

place to live, and all the other people who could understand a different language went somewhere else, until everyone, with his family, was spread out in different countries. That's how languages started."

"So God made them all up?" Sandy asked.

"Yes." Mother nodded. "God even understands the deaf people who don't use words but speak with their hands."

"What if I don't know someone else's language?" Sandy asked. "Like John. How can I be his friend?"

"There's one thing that everyone understands," Mother said. "Even if you can't speak their language, everyone understands a smile. Everyone smiles in the same language."

HAPPY HEARTS; HAPPY HOMES

The Bible says, "Serve the Lord with gladness." Psalm 100:2, N.I.V.

BARRY and Linden had to clean their room. With sour faces they slouched in to do what Mother had asked.

First Barry threw his red pickup truck into the toy box. His pajamas were on the floor, where he had dropped them when he had dressed that morning. He picked them up and stuffed them into a drawer without folding them neatly.

"I hate cleaning up this old room," he muttered as he bumped into Linden on purpose, making him fall down.

His brother started to cry.

"Oh, I'm sorry!" Barry mumbled as he helped Linden get up again. "But you were in my way. And you're not helping clean up this room very much!"

"Well, I'm picking up just *my* stuff!" Linden said. "And you can clean yours!"

"But some of it belongs to both of us!" Barry shouted.

"Well, I'm not doing it!" Linden declared. Before too long the boys were shouting angrily at each other. Their room was not getting cleaned up at all.

Then Daddy walked down to their room. "Well, well," he said. "You must be discussing something pretty important if it makes you talk that loudly!"

"Linden won't help me clean up the room!" Barry yelled.

"I'm cleaning up just *my* stuff!" Linden shouted back.

Daddy raised his hands to silence the boys. He sat down on the floor. "Barry, would you get my Bible for me, please?" he asked. "I want to read you something that King David wrote."

With a frown, Barry left the room and returned with the Bible. Quickly Daddy leafed through it and pointed to a verse. "Here it is in Psalm 100," he said. " 'Serve the Lord with gladness.' " He closed the Bible. "How are we to serve the Lord?" he asked, as though he had forgotten already.

"With gladness," Barry said quietly. "But we're cleaning our room—not serving the Lord!"

"Yes, you *are* serving the Lord," Daddy explained, "because serving the Lord means doing what He wants you to do. He wants you to have a neat room. But I'm afraid you didn't serve God with gladness this evening. Jesus and the angels don't like to hear fighting and fussing. They're much happier to be with us when we are smiling and helpful. And we're happier, too."

"I'm sorry," Barry said, and Linden agreed.

Everyone wants a happy home. But we can't have a happy home if we choose to fight. Your home will be as happy as the people who live in it. Are you making it happy?

THE DOLPHIN THAT LOVED CHILDREN

The Bible says, "There are three things that remain—faith, hope, and love—and the greatest of these is love." 1 Corinthians 13:13.

DO you like dolphins? Have you seen them do tricks at a sea show? Would you like to have one for a pet? I know of someone who had a dolphin for a pet.

It was in 1955, when your parents were babies or maybe not even born yet, that a 13-year-old girl named Joy Baker made friends with a dolphin. Joy lived in Australia, and her house was near the ocean. Every day after school, she and her friends would meet at the beach to play in the water and jump the waves and do all the other things that people like to do at the beach.

She and her friends didn't know it, but as they were playing, a dolphin was watching them from out in the ocean. He saw them tossing a ball back and forth and splashing one another, and he must have thought it looked like fun.

One day someone tossed the ball farther out into the water than Joy could swim.

"Oh, no!" she cried, "now we'll never get it—unless the waves bring it in."

"They will," her friend replied. "Look how they bring drift-wood up to the beach."

"Yes, but my ball could be miles down the beach before it comes back!" Joy stared after her ball bobbing on the waves. It was too far out for her to go after it safely.

All of a sudden the ball seemed to jump! It came flying over the waves and landed close to Joy, who just stared at it with her mouth open. She looked back at the spot where the ball had come from, and there she saw a dolphin nodding its head and squeaking a funny sort of laugh.

Joy tossed the ball out to the dolphin, and he threw it back to her. She named him Opo and played with him every day. Opo soon learned to play tag and ring-around-the-dolphin, and sometimes he even gave her rides on his back! He enjoyed being with her and her friends, and he did things for them because he loved them.

Who is somebody you love? Have you done something for him today to show you love him? Love does things. Love picks up your toys so Mother doesn't have to. It helps clear the dishes after meals. Love brings someone a drink of water if he is hot and thirsty. Love puts an arm around someone if they are crying and says, "I'm so sorry." Love is kind to animals and remembers that they have feelings, too. Love doesn't demand its own way. It tries to make other people happy. See how many people you can love today.

TODAY I FEEL LIKE DISOBEYING

The Bible says, "Young man, obey your father and your mother." Proverbs 6:20.

TIMMY was visiting his grandparents at their house in the country. How he loved exploring the woods, climbing trees, and floating little leaf boats in the creek.

"Just be sure you don't cross the creek," Father had said that morning. "Grandpa hasn't cleared that land yet, and you might get hurt."

So Timmy stayed on his side of the creek most of the morning and had a really good time. But then he spotted some fat and shiny, juicy-looking blueberries on the other side of the creek. "I'll bet I could cross the creek there and eat just a few without getting hurt," Timmy muttered to himself. "I don't see anything that could hurt me."

Even as he crossed the creek Timmy wondered why Father had told him not to go. "Probably doesn't trust me to take care of myself!" he said to himself.

The berries were delicious. Timmy ate one right after another and pressed into the bushes to get the biggest ones.

But after a while his ankles began to burn. And then his arms and legs started hurting. When he looked down he saw red welts forming on his legs where he had scratched himself. Oh, how it hurt! He thought he was on fire from the pain.

Quickly Timmy dashed back into the creek and tried to stop the pain by standing in the cool water, but it didn't help. At last he ran back to Grandma's house.

Mother knew immediately what was wrong. Timmy had brushed against some stinging nettle in the blueberry bushes. "That's why Father didn't want you going across the creek," she said. "If you had obeyed, you wouldn't be hurting now."

"I'm sorry!" Timmy cried, as Mother hugged him real tight.

"You're forgiven," Mother said. "But you still hurt, don't you? That makes me sad too."

Some children think that obeying means not having any fun. That's not true! If parents let us do anything we wanted, we might get hurt. Would it be kind if our parents let us crawl into the lion's cage at the zoo just because we wanted to?

Would it show they loved their baby if they let him burn his mouth on hot food just because he pointed to it? Sometimes they have to say No. When they do, it's because they love us. That's how God is, too.

WHO OWNS YOUR CHURCH?

The Bible says, " 'Keep my Sabbath laws and reverence my Tabernacle, for I am the Lord.' " Leviticus 19:30.

ONE Sabbath morning my son David asked me why the pastor always calls for money. "Why do we have to give an offering?" he asked. "Can't the pastor himself take care of his church?"

What do you think? Do you know why we give money in church? I'll tell you why: Some of the money goes to help build schools or pay for children to go to school. Sometimes the money buys Sabbath magazines for people or for special religious programs on TV. We give money for these things because we want other people to know about Jesus.

But sometimes the money pays for the things we use in church. Your church does not belong to your pastor—it belongs to you. It is a special house for God that you are responsible for. Every Sabbath your pastor preaches there to remind you about how much God loves you. And some of the tithe your parents give goes to the pastor so he can buy food and clothes and a car for his family. But he works for you. And some of your offering provides the electricity that makes the lights turn on while you are at church. Your offering helps buy the water you drink and wash your hands in, the hymnals, the benches you sit on, the carpet, and the piano and organ. Your church doesn't belong to your pastor—it belongs to you. You want to keep it nice because it's your gift to God. It shows that you think He is special.

How do you help your parents take care of the nice furniture in your house? Do you jump on it? Do you stand on it with dirty shoes? Do you bite on the wood and make marks in it? You are very careful with special things, aren't you? So you are careful with everything in church, too.

Some children don't have a special church building. But if they have church at home, then their home becomes extra-special while it's churchtime. They don't talk when they shouldn't; they sit quietly and remember that God and Jesus and all Their angels are really there too.

Have you ever visited someone very important? One time some children were visiting the President of the United States. They didn't run down the halls, but walked softly. Nor did they yell and shout to one another. Instead, they whispered quietly. When the President was talking to them, they listened quietly and didn't wiggle and squirm the whole time.

We are lucky. We get to visit with someone much more important than the President every week. Each one of us visits with a king—King Jesus—every Sabbath!

What do you do to sit quietly in church? Some children look at picture books. Sometimes they put Sabbath puzzles together or play with felts. One little boy I know puts animal stickers on pretty paper every time the preacher says "Jesus." It helps him to listen.

Church is special. God is special. By going to church and being quiet and reverent, we show God just how special we think He is.

BEING YELLED AT

The Bible says, "A cheerful heart does good like medicine, but a broken spirit makes one sick." Proverbs 17:22.

GERALD is a good boy. His parents tell him so. But sometimes he forgets things, just as everybody does.

One day Gerald rode his bike past Mrs. Crandall's house. As he went past he rang and rang the bell on his bike and shouted across the street to one of his friends.

Mrs. Crandall came running out of her house. "Come here, Gerald," she called sternly from her driveway, holding her hands on her hips in a way that made him nervous. She looked angry!

Instantly Gerald stopped riding and walked his bike toward

her. Scared, he felt like crying and racing home. But he was a good boy, so he went up to talk to Mrs. Crandall.

"I told you not to ring your bell or shout when you ride by my house," she said angrily. "I have a sick baby at my house, and I don't want him to wake up! If you can't be quiet, I'm going to have to talk to your mother. Can you remember that?"

He nodded. "I'm sorry," he said, as he turned and rode away. How do you suppose he felt now? What would you have done?

When he got home he told his mother what had happened and what Mrs. Crandall had said. Mother put her arms around him and told him he was a good boy. She said maybe Mrs. Crandall shouted at him because she was so worried about her own son. Sometimes people yell or frown at us because something else is bothering them. Even so, being yelled at is scary, isn't it? Even if you didn't do anything wrong. But especially if you did.

When you're upset your stomach gets all red and sore inside. But it isn't good to stay hurt and angry. It's better to talk with a friend or a parent about how you feel. Then you'll feel better. When you're happy your stomach changes back into a nice healthy pink again.

Some people like to be alone when they're feeling bad after someone yells at them. Others feel so sick to their stomach that they don't want to eat.

Everyone hurts when he gets yelled at. Bad feelings come to everyone. But such feelings go away, too. After a while, if you have talked with somebody and maybe even cried a little, your hurt feelings will vanish, and you will feel like playing again.

WHAT GOT INTO "STAR"?

The Bible says, "Thou understandest my thought afar off." Psalm 139:2, K.J.V.

WITH two fingers Melissa lifted a heavy gray sleeve of the coat Uncle Adam had given Mother and sighed. "It's a man's coat," she said, "and it's heavy. How will you ever make a coat out of it for me?"

"Little girls wear gray coats," Mother said. "You'll be nice and warm. We'll even put a fur collar on it for you, and nobody will ever guess that it used to be Uncle Adam's!"

As Melissa watched her new coat taking shape she began to get excited about it. It really did look lovely, and she could hardly wait for winter to come so she could wear it. Until then, Melissa kept busy riding Star, the colt that Uncle Adam had given her for a birthday present. Star was a calm and gentle horse, one of Uncle Adam's best—just right for a young girl.

At last the day came when it was cold enough for Melissa to wear her new coat. It felt warm and snug and not too heavy, after all. Melissa followed her father out to the barn to see if Star was warm enough, too.

As soon as she walked into the barn she knew something was wrong. Star became very restless. He started stamping his feet and blowing into his feed bin. When Melissa put out her hand to stroke his neck and calm him down, the horse knocked her arm away with his head and tried to bite her.

"Daddy!" Melissa cried. "What's the matter with Star?"

But Daddy didn't know. "He looks upset for some reason," he said. "Better go into the house. I'll be there in a minute."

Daddy watched Star carefully as Melissa left the barn. As soon as she had gone, the colt shook himself all over and started quietly nibbling his feed. When Daddy walked over to pet him, Star looked at him calmly as he chewed.

"I can't understand it," Daddy told Mother as he came into the kitchen. "As soon as Melissa left, Star became calm and gentle again, as he was yesterday. But while she was in there, he was wild! I don't know what's the matter with him. But I won't let her ride him if he's going to be mean."

After breakfast Melissa went out to the barn with Daddy again, all bundled up in her new coat, and Star acted wild again.

Daddy called Uncle Adam on the phone and asked him to come take a look at Star. "He's your horse. You know him better than we do," Daddy said. "Maybe you can figure out what's wrong."

Daddy and Uncle Adam went out to the barn together. Star looked at them quietly and calmly. Then Melissa walked into the barn, and the colt began snorting and stamping the ground.

Uncle Adam looked at Melissa, then back at Star. Then he stared at Melissa again for several minutes. "Is that the coat your mother made from mine?" he asked suddenly, as he started to laugh.

Melissa nodded.

"That's it! It's the coat! I always gave Star a treat of sugar cubes whenever I wore that coat into the barn. He's not mean—he just expects sugar cubes!"

Sometimes people don't always understand why we do the things we do. They sometimes get mad at us, and we don't know why. But even though *they* may not understand our reasons, we can be sure that God does. He knows all about us, because we are His.

WHAT'S STEALING?

The Bible says, "If anyone is stealing he must stop it." Ephesians 4:28.

WHEN Bobby was playing in his sandbox he found a little dump truck that was all rusty. But it worked. After filling it with sand, he dumped it out, pretending he was building a road. He knew the toy probably belonged to Justin, who lived next door, because the boy had been over to play the day before and had brought several trucks along.

"Finders, keepers!" Bobby thought as he decided not to tell his friend about the truck. "He left it in my yard, so I guess he doesn't want it anymore!"

The next day Bobby was riding his Hot Wheels tricycle down the sidewalk when he saw a little boy playing with a bright-purple beach ball.

"Hey, that's my beach ball!" Bobby said as he got off his tricycle and walked over to the boy.

"Prove it!" the boy said. "I found it lying in the street, so it's mine!"

"It has my name on it," Bobby explained. "Just look on it. You'll see!"

The boy didn't even try to look. He just kept throwing the ball up in the air and catching it. "Well, even if it is yours, you can't have it because it's mine now!" he said, and ran into his house.

Bobby started to cry. He knew that ball was his because he had seen his name on it as the boy threw it up in the air. It was a special ball, too, that his uncle had given to him.

What would you do if you were Bobby?

Bobby pedaled home as fast as he could and told his daddy about the boy.

"Can you talk to him for me, Daddy?" he asked. "He won't give me my ball!"

"I'll go with you in a few minutes," Daddy said. He was working on the car and was all dirty.

While he waited for his father, Bobby went to his sandbox and got the little rusty dump truck. He washed it off and made it look better. Then he took it to Justin.

"Here. I think you left this in my sandbox," Bobby said.

"Oh, thank you!" Justin said. "I wondered where it was! It doesn't look very pretty, but it's one of my favorites. Thanks for bringing it back!"

Bobby smiled. "I know how it is when other people keep your toys," he said. "Finders, keepers is sure an awful rule. I don't think it's fair at all!"

Daddy walked up to Bobby then. "Let's go talk to the neighbor about your ball," he said.

"Do you think he'll give it back?" Bobby asked.

"I don't know about him," Daddy said with a wink. "But I know you would!"

SECRET OF THE ROSES

The Bible says, " 'Give as freely as you have received!' " Matthew 10:8.

MR. Kittleson had the most beautiful rose garden that Jenny had ever seen. He had rows and rows of rose bushes, and so many roses covered each bush that Jenny couldn't count them all. Often Mr. Kittleson gave a bouquet of roses to each of the neighbors at the end of the week, but still his bushes had more and more flowers on them. There never seemed to be an empty spot left from where he had cut a flower.

103

One day Jenny decided to ask him what his secret was. She just had to know!

Slowly she walked down to his house. She watched him for a few minutes as he carefully watered the bushes and did a little digging around each one. Then he glanced up at Jenny as she stood there by the gate.

"Come on in!" he invited, smiling broadly. "The roses are extra sweet today. And you can choose just which one you want."

"Oh, thank you!" Jenny said as she walked into the garden. "I've been wanting to ask you a question, Mr. Kittleson," she began as she bent to smell a dark-red rose. "How come you are able to give so many roses away, but your rose bushes are always full of roses again? Why don't I see an empty spot from where you have cut them?"

Mr. Kittleson smiled. "Good question," he said. "And the answer always makes me smile. You see, I consider my roses to be special presents from God. They are perfect and beautiful, just as God is. The Bible tells us to give or share things with others like God shares His presents with us. And when it comes to plants, do you know what God does?"

"No," Jenny answered. "What does He do?"

"Well, every place that I cut off a rose, God makes more branches with many more roses on them. My plants get bushier and bushier. The more I cut off, the more God gives to me!"

"Does that work for everybody?" Jenny wanted to know.

"It certainly does! Whether a person loves God or not, the more roses he gives away, the more he will receive."

"God sure is nice!" Jenny said in awe.

"He certainly is!" Mr. Kittleson agreed. "You see if it doesn't work for you. The more love and kindness you give away, the more you will receive!"

SOMETIMES I HATE MY SISTER

The Bible says, "For jealousy and selfishness are not God's kind of wisdom." James 3:15.

KAMI thought the new little baby at her house was a big bother. Ever since Mother had gone to the hospital to have the baby she seemed too tired to play with Kami anymore. To her it appeared that all Mother did these days was feed the baby, bathe the baby, cuddle the baby, then feed the baby again, put the baby down for a nap, and take a nap herself. Grandma read stories to Kami while Mother and the baby slept. And Daddy took her to the park when he got home from work. But she wanted to be with Mother! It seemed that maybe Mother didn't love her anymore since she had the baby. She used to spend lots of time with Kami. But now the baby took all her time.

Sometimes Kami wished the baby had never come. Why couldn't it be just Mommy and Daddy and her, as it used to be? At church everyone looked at the baby and not at Kami anymore. Everybody asked her about "the baby" and told her how pretty it was and such stuff. Kami wondered what was so great about the baby, anyway. It couldn't talk or walk, or do anything. All it did was sleep.

One day while Mother was feeding the baby, Kami played on the floor with her toys. She didn't like to watch her mother smiling at the baby and talking to it, but she didn't want to miss being with Mother, either.

"Oh, look, Kami!" Mother said happily. "The baby smiled at me! Come here, honey. Maybe she'll smile at you, too!"

Slowly Kami got up from the floor and stood beside the rocking chair. Mother tried to get the baby to smile again, but the infant just closed her eyes and went back to sleep. Feeling very angry inside, Kami went back to her playing. "Well, then, if Mother thinks her baby is so cute, I'll just keep it awake so it can smile some more at her," Kami said to herself. She began to bang her toys together and make a loud racket. The baby woke up and began crying, and Mother told Kami to go to her room.

Feeling a little bit happy that she had made the baby cry, Kami walked to her room. Now Mother would spend some time with *her.* She had promised to come talk to her in a few minutes.

But when she reached her room, Kami felt bad about what she had done. So when Mother came in she found Kami crying, with her face to the wall.

Mother put her arms around her. "Honey, I know that you think I don't love you anymore since the baby came," she told the girl gently. "But I do love you! No baby can ever take your place. Everything I do for the baby, and all the time I spend with her, is the very same I did for *you* when you were small!"

"But you never get angry at the baby, and you get angry at me!"

"I get angry at the things you do, but I always love you. I don't get angry at what the baby does, because she doesn't know any better. But she'll grow up just as you have, and she'll get her share of spankings then. It won't always be this way. The baby is special, and so are you. She doesn't know much yet. You will need to teach her all the things you know."

Have you ever felt the way Kami did? Everyone does sometimes. Everyone feels jealous now and then. Next time you feel jealous, think about three people who have done special things with you and remember those things. You are special. Lots of people love you very much!

YOU CAN'T HIDE!

The Bible says, "I cannot behold him: . . . but he knoweth the way that I take." Job 23:9, 10, K.J.V.

A SOFT, white bunny hopped across the snow in the forest one day. Every now and then he stopped to listen to something and wriggled his little pink button of a nose in the air. When he stopped I could hardly see him. His fur was the same color as the snow. Then he hopped again. He just seemed to fly right over the snow so fast that I wondered how anything could catch him. If I tried to walk in the snow, I would sink up to my knees in it. But the little rabbit's feet are wide like snowshoes, so he had no problem. Landing with his back feet first every time, he seemed to float on the snow.

Have you ever looked at rabbit footprints? If we didn't know better, we might go in the wrong direction trying to track him. Hunters and trappers know better. They can find the rabbits because they know how to follow their footprints.

Leaving footprints behind can be dangerous to some animals because their enemies can find them and kill them. If they don't leave footprints, they are safer, because their enemies don't know where they are.

Sometimes we think of turkeys as not being very smart. But one kind of wild turkey is, I think, quite intelligent. When this mother turkey lays her eggs, she tries to hide them under a thick bush. And then, when she leaves them for a while to find food, she doesn't walk away from her eggs or babies. Can you guess how she gets away so no one can follow her footprints? The mother turkey *flies* away. If mud or snow is on the ground, she doesn't worry, because she doesn't leave any footprints behind. Nor does she worry about dogs that might sniff their way to her nest, because they can't find her trail when she's in the air.

When we leave muddy footprints on the rug or in the kitchen, Mother can tell where we are, can't she? She just follows the mud.

Sometimes we don't want to leave footprints behind. But other times we're glad we have. If you were lost, your parents would have trouble finding you if you left no footprints. But if they can follow them, they can know where you are.

Remember the rabbit I told you about? I followed his footprints carefully and quietly, and I found his little home. It was under an old log in the woods. He couldn't see me, but I knew where he went because of his footprints.

Jesus knows where we are all the time. He doesn't need snow or mud or footprints to find us. We are never hidden from His kind, loving care. He knows what we're doing every minute—even though we can't see Him! That makes me feel good.

WHEN CINDY WAS LOST

The Bible says, "The policeman is sent by God to help you." Romans 13:4.

IT seemed as though Cindy had been riding her tricycle a long time. She stayed on the sidewalk, for that was what her mother had asked her to do. But the sidewalk never seemed to come to an end. It just curved this way and that way, and turned one corner after another. After a while, she didn't know where she was at all. None of the houses looked familiar to her.

As a tiny tear slipped down her cheek she remembered to pray. She felt all alone. And so lost! But in worship that very morning Mother had read to her from the Bible that Jesus knows everything about us and cares about us. So Cindy prayed. "Dear Jesus," she said, resting her head on the handlebars and closing her eyes, "I've been ever so careful to stay on the sidewalk and look for cars coming out of the driveways as Mommy asked, but now I don't know where I am! And I'm so scared. Can You send an angel to help me get home? Thank You, Jesus. Amen."

After she prayed she felt much better, but she kept her head down and cried, just the same.

All at once she heard a car door open beside her. She looked up and saw a policeman standing beside his police car. "Need some help, young lady?" he asked.

Cindy nodded. "I'm lost," she said. "But I've asked my angel to help me." She paused a minute. "You aren't my angel, are you?"

"No." The policeman chuckled kindly. "But I can help your angel to help you! Why don't you and your tricycle get in the front seat with me, and we'll drive around until you find your neighborhood?"

"Oh, thank you!" the girl said as she stood up to get in the car.

The policeman drove slowly around the block.

"There's my house there!" Cindy said suddenly. "And oh, I almost forgot." She folded her hands quickly and closed her eyes.

"Thank You, Jesus, for sending the policeman to help me. Amen."

ABOUT YOU

The Bible says, "God said, Let us make man in our image" Genesis 1:26, K.J.V.

HAVE you ever made animals or people out of clay? Wouldn't it be fun if you could make them come alive? That's what God did!

One day Chad and his daddy were watching the monkeys in the zoo. The monkeys seemed to have such fun swinging from tree to tree with their tails and long arms.

"Have you ever wished you were a monkey?" Daddy asked with a laugh.

Chad shrugged. "Sometimes, I guess." He solemnly watched the monkeys for several minutes, and then he asked a very serious question. "Daddy," he began, "Mikey's teacher told him that we used to be like monkeys. Is that true?"

"It's not what the Bible says," Daddy told him. "The Bible says that God and Jesus made people to be like Them. I don't know about you, but I don't think God and Jesus look like monkeys, do you?"

"No!" Chad agreed, shaking his head. "Monkeys can't even talk!"

"Monkeys have noses and mouths and arms and legs just as we do," Daddy said, "but the Bible says there's one big difference in how God made us."

"There is?"

Daddy nodded and looked far away as though he were thinking. "If you were drawing two pictures, one of a tree, and one that was supposed to look like you, which picture would you take the most time on?"

"The one that looked like me," his son said quickly.

"That's just what God did," Daddy told him. "When He made the monkeys and other animals, God just spoke and there they were. But when He made Adam, God took His time. The Bible says that God formed Adam out of clay—"

"I like to make animals out of Play-Doh!" Chad said quickly.

"Yes, and that may be close to what God did, except that He had a really big lump of it to work with! I imagine God smiling as He carefully formed a handsome face and made eyes to see, a nose to smell, ears to hear, and a tongue to taste things with. Then He made a body with arms that bent so

109

they could hug, or draw, or help others. Fingers that could do so many things. Strong legs, and feet with toes on the end for balance. When that person, Adam, was exactly as God wanted him to be, God knelt down and gently breathed into his nose the 'breath of life,' and Adam became alive.

"Can you imagine how exciting that must have been for God to see the person He had made come alive and blink his eyes and stand up? Probably Adam opened and closed his hand and watched it. Maybe he wiggled his toes in the grass and laughed. I'm sure he looked around in awe at the beautiful world God had made for him."

Chad smiled as he imagined it too. Then his face sobered. "I wonder why Mikey's teacher told him that people used to be like monkeys."

"Well," Daddy suggested, "maybe Mikey's teacher doesn't believe the Bible. Ever since Satan lied to Eve in the Garden of Eden, he has been lying about God. Satan wants us to think that we are related to monkeys. He doesn't want us to know that God made us special—much more special than monkeys!"

"Well, I believe what the Bible says more than I believe Mikey's teacher," Chad said firmly.

"I do too!" Daddy agreed.

THE DOLL THAT JUMPED

The Bible says, "The lame man will leap up like a deer, and those who could not speak will shout and sing!" Isaiah 35:6.

WHILE helping her daddy clean out the attic one day, Maryanne found an old rag doll that somebody had forgotten, tucked back in one corner. It was limp and dirty, and most of its face had faded away. Much of its yarn hair had rotted, and it smelled like a wet mop. But somehow Maryanne didn't feel right about just throwing it away. Daddy said it would have to be washed before she could play with it, and even then only if Mother said so.

"Where did you find that awful thing?" Mother asked as soon as she saw it. "It looks awful. And it stinks. Please throw it away!"

"But, Mother," Maryanne pleaded. "We can't just throw this baby away! Just because it's dirty doesn't mean we can't keep it. Please? I'll wash it up nice and you can draw another face on it for me, Mother. Please?"

Maryanne's eyes looked so serious that Mother finally agreed. "Well, all right. But first it needs a good bath! Outside!"

Nodding happily, Maryanne ran inside to get the shampoo. Soon the doll smelled nice and clean, and she was eager to get it dry and dressed in some new clothes.

After placing the doll on the back of the woodstove so it could dry slowly, she went upstairs to find a dress and bonnet for it.

Maryanne's big sister, Lynne, came into the house a little while later, sniffing around. "What's that horrid smell?" she asked. "Smells like a gunnysack smoking. And what's this on the stove? . . . Mother!" Lynne screamed. "It's alive!"

Mother hurried into the room to see what was burning. When she saw the doll she nearly froze on the spot. For there on the back of the stove Maryanne's doll was jerking its arms and legs up and down and sideways.

"Maryanne!" Mother called. "Come quickly!" The girl rushed into the room and stopped.

"My doll!" she breathed softly, watching the doll's head flop and jerk as its arms flew up and down. "She's alive!"

"She's not alive," Lynne said, snatching it from the stove. "She's . . . she's . . . " Lynne drew in a long breath. "She's filled with popcorn! I can smell it!"

"Well, if it isn't," Mother said slowly. "I'll take that popcorn out and fill her with rice, instead." She glanced at Maryanne, who was still eyeing the doll with awe.

"That's the only doll I've ever owned that could move itself," the girl said wonderingly. "She was alive."

When Jesus comes, people who are in wheelchairs now and people who can't walk or talk now will be healed. People who were dead He will make alive. It will be much more exciting than if your dolls came to life. Can you imagine how wonderful that is going to be?

SPECIAL TIMES
FOR SPECIAL THINGS

The Bible says, "There is . . . a time to be quiet; a time to speak up." Ecclesiastes 3:1–7.

JASON loved to sing in Sabbath school. He knew almost all the songs and all the words, and he liked to see his teacher smile when she saw him singing.

But teacher didn't always smile. Sometimes she looked at him very seriously, holding her finger to her lips to show him it was time to be quiet. You see, Jason loved to sing so much that sometimes he sang even while the teacher was trying to talk. And then nobody could hear her.

One Sabbath morning after they had sung a few songs, he kept right on singing while the teacher started to talk. He looked over at the little boy beside him and sang right into his face. But even though it was hard to listen, the other boy kept his eyes on the teacher and tried his best to hear her.

Jason did not stop. He was having too much fun. And teacher hadn't asked him to be quiet yet, so he sang song after song.

But then he noticed something. Some of the children were saying something to the teacher, and she was handing out special animal stickers to them.

He stopped singing. "May I have one too?" he asked.

His teacher shook her head. "I'm sorry, Jason, but you didn't answer the question I asked."

"Well, what was it?" he wanted to know. "I can answer it now!"

"No, I'm sorry. The stickers are a special prize for the children who were quiet and listened to what I was saying. But if you are ready to be quiet, you will hear my next question, and if you know the answer you can get another surprise I have for children who listen."

Jason nodded. "I'm through singing," he said.

"Good. You know, the Bible says that there is a time to be quiet and a time to speak up. Two of the times to be quiet are whenever we're in church and whenever someone else is talking. Isn't that right?"

Jason nodded. He'd decided it was sometimes better to listen.

Have you ever hurried home with something very exciting to tell Mother, but she was on the phone? You had to wait until she hung up. It's hard to wait for your turn to talk, but you can wait. That shows you are growing up.

And when your parents are talking to their friends and you want to ask them something, you don't just interrupt, do you? You touch their arm gently and then wait till they finish speaking.

You have many important things to tell your parents. And they like to talk and listen to you. But make sure you choose the right times.

WHY I LOVE JESUS

The Bible says, " 'The greatest love is shown when a person lays down his life for his friends.' " John 15:13.

ELLEN was fast asleep in the middle of the night when loud sirens and bells and people shouting in the street awakened her.

"House on fire! Get out! Get out! House on fire!"

Sitting up in bed, she rubbed her eyes. Whose house was on fire? she wondered. Bright lights outside flashed on and off onto the walls of her room as she ran to the window. Down below in the street were fire trucks and firemen scrambling around to get their hoses connected and spray out the fire. For a moment Ellen watched them. They seemed to be running toward *her* house! And then, as she looked over at the garage, she saw that it was burning. Bright, orange flames curled out through the window on the side.

Ellen's bedroom door was closed. She wanted to run across the hall to see if Mother and Daddy were all right, but she had learned fire safety and knew that if the door was hot, she mustn't open it.

Quickly Ellen rushed to the door and patted it all over. It was too hot. Might be a fire on the other side. She crawled back to the window and shouted to the firemen below.

"Help!" she cried. She waved her arms at them. "I'm up here! Somebody get me down!"

One fireman was already hurrying to her window with his tall ladder. He climbed up to her. Then, putting her on his back, piggy-back style, he carried her down to safety.

"Mommy! Where's Mommy? And Daddy?" Ellen asked the firemen who wrapped her in a blanket. "Have you seen my mommy or daddy?"

"Yes! They've been watching your window. Here they are!" the fireman said as her parents rushed over to her.

"Are you OK?" Mother said as she hugged Ellen close.

Ellen nodded. "I'm OK. But how's Toby? Where's my Toby? My dog?"

"He was a faithful dog," Mother told her gently. "He woke me up by barking, and then he bounded across the hall to your room to get you. But he breathed too much smoke and hot air. He died just outside your door."

"If it weren't for Toby, we would all have died, wouldn't we?" Ellen said soberly a little bit later. She loved him more than ever for what he had done, and now she would miss him terribly.

We love Jesus, too, for what He has done. He died to save us from more than a house fire. Jesus died so we could go to heaven and live forever. It hurt Jesus to have nails put in His hands and feet just as much it would have hurt you. But He did it anyway because He loves us so much and wants us with Him in heaven.

The Bible says that dying for a friend is the most loving thing anybody can do. And that is why I love Jesus so very, very much. Don't you?

114

JUST TWO PUMPKINS

The Bible says, "All that happens to us is working for our good if we love God and are fitting into his plans." Romans 8:28.

"MOTHER!" Linda shouted from the garden. Then she turned to face her little brother Benjamin. "You—you—" She was so angry that she couldn't even think of what to say. "You little pest!" she finally blurted out.

Benjamin was 2. He looked up at her with big, round eyes. He had been enjoying himself picking the pretty yellow flowers he saw in the garden, not knowing that they were special pumpkin flowers that were important to his sister. You see, she was trying to grow some pumpkins. Her father had told her that flowers were necessary if she was to have any.

Mother ran out to the garden. "What's wrong?" she asked, worried.

"Benjamin picked all my pumpkin flowers!" Linda cried. "Now I won't have any pumpkins at all. And it's all Benjamin's fault!"

"Well, let's look," Mother said. "Maybe he missed some flowers that were tucked under the leaves." Carefully, she separated leaves. She found a few yellow flowers that still remained.

"Now I'll have just one or two pumpkins," Linda said with a sigh. She looked down at her brother. "Thanks to you."

Mother took him by the hand and led him back into the house with her.

"I'm going to water the few flowers I have left," Linda said. She had wanted to have lots of pumpkins to sell. But now she would be lucky if she got just one.

Summer passed quickly. Sure enough, Linda didn't have very many pumpkins, but she was surprised by the two that did grow. They were amazing! Every day they seemed to be getting bigger and bigger until they were soon almost as high as her waist!

"I think we should enter your pumpkins in the state fair," Daddy said one day. "They're the biggest ones I have seen in a long time."

"How did they get so big?" she asked.

"Well, when Benjamin picked those flowers the plants

115

couldn't make lots of pumpkins, but they did what they could and used all their energy to make one apiece. If you had had all the pumpkins you wanted, you might have had a lot of them, but they would have been small ones. But, thanks to Benjamin, you grew two huge pumpkins that I think could win a blue ribbon at the fair!"

Linda's eyes shone. "Thanks, Benjamin!" she said as she tousled his hair. "I'm sorry I got mad at you. You did me a favor."

Sometimes we think things are going all wrong. But God can make good things come from anything if we let Him. Trust Him and see.

KEEPING HEAVEN CLEAN

The Bible says, "Wash me, and I will be whiter than snow." Psalm 51:7, N.I.V.

MOTHER was making some pudding as a special treat for supper. Loretta heard the electric mixer and hurried in to help.

"Can I do that?" she asked eagerly, reaching to take the beater from her mother.

"Oh, not with those hands!" Mother said. "They're stained with dirt! Go wash them, and then you may help."

Loretta ran to the bathroom, then hurried back quickly. "Now can I help?" she asked.

"Let me see your hands," Mother said. They were still dirty. "You didn't use soap, did you?"

Her daughter shrugged. "No, I didn't."

"Well, go and use soap and really scrub in between your fingers and everywhere. We don't want dirt in our pudding!"

When Loretta came back this time her hands were clean.

"It really helps to use soap, doesn't it?" Mother said as she handed the beater to Loretta.

The girl nodded. "I didn't realize how dirty my hands were until I saw the soapy suds turn brown. I wouldn't have wanted that dirt in the pudding!"

Would you like to have dirt in your pudding? Me neither!

Jesus is preparing a special treat for those who love Him. We don't want it spoiled by dirt either, do we? Some people will not be allowed into heaven because they would spoil it. What kind of people do you think won't be there? Do you know why? Heaven wouldn't be a very happy place if Jesus let killers and robbers up there, would it? Some people *used* to be killers and robbers but stopped doing those bad things when they started loving Jesus. They will be in heaven. But those people who want to keep on killing and stealing will not get to enter.

I used to think that it wasn't fair that those people wouldn't get to go to heaven. So I asked my daddy why God would keep them out. He said that God gives them the same chances that we have of choosing to love Him and be kind and good, but they don't want to change. God knows that they wouldn't be happy in heaven, so He lets them do what they want to do. He never makes us do anything we don't want to do—He lets us decide.

Have you ever gone to eat at somebody else's house, and they served food that you weren't used to? You didn't know how to eat it, and you didn't feel very comfortable. You felt strange. That's how heaven would be for killers and thieves. They wouldn't be happy there. But we would! So we'll get to go if we love Jesus!

SOMETIMES I FEEL SHY

The Bible says, "Be strong and of a good courage." Joshua 1:6, K.J.V.

SOMEONE you know is funny sometimes and likes to have fun and laugh about funny things. Someone you know is quiet sometimes and likes to think about nature and Jesus. And someone you know is someone other people would like to know, but they won't be able to unless you let them. Do you know who that somebody is? It's you! People want to know you.

Everybody feels shy sometimes. When I was a little girl I used to feel shy when big people would talk to me and tell me how much I had grown, or that they used to change my diapers. I wanted to curl my shoulders up to my ears, and look down at my toes, or run away, I was so shy and embarrassed. I didn't know what to say next.

I used to think that only children felt shy, but as I grew up I learned that sometimes grown-ups feel shy, too. When you grow up, you can't just look down at your feet when you're shy. Grown-ups who feel shy usually just smile and listen quietly.

Sometimes you feel shy, and other times you don't feel quite so bashful, do you? Shyness comes and goes according to whom you're with. That's OK! It's often hard to talk to people you hardly know. What will they say? What will they think about what you say? How will you sound?

One thing everybody likes to hear is something nice about himself. If you have just met someone, and you are feeling shy, and neither of you knows what to say next, try saying something nice about him, or ask him a question.

You can tell him that you like his shoes, or his shirt, or his car, or his glasses. Or you can ask him where he lives and what he likes to do for fun. Then you can tell him what *you* like to do. After the first few words, it becomes easier to talk. And as you grow older you will find that you are shy less often. You will have learned how to talk to people without being so shy.

Remember that everyone likes to hear nice things about themselves, and everyone likes people who say nice things about them. By telling other people you like them, you will make lots of friends.

Friends are presents we give to ourselves. Give yourself a present—share yourself with a friend!

(Adapted from *Today I Feel Loved* by William Coleman.)

ABOUT ASKING

The Bible says, " 'Ask and it will be given to you.' " Luke 11:9, N.I.V.

GARY's neighbors had some brand-new baby puppies. They were tiny, with long, soft brown ears, and he loved to watch them squirm and tumble over one another as they snuggled up to the mother dog.

"I sure would like one of those puppies," he told his daddy one day. "Do you suppose Mrs. Jewett would let me have one?"

"I don't know," Daddy replied. "Why don't you ask her? If she says Yes, then you may."

But Gary was afraid to ask for a puppy. He worried that Mrs. Jewett would say No, and then he would be embarrassed. Or he worried that Mrs. Jewett would say he had to buy a puppy, and it would be too much money. So every day he visited the puppies, but didn't ask for one.

One day Gary noticed that one was missing. He asked Mrs. Jewett about it.

"Oh, I gave that one to my little nephew, Jonathan," the woman said.

Gary nodded. He wanted to ask for a puppy of his own, but he was too afraid. Maybe she was giving them only to her relatives.

That evening he told his daddy that Mrs. Jewett had given one of the puppies away.

"Oh, they must be old enough to leave their mother now," Daddy said. "Did you ask for one?"

"No, I'm too scared," his son said with a shy smile.

"Well, Mrs. Jewett can't know that you want a puppy unless you ask for one," Daddy explained. "Why not ask her tomorrow?"

The next day another puppy was gone. Gary decided he *had* to ask for one today before Mrs. Jewett had given them all away.

"Uh, Mrs. Jewett," he said softly as he stroked a puppy behind the ears. "Could I have this puppy? Or are you going to give it to somebody else?"

"Oh no! You can have him! I didn't know you wanted a

puppy, Gary," she said. "If your parents say you can have him, it's fine with me."

"Really?" Gary laughed. "Well, my dad said I could have one if *you* said I could!"

"Then it's settled! Take that puppy home and love him for me."

And that's just what Gary did.

Suppose he hadn't asked for a puppy. Do you think he would have gotten one from Mrs. Jewett? God always knows what we want, but sometimes people don't. Sometimes we feel like being held and rocked, and we expect our parents just to know. But they don't always know. If you feel sad or lonely or afraid, tell them. Tell them what you need. If you need a hug or a kiss, or a word of encouragement, let them know. They'll be very glad to help you feel better, because they love you.

VOICE IN THE FOREST

The Bible says, " 'Do for others what you want them to do for you.' " Matthew 7:12.

BILLY was visiting his uncle on the farm. There were so many fun things to do that he almost hated to stop playing and come in for meals. But he did, and he always hurried back outside as soon as possible. The farm had trees to climb, an old treehouse with a rope to slide down on, and a tall swing that hung out over a hillside and made Billy feel as though he were really high up in the air when he swung out over it. Then there was the creek—

One day Billy was pretending to be riding a horse along the creek. "Whoa!" he called to his pretend horse as he stopped to take a drink. Then he yelled, "Giddyap!" and was about ready to start riding again. But first he stopped to listen. Someone else had said "Giddyap!" too. Thinking someone was watching him and making fun of him, he crouched beside a large rock.

"What's your name?" Billy yelled.

The other voice replied, " . . . your name?"

"I'm not telling!" Billy called back over the top of the rock.

" . . . not telling!" he heard the other voice answered.

"Go away!" Billy said.

"Go away!"

Angry, Billy yelled, "I'm going to punch you!"

" . . . going to punch you!" the other voice repeated.

Afraid of the other boy, since he didn't know how big or how mean he was, Billy ran back to the house to tell his mother.

"Mother! There's a mean boy over by the creek! Whatever I say, he says. I told him to go away, but he told *me* to go away. I asked him what his name was, and he wouldn't tell me. Then I said I was going to punch him, and he said he was going to do it to me!"

"Was he laughing?" Mother asked.

"No, I didn't hear him laugh. I didn't see him at all. I just heard him."

"But he said the very same things you said?"

"Yes!"

Mother laughed gently. "Billy, that wasn't another little boy; that was your echo. It said only what you said."

"Really?" He felt a little embarrassed.

Mother nodded again. "Echoes are a little bit like people," she said, "because they talk back to us just as we talk to them. I want you to try something. Go back out to the creek and say something nice. Shout it out just as loud as you said the mean words, and see what happens."

Billy ran back to the creek and cupped his hands around his mouth. "Let's be friends!" he yelled. And the little echo replied, " . . . be friends!"

It works with people, too.

(Adapted from *More Little Visits With God* by Allan Hart Jahsmann and Martin P. Simon.)

ABOUT BEING PUNISHED

The Bible says, "For when he punishes you, it proves that he loves you. When he whips you it proves you are really his child." Hebrews 12:6.

JACK looked out between the bars of his jail cell and thought of all the bad things he had done.

First he had started copying his friends' papers at school. Then he began to sneak erasers and pencils from their desks. Nobody ever saw him; nobody ever spanked him; and nobody seemed to care.

As Jack got older he took food from stores. Then he started stealing clothes. Once he got caught, and he had to return the shirt he took. But his parents didn't spank him or punish him in any way. They didn't seem to care.

After Jack grew up and learned to drive a car, he decided he would try to steal somebody's car. So one day when he saw a car parked along the street with the windows rolled down and the keys in it, he just jumped in and drove away.

But the police caught him. Finally they put him in jail. Jack would be there for a long time. Now he thought about all the things he could be doing instead if only he hadn't been bad. But nobody had cared enough to teach him what was wrong to do.

Robbers and killers and mean people all started out as sweet, little babies just as you did. They were cute and lovable, just like you. But their parents didn't teach them what was right and what was wrong. Maybe their parents didn't tell them that they loved them. So they did bad things for attention.

Some children never get spanked or sent to their room, or never have to stand in the corner. They never get punished. But if their parents never help them learn what is right and wrong, they could get in big trouble someday, as Jack did.

Parents who love their children want them to do what is right. Punishment means somebody cares about you. Your parents don't punish visitors, do they? Instead parents punish their children because they love them more than they love visitors.

It is hard for parents to punish their children. Your parents would like to just hug you and let you do whatever you want to do. But they know that if they did that, you would probably grow up to be a selfish, unhappy person without many friends. And they want you to be happy.

Would it be kind if parents let their children burn their fingers just because they wanted to touch a hot stove? Would you think your parents loved you if they let you eat some poison just because you wanted to? Even if you really wanted to? Sometimes the most loving thing is for parents to say No.

Your parents love you. You are special to them. That's why they want to teach you to do what is right. Someday, when you're bigger, you'll understand why they said No.

ABOUT WORDS

The Bible says, "Don't use bad language. Say only what is good and helpful to those you are talking to, and what will give them a blessing." Ephesians 4:29.

A LITTLE piece of green lettuce clung to the scoop of cottage cheese on Beverly's plate. "Oh, look!" Tony cried, pointing across the table to the little green thing. "There's a worm on your cottage cheese!"

"Where?" Beverly turned her plate around slowly. When she saw the green thing, she shivered and put her hand up to her mouth. "I can't eat," she said, shoving her plate away from her.

Mother pulled the plate over to her place and looked at the little green thing on the cottage cheese. "Honey, that's just a piece of lettuce," she said gently. "You can finish. It's not a worm!"

"But I have wormy thoughts in my head now," Beverly complained. "Even though you say it's lettuce, I'll think it's a worm."

Poor Beverly! Just one word ruined her whole meal. That's how powerful our words are.

Once I heard a story about a little boy whose big sister always told him he was dumb. She said he couldn't do anything right. And she told him he was ugly and that he would never have any friends. Because she was his big sister, the little boy believed her, and he thought she knew better than he did. So he never tried to learn his memory verse—his sister had said he couldn't. He never smiled at people or tried to make friends—his sister had said nobody would like him. Instead he just stayed at home and played by himself. But he was so lonely!

Finally he was big enough to go to school. His teacher started telling him that he was smart. She said that she liked to be with him and teach him. Sometimes she brought children to his table and said they needed a friend. Pretty soon that little boy discovered that he wasn't dumb after all. And he wasn't ugly, and he wasn't without friends!

That's what can happen when we call other people bad names. Often they believe us, and we make them sad and unhappy. When we talk about sickening things during a meal, we can make somebody go hungry.

Words are very powerful. Try to use words that make other people feel good today, OK? You'll feel good too.

FEELING LAZY

The Bible says, "A lazy fellow has trouble all through life; the good man's path is easy!" Proverbs 15:19.

SOMETIMES I think I'd like to be a kitty. Do you know why? Because kitties sleep so much. They play when they want to, eat when they want to, and then, if they feel like it, they sleep. And sleep. And sleep. Kitties sleep anywhere! In trees, on pillows, under beds, in drawers or closets, on top of cars. One kitty we had always napped on top of one of our truck's tires. We learned to wake him up and move him before we went anywhere.

The days I want to be a kitty are the times when I don't feel like doing anything. Everybody has days when he doesn't want to make up his bed. Everybody has days when he doesn't want to pick up his clothes and straighten his room. And everybody has days when he doesn't want to help anybody with anything. He just wants to sit and rest ... and rest ... and rest.

Sometimes we feel lazy because we're sick. If we're sick, then we *should* rest. We should lie in bed or on the couch and drink lots of water and juice and get lots of rest so our bodies can fight the infection.

Other times we feel lazy because we stayed up too late the night before, or we ate too much sugar, or not enough of the right foods. We need to take care to change that if that is the reason we feel lazy.

But if we're not sick, and we're not tired, and we're just feeling lazy, we need to say No! to laziness. When it is time to get the job done, don't just stand there and stare at it—start humming. Take one thing at a time and put it away without looking at the whole mess and thinking about what a big job it is. By putting away one thing at a time, pretty soon you'll discover that the mess is gone!

You might think you want to be a lazy person, but it's not really all that much fun. Lazy people have trouble all through life. They are often lonely because their homes are always too messy to invite anybody over. Or they are afraid that someone might ask to come inside and would see the mess. Lazy people don't like to go to work, so they don't have much money to buy things or go places with. Instead, lazy people just have to sit around and watch others have fun. You would rather be the one having fun, wouldn't you?

The Bible tells us that Jesus was not lazy. He likes neatness. Scripture says that when Jesus was raised to life from His tomb, He folded His graveclothes neatly and laid them on the table where He had been lying, before He left the tomb. Jesus likes to have things neat. I'm sure you do, too. Don't let laziness win today!

WHY CAN'T WE
SEE THE ANGELS?

The Bible says, " 'Yet I will not be alone, for the Father is with me.' " John 16:32.

HOW can angels be with us when we can't see them? Jeanne wondered to herself as she lay in bed with the covers tucked up to her neck. Her room seemed dark, and she felt so alone. It was nice, in a way, to be alone. She could think about what had happened that day without any interruptions. She didn't have to worry about anybody else. Now she could just think and talk to Jesus without anyone else listening in. Daddy had told her that angels were in the room with her, but how could they be? She couldn't see them. Maybe you wonder that sometimes, too.

Angels aren't the only things that are with us even though we can't see them. Does your mother ever tell you to go wash your hands before you eat? Do you know why? Germs! Germs live everywhere on our skin, even though we can't see them, unless we use a microscope. Some of the germs are friendly ones that we want to keep. But we don't want to eat them! They're supposed to stay outside our bodies! So we wash them off our hands before we eat.

Have you ever seen the water in celery? It moves! We can't see it move unless we color it, but it's moving, nevertheless. Try this experiment sometime: put some food coloring in a glass of water, and then break off the end of a stick of celery and place the broken end in the water. The celery will suck the colored water up and it will have colored streaks in it. Then you will see that the water really does move.

Do your parents have a radio with speakers on each side? Did you know those speakers tremble and move when the music is on? You can't see them move, can you? But they do. Sprinkle a little bit of salt on the tops of the speakers when the music is on. The salt will start to bounce around. The sound waves make the speakers move, but you can't see sound waves, either, can you?

Germs and water moving in celery and sound waves vibrating in the air are things we can't see, but they are there. You just have to know what to do to see them. Angels are there,

126

too. When we get to heaven we'll learn what it takes to see them. Your angel will have all sorts of exciting stories about how he protected you while you lived here on earth—even though you didn't see him!

BUT *WE* WOULD

The Bible says, "For our conscience is clear and we want to keep it that way." Hebrews 13:18.

OF all the things Emily liked to do, going shopping with Mother for new clothes was her favorite. Mother always looked at the racks that had the lowest prices first, and then if she didn't find anything there, she would look at the more expensive things.

One day Emily spotted a beautiful, soft sweater the color of purple grapes under some things on the sale table. "Oh, Mother! Look!" Emily squealed. "Isn't it beautiful?"

"It is," Mother agreed as she picked it up and started looking for the price tag. "Uh, oh. I don't believe it's on sale, honey. It costs too much money."

"But it was on the sale table!" Emily said. "Can't we ask the lady about it before we put it back? Please?"

"Well, all right," Mother said. "Let's find the things we need, and then when we go to pay for them, we'll ask about the sweater."

Emily busied herself choosing a matching blouse and skirt. Mother found some other things for her, too, and pretty soon they were finished.

Mother asked the saleslady if the sweater was on sale.

"Oh, I'm sorry. Someone must have put that sweater on the sale table when she passed," the woman said. "It's not on sale. It costs $45."

"Well, I'm afraid I can't afford to pay that much for a sweater," Mother said. "But it sure is beautiful, isn't it?"

The saleslady nodded as she quickly folded all the things Mother had bought and stuffed them in crisp, paper bags as Mother wrote out her check.

Emily could hardly wait to get home and try on her new

clothes. She couldn't forget that sweater, though. As soon as the car stopped in the driveway she jumped out and hurried to her room with one of the bags.

She dumped it out on her bed and gasped as the beautiful, grape-colored sweater fell out of the bag.

"Oh, Mommy!" she cried as she hurried down the hall. "You bought it after all. Thank you!"

Mother looked puzzled. "How did that sweater get in our bag?" she asked. "I told the lady I didn't want it. I know I didn't pay for it! We'll have to take it back!"

"But the lady gave it to us, then!" Emily said stubbornly. "We get to keep it because she put it in our sack. She'll never know that we have it!"

"But *we will know,*" Mother said. "I'll take it back this evening."

Many times it might be easy to keep things that aren't ours. Storekeepers may not know if you snitch a grape from the box. They may not know if you slip some gum into your pocket. But *you will know.* And God will know. And you won't feel very good about yourself. Be good to yourself. Be honest!

TODAY I FEEL LIKE LEARNING

The Bible says, "Learn of me." Matthew 11:29, K.J.V.

ALLISON and her parents were driving through the mountains. Many tall trees grew along the road, and when Allison glanced out her window at them, they seemed to zip past.

"Watch out the front window, Allison," Mother suggested. "When I look carefully at the trees, I can see two types of evergreens on this mountain. One kind has bushy pine needles, and the other kind has long, flat ones. Can you see the difference?"

Allison leaned forward and studied the trees. "Oh, yes! I can see the difference, too! Are there any bears in these mountains? And do they sleep under the trees?"

Mother nodded. "Yes, there are bears in these mountains. But it's wintertime now, so they are all sleeping in a special deep sleep called hibernation. You see, God knows that the bears need berries and insects and honey for their food, but that kind of food is just not around in the winter, so God lets the bears sleep until spring."

"But won't the cars wake them up?" Allison asked.

"No. Hibernation is such a deep sleep that nothing wakes the bears. Their bodies become cooler, their hearts don't beat as often. They even breathe less. But once spring comes and the weather gets warmer, that will wake them up—when there are fish in the streams, and berries on the bushes, and lots of insects under the fallen logs."

"God sure takes good care of His animals!" Allison said.

"Yes, He does. And when we study nature and see how He cares about the animals, and how He makes so many kinds of trees and flowers, we are learning about what God is like. He could have made one kind of tree, and one kind of flower, and one kind of animal . . . but He wanted this to be a pretty, exciting world for us to live in."

"God sure went to a lot of work for us," Allison replied.

"And we'll never know all there is to know about nature!" Mother told her. "Even when we're in heaven, we'll be learning about God. There is much to know!"

"The more I know about God, the more I love Him," Allison said.

Don't you?

WHAT GOES IN COMES OUT

The Bible says, "For as he thinketh in his heart, so is he." Proverbs 23:7, K.J.V.

THE wind blew snow flurries around Cory's legs and made his cheeks tingle as he ran outside to play one wintry day. The snow came up almost to his knees, and he felt like an explorer in Alaska as the snow flew out in front of his boots.

"Hey, Denny!" he called to his neighbor who was watching from inside his house. "Come on out and play!" Cory waved and then began making a snowman.

Denny waved back and jumped down from the sofa in front

of the window. Before long he was outside, too, all bundled up like Cory in his coat and hat and mittens and warm boots.

If you have snow where you live, then you know how cold it can make you when you play in it.

The boys played all morning long. Pretty soon their cheeks were pink, and their noses looked like little red cherries. Hard, crusty snow covered their hats and coats and mittens.

"Oooh, my fingers are tingling!" Cory laughed.

"So are mine!" Denny replied.

"I think I'm going to go inside," Cory said as he started for his house. "See you later!" He kicked the snow from his boots and tried to open the front door. Mother was watching at the window and hurried to open the door for him.

"Oh, you're so cold!" she said as she put her hands on his cheeks.

"And you're so warm!" he squealed. "I don't think I'll ever be warm again!"

"Oh, yes, you will," Mother said, stripping off his wet clothes. "Here." Gently she pressed a mug of warm cocoa into his hands. "Just sip it slowly, and it will warm up your insides real fast."

Cory wrapped his hands around the mug. He felt the tingling stop, and soon he could wiggle his fingers as before. Before long he began to feel warm inside, and even his ears felt better.

Now, how do you suppose putting that hot cocoa into his *insides* made Cory feel warm *outside?* Because that's the way God made us. We can't be right outside until we are right inside. It works the same with what we put into our mouths or into our heads. If we read and think about kind, good things, then that is the kind of person we will become. If we drink warm cocoa, we will become warm; if we read and think about Jesus, we will become kind.

WHEN JESUS COMES

The Bible says, "For the Lord himself will come down from heaven with a mighty shout and with the soul-stirring cry of the archangel and the great trumpet-call of God. And the believers who are dead will be the first to rise to meet the Lord." 1 Thessalonians 4:16.

ON a dark night in southern California, several people waited along the beach with buckets and shovels and flashlights. Some of them had shorts on, others just rolled up their jeans, but everybody was barefoot. The waves rolled in and then seemed to whisper "Sh-h-h-h" as they swept back off the sand into the ocean. Higher and higher onto the beach the waves crept, and the people stood silently, watching.

All at once somebody shouted, "There they are!" as his flashlight shone onto something silver, twisting and wriggling on the sand.

More people turned their flashlights onto the sand and saw on the beach a mass of flopping, silver grunion fish waiting to ride a wave into the ocean.

Two weeks before, the mother grunions had come up onto the shore and wiggled their tails into the sand, sticking their heads almost straight up. They laid thousands of eggs, and then they wriggled out of the sand and rode the waves back into the ocean. Now their babies were hatching, some of them seeming to pop right out of the sand headfirst.

They were easy to catch, if they didn't flip out of somebody's hand. The little fish were popping up everywhere, and people raced to scoop them up by the handfuls.

Before long some of the fortunate grunion babies had been washed into the ocean by the waves and were safe. The not-so-fortunate ones were in somebody's bucket, on their way to the freezer.

When Jesus comes to take us to heaven, He is going to raise the dead people from their graves and make them alive again. I can imagine it might look something like the grunions coming out of the sand. People who were buried in the ocean or died at sea will come up out of the water. Those in graves will rise up out of the ground. It will be wonderful to be with our grandmas or grandpas or friends who have died, won't it?

When the grunions started coming out of the sand everybody shouted and was very excited. When Jesus comes, God Himself will shout "Come forth," and angels will blow their trumpets as the people who were dead leave their graves. Even though we are sad when someone we love dies, we can remember that he won't stay dead forever. We will see him again when Jesus comes!

BEING FROWNED AT

The Bible says, "A happy face means a glad heart; a sad face means a breaking heart." Proverbs 15:13.

"HI, Carla!" Vera called from her front porch as Carla walked along on the sidewalk.

Carla looked up at her, then frowned and kept on walking.

"Carla!" Vera called again. But the other girl started running away as fast as she could.

Vera picked up her doll and looked at it. "What's the matter with Carla?" she asked it softly. "What have I done to make her mad at me?" But the doll just continued smiling and said nothing.

Sitting down, Vera began dressing her doll. She thought about the things she and her friend had done together. Vera had had fun with Carla just the day before. She couldn't remember making her angry or hurting her feelings. Vera felt bad that Carla didn't want to be her friend anymore. What have I done to Carla? she wondered.

After a while Mother came out to see what Vera was doing, and Vera told her that Carla had frowned at her.

"Did she tell you why she was frowning?" Mother asked.

Vera shook her head. "She won't talk to me today. I think she's mad at me."

"Maybe she's just sad about her grandpa," Mother suggested. "Carla's grandpa was very sick, and he died last night. I think that could be why she was frowning. She feels bad inside."

"But I didn't say anything about her grandpa!" Vera said defensively.

"Maybe not," Mother said, "but Carla was so sad that she didn't feel like smiling or being friendly."

We feel bad when we want to be friendly and someone else doesn't want to be, don't we? Sometimes other people frown at us or run away from us. But that doesn't always mean that we have done something wrong or made them mad. People frown for many reasons. Many of their reasons have nothing to do with us.

Maybe the person just got yelled at by somebody else and is about to cry. Maybe he didn't get enough sleep last night and feels grumpy. Or maybe he lost something that was very special to him, and he feels sad. It's OK if he frowns at you. He is just showing you how he feels.

Sometimes it's best just to smile at other people and then leave them alone till they're ready to smile back. The people who frown sometimes are the same people who smile when they're happy. Sometimes you can help them be ready to smile sooner by smiling and being friendly, even when they're frowning at you.

It doesn't feel good to be frowned at, especially if you didn't do anything wrong, but it happens to everyone. Everyone gets frowned at sometimes. Even Jesus got frowned at, though He was always good and kind. Being frowned at doesn't mean you're bad.

TODAY I FEEL LIKE HUGGING

The Bible says, "And they brought young children to him, that he should touch them." Mark 10:13, K.J.V.

IF you closed your eyes and your mother put a feather and a crunchy leaf into your hand, could you tell which was which? You could? How? Does one feel soft and smooth, and the other dry and crumbly?

What if you petted a bunny rabbit and a dog with your eyes closed, but nobody told you which one you stroked first? Could you tell just by touching their fur? How?

Try this sometime: Have your mother take a paper bag and put three or four things in it without letting you know what they are. Don't peek while she does it, now! Then reach in without looking and try to discover what she put in there just by how each item feels.

I'm glad Jesus gave us fingers to touch with. I work as a nurse in the part of a hospital where babies are born. All parents do the same thing with their baby as soon as it is born. Your mother and father did it to you, too, I'm sure! All parents reach out their arms to hold their baby. They stroke its tiny nose and soft cheeks and kiss its tiny head. Parents love to touch their baby! But one thing makes them happiest of all. Can you guess what it is? While they are stroking and cuddling their baby they often hold onto its hand ever so gently and stroke its tiny fingers. And usually their baby grabs on to their fingers and squeezes them tightly.

"Look! He's holding onto my finger!" the parents say proudly. It makes them happy to feel their baby touching them, too.

Maybe you have seen a tiny baby. Maybe you have a tiny baby brother or sister. If you put your finger into the baby's hand, he will probably tightly grip your finger. You just see how it makes you smile.

You're not a baby anymore, but your mother and father still like to feel you holding on to their hand. They like to have you hug them with your arms around their neck. And they like to hear you say, "I love you!" Even though you're getting bigger, your mother and father still like to have you sit on their lap or up beside them so they can hug you while they read you stories.

When Jesus was here mommies and daddies brought their children to Jesus so He would touch them. It feels good to be touched. It makes everybody happy when you hug them nicely.

PINCHY SHOES

The Bible says, "Pride goes before destruction and haughtiness before a fall." Proverbs 16:18.

THEY were the most beautiful shoes that Briana had ever seen! Brown, with shiny toes and satin ribbons that twisted and tied around her ankles.

"Oh, Mommy," she exclaimed as she watched the salesman

tie the ribbons, "aren't they beautiful? I want these shoes. Please? I don't even want to look at any others!"

"Walk around in them and see how they feel," Mother suggested.

As Briana started to walk she could feel her toes bumping into the front of the shoes, but she tried not to notice.

"Do they pinch?" the salesman asked.

"Pinch? Oh, no! They're just right!"

"Remember, I have just enough money for one pair of shoes," Mother reminded her. "If your feet get too big for these, I can't buy you another pair until next year."

"Oh, they're fine!" the girl insisted. She was sure they were the most beautiful shoes anybody had ever seen. And she just couldn't wait to wear them to church so all her friends could admire them and tell her how lucky she was to have them.

But Mother was doubtful. She turned to the salesman. "Do you have any in a larger size?" she asked. But all the salesman had in a larger size were some black ones just like Sue-Ann wore. Briana didn't want shoes like Sue-Ann's—she wanted something different so everybody would notice.

"I want these, Mother. They're fine! Really!" the girl declared. For a moment she knew she really should tell Mother that her toes bumped into the front of the shoes, but her desire to have them won out, and she didn't mention it.

Mother paid for the shoes, and Briana carried them home proudly. She just couldn't wait for Sabbath.

It was just as she had hoped. The other girls stood around and admired her shoes and told her how lucky she was. They envied her.

The shoes felt pretty comfortable for the first few Sabbaths, till Briana's feet began to get too big. Then the shoes really started to pinch. Briana found she could hardly stand wearing them unless she was sitting down, so she sat whenever she could. All her friends started laughing at her. She sat down in the hall and on the stairs. Whenever they stopped to talk, Briana would sit down wherever she was.

Finally, she could stand it no longer. She told Mother that her new shoes were really too tight, and that she was sorry she hadn't told the whole truth in the beginning.

"I don't have money for another pair of shoes," Mother said solemnly. "You'll have to wear your tennis shoes to church till next spring when we get some more money from our wheat sales."

Now, instead of having the prettiest shoes in Sabbath school, Briana had the plainest ones. She tried to tuck her feet under her chair. Now she wished that she had those plain black shoes like Sue-Ann's. At least they would fit. And they would have been better than tennis shoes for church.

Sometimes being proud and wanting to show off brings more trouble than it's worth. God wants you to be happy. That's why He tells us not to do that. In the end, being proud makes us unhappy.

TURN ON THE LIGHTS!

The Bible says, "Thy word is a lamp unto my feet, and a light unto my path." Psalm 119:105, K.J.V.

IT was very dark in the cave where Jessica stood holding Mother's hand as tightly as she could. Just a few minutes before, their guide had turned out all the lights. "Do you see how dark it is in a cave before people come in and put up lights?" the man asked.

Jessica nodded. But nobody saw her nod. She couldn't even see her own hand—not even when it touched her face.

For several minutes the group of people stood silent, listening to the roar of an underground waterfall somewhere off in the distance. A superhighway stretched somewhere above them, but they couldn't hear the cars whizzing past.

Soon the guide asked, "Is there anyone who would like to continue the tour without lights?" He laughed.

"Not me!" someone answered.

"Me neither!"

"Turn on the lights!" Jessica shouted with the rest. All at once the lights came on, and she could see again. Now she could see the dangerous drop-offs which she should stay away from, along the cave trail.

"I sure like being able to see!" Jessica told her mother as they walked back to the opening of the cave and daylight. "What if the cave lights hadn't come back on?" she wondered. "How would we have gotten out?"

"It would have been very hard," Mother replied.

Do you get afraid when it's dark all around you? I don't

mind if it's dark when I go to sleep, but I don't like to take walks at night without a flashlight.

Some people who don't know about Jesus are afraid all the time, just as we would be if it were dark all the time. They don't know that Jesus is preparing heaven for them. Such people think that they will just be sad and hungry and unhappy all their lives until they die, and that's all. They don't know that when Jesus comes He will make them alive again and take them to heaven if they love Him. Would you be happy if you were like them?

The Bible says that knowing about Jesus and following what He says to do is like having a light that shines in front of us, behind us, and all around. We can see where we are going, and what we should not do so we don't get hurt.

Right now you are making Jesus very happy by learning about Him. Why not tell somebody else about Jesus too, and about heaven, so they don't have to be sad?

SEAN'S PRAYER

The Bible says, " '[God] sends rain on the just and on the unjust too.' " Matthew 5:45.

IT was so hot that even the rocks seemed thirsty. They looked dry and cracked, and Daddy said something about frying an egg on them. "I'll never get Sean's playhouse finished if it stays hot like this," he said when he came inside that afternoon. "It's just too hot to work."

Not finish his playhouse? Sean turned the problem over in his mind. He could do nothing about the heat. If Daddy said he couldn't work on the playhouse, then that was that. No playhouse until the weather cooled off. But Sean did so want to have it finished by his birthday!

At worship that night Daddy read from his Bible that if we ask anything in God's name, He will do it.

"That's it!" Sean said to himself. "I'll pray for cool weather tomorrow!"

While Daddy prayed for God's blessing and protection on their home, Sean was praying for cool weather.

The sun woke up Sean the next morning. He ran to his window and looked out. Not a cloud was in the sky. It looked as if it was going to be another hot, dry day, like yesterday. No way Daddy could finish the playhouse today, either.

Often that day Sean returned to his room and knelt down by his bed to pray for cool weather. He promised to be obedient and kind if only God would answer his prayer.

Shortly after lunch, Sean felt the air beginning to turn cool. Mother looked out the kitchen window. "Looks like we have a storm coming, Sean. Hurry upstairs and close the bedroom windows, would you? I haven't seen black clouds like those in a long time!"

Sean watched the results of his prayers in quiet fascination. He was becoming a bit worried. This was no ordinary storm! Hailstones as big as walnuts were soon bouncing off the porch and off the car, and Sean's dog came running to the door, yelping.

And then the storm ended as quickly as it had started.

That evening when Daddy came home, he told Sean that the hailstones had melted inside the playhouse, and when the floor dried it would be warped. Some of Daddy's tools had been ruined, too.

Suddenly Sean ran from the room and hurried upstairs. He threw himself down on his bed and cried. His playhouse was ruined, and Daddy's tools, too. What would Daddy do to him when he found out it was all his fault? Sean had just prayed for cool weather, not hail!

Daddy followed him upstairs. He took him on his lap, and Sean told him the whole story in between sobs.

"Why Sean, this hailstorm wasn't your fault!" Daddy assured him. "A hailstorm like this often comes after hot, dry weather such as we've had. God sends rain to all of us, whether we've prayed for it or not. Sometimes, because of the weather, the rain changes to hail. It's just part of nature."

With the back of his hand Sean wiped his eyes. "You aren't angry, then?" he asked.

"No." Daddy shook his head. "The hailstorm wasn't your fault. But next time you pray, remember to pray as Jesus did: Always ask that God will do what is best."

COALS OF FIRE

The Bible says, "Feed your enemy if he is hungry. If he is thirsty give him something to drink and you will be heaping coals of fire on his head.' In other words, he will feel ashamed of himself for what he has done to you." Romans 12:20.

"AND you give me a pain, Elaine!" Susan shouted to her friend as she stomped into the house.

"What's the matter?" Mother asked.

"Elaine won't play with me. And she ripped my doll's best dress on purpose just because she was mad at me. I hate her! I wish she were dead!"

"I heard you shouting at her," Mother said with a frown. "Don't you think you hurt her feelings?"

"I want her to feel bad," Susan said tartly. "She's mean."

"Why don't you put coals of fire on her head?" Mother suggested.

Susan looked up suddenly. "Coals of fire? But I don't really want to hurt her!"

"I don't mean real coals of fire," Mother explained with a smile. "Jesus talked about another kind of fire. He said we shouldn't try to get even with those who hurt us. Instead, we should be kind to them. If someone does something mean to you, don't be mean back—do something nice for him. It will make him feel ashamed of himself for being mean to such a nice person as you, and he will be more sorry than if you put fire on his head."

"But Elaine's mean!" Susan insisted.

"She won't stay mean long if you are nice to her," Mother replied. "It won't be any fun for her to be mean if you are not mean back. Maybe she likes to see you angry. She won't know what to do if you do nice things for her, instead. Try it and see!"

Susan almost smiled. She agreed that it would be kind of fun to surprise Elaine. "Can I give Elaine one of my coloring books?" she asked, and Mother agreed.

After choosing her newest book, Susan picked up her crayons, too. She knocked on Elaine's door and waited.

Soon Elaine came to the door. "Wha' do you want?" she growled angrily.

"I just wanted to give you something," Susan said as sweetly as she could. She held out the coloring book. "You can have it. And maybe we could color together for a while."

Elaine looked down at the coloring book, then up at Susan with a puzzled expression on her face. "Really?" she said, a smile beginning to form at the corners of her mouth.

Susan nodded eagerly.

"All right," Elaine said slowly. "Come in."

After they had colored together for a while, Elaine said, "I'm sorry I tore your doll's dress. Shall we ask my mother to make a new one? Mother always makes new clothes for my dolls. Come on! I'll show you!" Elaine hurried to her room, with Susan following happily behind.

Jesus really does know the best way to be happy, Susan thought to herself with a smile.

THE ANT BOY

The Bible says, "Whatever you do, do well." Ecclesiastes 9:10.

AUGUSTE Forel was 11 years old. Just like all the other boys in his neighborhood, he went to school every morning and came home every afternoon. But when the other boys met in the park to play baseball, he wasn't always with them. Usually he was in his own backyard, squatting down and watching something on the ground very closely.

Auguste studied ants. Hundreds and hundreds of ants lived in his backyard, and he was fascinated in watching them crawl in almost a straight line from one hole to the other. Then, one by one, they would disappear into the hole.

He wondered what they did in those holes. Carefully he scraped away some of the dirt. And there, deep in the dirt, he found the ants' hallways and round rooms. Some had rotten leaves and dead ants, others were filled with motionless ants in white cocoons. They looked sort of like babies in blankets. Auguste noticed that as soon as he scraped away the dirt, special ants he called "nurse ants" hurried to those cocoons and carried them away, one by one, from danger.

Day after day he studied the ants. He discovered that there

140

were big ants and little ones, ants with wings, and black, red, and yellow ants. Each ant had a job to do. And they seemed to do their work without any rest.

One day, when Auguste was pretty familiar with his ants, he noticed that inside the nests of the big black ants were tiny passageways that belonged to little red ants. The little red ants were sneaky. They used their tiny size to get what they needed.

The little red ants would slip into the big black ants' tunnels and snatch away some of the food that the larger ants were storing away. When the big ants would try to stop the tiny red ants, the tiny ones would get together and bite the big ants so hard that they would soon flee. Then the red ants would run with the food into their tiny passageways, where the big ants couldn't follow.

It made Auguste think that even though he was just a little boy—just as the ants were little—he could do things that big people couldn't. He had time to study ants, but the big people didn't. So everything he saw, Auguste wrote down in a book. And when he was older, people listened to what "the Ant Man" had learned about the insects. He soon became famous. Remember, he was only eleven, and he was just studying the ants in his backyard when he started. But he did the very best he could do, and that's how he learned things that even grown-up scientists didn't know. You see how good things happen when we do the very best we can?

TODAY I FEEL LITTLE

The Bible says, " 'And the very hairs of your head are all numbered.' " Matthew 10:30.

"GOD must be a very busy person," Alice said one evening as she and her daddy were walking outside under the stars. "He has all those stars to worry about, and all the people or angels who live there . . . He is so busy, I'll bet He is too busy to take care of me!"

"Oh, why do you think that?" her daddy asked.

"Well, because I'm so little. I'm just a little girl. God probably can't even see me when He looks down here at this earth. Probably I blend in with the dirt and the trees!"

"Oh, I'm sure you're much more important than that, Alice," Daddy said. "How many birds do you think there are in the world?"

"I don't know! Hundreds of thousands! Robbie says he has a whole family of sparrows living in his barn, and there are too many to name, even!"

"That's a lot of sparrows," her father agreed. "Did you know that God sees when even one of those sparrows dies and falls to the ground?"

"He does?"

"He sure does! And He tells us 'Don't worry. You are worth more than many sparrows.' And something more—the Bible says that God knows how many hairs we each have on our head."

"Oh, my! It must take Him a lot of time to count all the hairs on everybody's head!" Alice exclaimed.

"Well, God doesn't have to count them as we would—He just knows everything. He knows all about us, and what we need. And He is very able to take care of us if we want Him to."

"I guess if God knows all about the sparrows and takes care of all of them, He will take care of me, too—especially since I'm bigger and worth more than the sparrows!" Alice said. And her daddy agreed.

EVERYONE MAKES MISTAKES

The Bible says, "A man who refuses to admit his mistakes can never be successful." Proverbs 28:13.

ANITA was riding her bike past her mother's flower beds one day when she lost her balance and fell right into the dirt, landing on Mother's pretty flowers.

Carefully Anita got up and looked at what she had done. The flowers were all crushed and flat where she had fallen, their stems broken and bent at odd angles.

"Oh, no!" she gasped as she held her hand over her mouth. She looked toward the house quickly to see if Mother had seen her. But she saw no sign of her mother at the window. Sooner or later, though, Mother would come outside and would find her beautiful flowers ruined.

"What should I tell her?" Anita wondered. "I could tell her the neighbor's dog got loose and dug up her flowers... No, she knows the dog is too small to make this much damage, and there aren't any dog prints in the dirt.

"I could tell her that Mrs. Baxter backed her car into the flowers and her tires crushed them... No, there aren't any tire prints, either."

She didn't know what to do. "I know!" she said to herself. "I could tell Mother that Johnny fell off his bike and landed on the flowers. Then she would be mad at Johnny and not at me!... But that wouldn't be fair, I guess."

Just then Mother came walking down the sidewalk toward her.

"What's wrong, honey?" she asked. "Why are you standing ... oh, look at my flowers! What happened?"

Anita swallowed hard. "The neighbor's dog... I mean, Mrs. Baxter's car... I mean Johnny..."

"Do you know what happened?" Mother asked again, looking straight at her.

"I'm sorry, Mom. I fell off my bike and landed in your flowers. Are you mad?"

"Not if it was an accident," Mother said as she pulled her toward her and hugged her. "People are more important than things. Everybody makes mistakes, and you did the right thing by telling me the truth and not lying—even if it was hard to do."

Have you ever done something by accident and then were afraid to tell anybody? Everybody makes mistakes. Even grownups! It's usually better to tell what happened right away and apologize than to wait until somebody finds out and gets angry because nobody told him about it. Tell the truth right away at the beginning. Then you'll feel better sooner.

ABOUT MERCY

The Bible says, " 'Happy are the kind and merciful, for they shall be shown mercy.' " Matthew 5:7.

IF somebody found your favorite doll lying in the rain and getting all ruined, you would want them to pick it up, dry it off, and bring it to you, wouldn't you? Or if somebody saw mean children hurting your puppy, you would want that person to help your pet and take care of it, wouldn't you? All of us are special to Jesus. He wants us to take care of each other for Him.

Jesus told a story about a man who was walking along the road when robbers jumped out from behind some bushes and knocked him down. After taking all his money and clothes away from him, they beat him up. Then they left him by the side of the road in a ditch, bleeding and crying in pain. The man couldn't get up because he was hurt so badly. He hoped somebody would walk by and help him.

Soon he heard footsteps. He started calling, "Help! Help! Please help me; I'm hurt!" so the person walking by would stop and take care of him.

But the person just stared at the injured man. He saw how dirty the man was, lying in the ditch. Not wanting to get his nice clothes all dirty, he just walked on down the road.

How do you suppose the wounded man felt? Probably he closed his eyes and waited for someone else to come by.

Pretty soon he heard more footsteps and again pleaded, "Help me! *Please!* Won't somebody help me?"

The man passing by heard the sick man. But he was in a hurry, so he pretended he didn't notice him. He crossed over to the other side of the road and looked straight ahead as he hurried by. Now, how do you think the hurt man felt? Perhaps he thought he would just die there. He must have been getting very cold and thirsty. But nobody seemed to care about him.

Finally the hurt man heard someone else approaching. He called out again, "Help! *Please!* Help me! Have mercy on me!" By now he may have been too weak to even open his eyes. And if so, he was probably surprised to feel somebody touch him gently and hold his head up so he could drink. The nice man washed off the man's cuts and put medicine and bandages on them. Then he wrapped him in a clean, soft blanket, helped him up on his donkey, and gave him a ride into town. There he found a place for the wounded man to stay until he got better, and he paid his own money for the room. Then, once the injured man was taken care of, the nice man went on his way.

Jesus said we are to be like the nice man. We are to show mercy. Mercy means treating others as we would like to be treated. It means not laughing at somebody else when he gets hurt, but helping him. Mercy means being friendly to people who are shy or not talking bad about somebody to others. It means not whispering in front of others without telling them, too. Mercy means treating others the way we would like to be treated. Mercy means taking care of one another for Jesus.

WHO STAYS AWAKE IN THE NIGHT?

The Bible says, "There shall be no night there." Revelation 21:25, K.J.V.

IT was a night just like any other. After supper and worship Marc and David took their showers, put their pajamas on, and went to bed.

Mother sat on David's bed to talk with him for a few minutes as she always did before he went to sleep. Then she sat with Marc for his turn.

"OK, boys, you go right to sleep, now," she said as she started for the door. Then she turned out the light and left. It was dark in the room.

"Witches!" David shrieked. "There's witches in this room!"

"Witches?" Mother said, surprised. "We don't have witches in our house! Why do you think there are witches in your room, David?"

"Because it's dark and I can't see anything!" he told her.

"Well, you have your night-light."

"I can't see it!" David said.

Mother stepped into the room again to check. Sure enough, the night-light had burned out. "I'll get you another one," she said, "and then we'll talk."

As she screwed another bulb into the light socket Mother spoke quietly, "You know, when I go to sleep, I like to think of happy thoughts, because happy thoughts make happy dreams. One of my favorite things to think about is heaven. Did you know that there is no night in heaven?"

"No night?" Marc asked.

"That's right! The Bible says there is no night in heaven. We will always have the light from God's throne. And we'll never get tired, so we won't need the darkness to sleep. Heaven is a present that God has promised us. And every night we sleep down here on this earth brings us one day closer to heaven, where there will be no more night, no more getting hurt, and no more crying. Close your eyes and think about heaven. Before you know it, morning will be here!"

Everybody is afraid sometimes. Many people are scared to go outside in the dark. Nobody wants to get hurt. But all day and all night people are awake to take care of you if you do get hurt. Hospitals always have doctors and nurses there at night, awake and ready to treat people who get sick or hurt. Your town, like every other town, has firemen and policemen who are ready to help keep you safe—even in the middle of the night.

Special animals that sleep in the daytime come out to play in the night. Listen to the night sounds. Nighttime is special.

WHY GOD LOVES YOU

The Bible says, "How great is the love the Father has lavished on us, that we should be called children of God!" 1 John 3:1, N.I.V.

CHUNDRA was a little girl who lived in India. When she was born, her parents had so many other children that they didn't have enough food for her, so they took her to an orphanage to live. She was an orphan.

Do you know what an orphan is? An orphan is someone

who doesn't have a mother or father to care for him. The people in an orphanage do their best to care for the children, but it's not quite like growing up in a family. Sometimes an orphanage does not have enough grown-ups to rock and hug and kiss all the children as much as your parents do with you, so some children there are very lonely.

Chundra was one of those lonely children. You remember she had been in the orphanage since she was a baby. Now she was four years old and wondered if anyone would ever come to adopt her. Oh, how much she wanted to have a mother and a father—maybe even brothers and sisters!

One day the lady at the orphanage received a letter from some people in America, asking for a little girl who was four—Chundra's age.

She quickly sent a letter back to them, enclosing a picture of Chundra and telling them all about her. In a few weeks the girl was on an airplane headed for America and her new home. At last she would have a real family of her own.

When the plane landed in America, Chundra stayed close to the stewardess until she met her new family. They were so happy to see her. Chundra's new mother held out her arms to her and hugged her. Then she showed her some new clothes she had brought for her and pictures of her new home, her brothers, and her very own room with stuffed animals on the bed.

Chundra was shy, but inside she was very happy. She couldn't believe that she had a real family of her own at last—and their house, and food, and toys belonged to her, too! It didn't matter what color her skin was, or what language she spoke, or how she used to live before. These people loved her because she was now their child.

God loves us that way, too. He loves every boy and girl, and every Mommy and Daddy, whether or not they're smart or pretty; nice, or bad; black or white. God loves *you* because you are His child.

TODAY I FEEL LIKE SHOUTING

The Bible says, "But even so, the quiet words of a wise man are better than the shout of a king of fools." Ecclesiastes 9:17.

HAVE you ever been to a baseball game? The batter hits the ball as hard as he can and begins running. He races to first base—the ball is still flying. Second base. Now everybody is shouting. Third base—the people are yelling. The batter runs to home base—a home run! Now all the people are standing, throwing their hats up in the air and shouting and clapping. They're making a lot of happy noise! Oh, it's fun!

We like to yell and shout at baseball games. But once we get into the car and drive home, we don't keep on yelling, do we? When we are inside, it hurts our ears.

A little boy I know was talking to his mother one day. He told her things that he had done with his friends and then asked her a question. She didn't answer right away since she was busy cooking.

"Mommy," he said, "did you hear what I asked you?"

Now, sometimes mommies think while they cook. His mommie was doing just that, and she was thinking so hard that she didn't hear him just then.

The little boy took a deep breath. He puffed up his cheeks till they looked as though they would burst. "Mommy!" he shouted.

Well, that got her attention!

"What, honey?" she asked, startled.

"I said, did you hear what I asked you?"

"No," she said. "What did you want to know?"

Yelling was the only way he knew of to get his mother's attention. Nobody had told him about other ways to get people to notice you when you want to talk to them—ways that are nicer and don't make people angry at you.

Sometimes you can walk up to the person you want to speak to and touch his arm gently while you say his name. If he is talking to somebody else, then you can stand there and wait until he finishes. That is the polite way.

If we don't take our turns talking at home, our homes can sound like noisy restaurants. Or worse, they can sound like baseball games. I don't think we are happy when we hear lots of shouting in our home.

Sometimes children yell because they can't find something. They holler for help from Mother, who is in another part of the house. What would be a better way of getting her to come? By going to where she is and asking for help.

When we shout all the time, people don't like to listen to us. Sometimes they don't want to even be around us. It is better to talk pleasantly and make everybody—even ourselves—happy!

TODAY I FEEL LIKE SINGING

The Bible says, "And when they had sung a hymn, they went out to the Mount of Olives." Matthew 26:30.

IT was a hot, muggy day in summer. Alisa and her mother were going downtown to do some shopping. Since they didn't have a car, they had to ride in the city bus. They had waited a long time for it, and it was so hot in the sun that Alisa was glad when they finally stepped into the bus.

But the bus was so crowded that she and her mother had no place to sit down. They had to stand with all the other people in the middle aisle, holding onto the seats or the straps that hung down from the ceiling. Alisa couldn't reach the straps, so she just clung to her mother. She watched the people sitting in the seats. No one was smiling. They just stared solemnly out the window or straight in front of them. Some looked grouchy. Many of the people in the aisle frowned and shoved each other. It made Alisa afraid.

Alisa did something when she was afraid—she sang. Almost without thinking, she began to sing a song from Sabbath school as she stood there crushed between big people's bodies, and looking right into unhappy faces in the seats.

"Jesus loves the little ones like me, me, me, Jesus loves the little ones like me, me, me. Little ones like me sat upon His knee, Jesus loves the little ones like me, me, me."

As she sang, the grouchy faces turned into smiling ones. People quit shoving to listen to her song. Everyone who could hear Alisa, stopped being mad. Just one little girl in a great big bus had made many people she didn't even know very happy.

Singing makes us happy. The Bible tells us that Jesus sang hymns. Jesus felt scared, sometimes, just as you do. He felt sad and lonely. But He sang when He felt that way, and it made Him feel better.

Have you ever tried singing for your mother or daddy? Try it! Some day when mother is tired and doesn't smile as much as she usually does, try taking your toys where she is and singing some happy Sabbath school songs while you play. Even though you aren't as big as your mother, you can make her do something when you sing. You know what it is? You can make her smile. And when Mother smiles and gives you a hug, the whole house is happier, isn't it?

SOMETIMES I FEEL TIRED

The Bible says, "Then I lay down and slept in peace and woke up safely, for the Lord was watching over me." Psalm 3:5.

DENISE sighed loudly and knocked over the tower of blocks she had made. "I'm just dumb!" she mumbled to herself.

"What's the matter?" Mother asked. She had heard the blocks tumble to the floor and came in to see what was the matter.

"Oh, I can't build a decent tower of blocks. I'm just a dummy."

"I don't think you're dumb," Mother said.

"Well, you just don't know me, then."

"I don't think you're dumb, honey. I think you're just tired," Mother said gently. "Everyone feels grumpy when he's tired. Good boys and girls sometimes act naughty when they're tired."

"But I'm not tired!" Denise shouted. She stood up, then flopped down on her bed and pouted.

"Why don't I get a book, and we'll read together before you go to sleep," Mother said.

"I don't like naps."

"Well, I don't like to see you grumpy. I know that there's a happy Denise in there, and she'll be here after you take a nap."

"But what if I never wake up again?" Denise asked suddenly. "Vicki's grandma went to sleep and never woke up. She died while she was asleep."

"That sometimes happens to old people, or to those who are very, very sick," Mother explained. "But it won't happen to you. Young, healthy boys and girls just don't suddenly die in their sleep. But if they did, there's nothing to be afraid of, because when they woke up, the first thing they would see would be the lovely face of Jesus."

"Oh," Denise said slowly. "That would be nice. Then it doesn't hurt to die? I guess Vicki's grandma is lucky, then."

"If she was sick and couldn't get better, maybe she *was* lucky in a way," Mother agreed. "Now she's not hurting anymore. But we're lucky we can be alive, too. Sometimes playing is so much fun for boys and girls that they get tired. They need to take a little rest so they can enjoy playing again.

"Whenever I find myself getting grumpy, I just lie down for a few minutes if I can, and then I feel happier again. And did you know that you grow the most while you're asleep?"

Denise shook her head. "Read the book, Mommy," she said. She snuggled up against her mother. It was kind of fun to feel sleepy and go to sleep.

If God made us to sleep, it must be good for us. Try taking a rest next time you begin to get grumpy or noisy and rowdy. Pretty soon you'll be your nice, pleasant self again. And that's a sign of growing up smart!

HOW TO LOVE OTHERS

The Bible says, " 'Love your neighbor as yourself.' " Romans 13:9, N.I.V.

HAVE you ever known anyone who was a tattletale? Someone who ran in to his mommy all the time to tell her what you were doing to him? Sometimes it is important to tell your mother what a friend of yours is doing if you think it might be dangerous. But a tattletale is a person who will run in just to say things like "Johnny won't share his trucks!" Or "Billy threw my toy on the ground!" or other things that he and his friend should take care of between themselves.

Once I knew a little tattletale by the name of Beth. That's not her real name, of course. I wouldn't want to use her real name because it might embarrass her, but this little girl we'll call Beth was always running in to tell her mother the little things that her friends were doing that made her angry.

"Mother! Jeremy won't let me swing! Heather isn't sharing her bike with me!" and so on.

One day, when she had been coming in all morning with little stories like that, her mother decided she had to do something about her tattling. She took out a large piece of paper and drew a line down the middle.

"Now," Mother said, "why don't you tell me all the things that you want your friends to do for you."

Beth took a big breath and began her list. Mother wrote each wish down on one side of the paper.

"I want Jeremy to let me swing as long as I want. I want Heather to let me ride her bike as many times as I want to. I don't want Johnny to hit me anymore. I don't want him to pinch me, either. And I want Heather to stop calling me a fatso."

There were many more things that Beth wanted, too, and her mother wrote down each one carefully. When she had finished the list, Beth's mother said, "OK, these are all the things you're going to do for your friends."

"But I thought this list was all the things they would do for me!" the girl said at once.

"The Bible says to love our neighbors—that means everybody else—as we love ourselves," Mother said. "We are to do to them what we want them to do to us. That is called the golden rule. If you treat others as you would like to be treated, I think you'll find that you have lots of friends and won't need to tattle anymore."

Beth tried it. And it worked! Jesus knows what He is talking about!

TODAY I FEEL FRIENDLY

The Bible says, "A man that hath friends must shew himself friendly" Proverbs 18:24, K.J.V.

"HEY, retard, we don't want you playing with us!" the boys called out as Bill Jonas followed them onto the playground.

"Yeah. Go away, dummy!"

Bill dropped his head and scuffed his feet. Finally he stopped and just watched the boys run to the swings. He wasn't dumb; he just didn't do well in school. The boy had a hard time remembering memory verses and poems and numbers and the alphabet and things like that. But for a 9-year-old he could fix bikes and other broken things really well.

His only friend was Fred Markham. Fred never called him names or pushed him around. Bill felt safe with Fred and liked to watch him play basketball and baseball. Fred was 12, and to Bill, he was a hero.

But Fred's friends couldn't understand why he was so friendly with Bill. "He's just a retard," the boys said. "How can you stand having him hanging around all the time?"

"Because I like Bill. He does some neat things that I bet you can't do. Why don't you give him a chance?"

But nobody did. Sometimes even Fred got tired of Bill, and for a few days Bill would leave him alone. But then he always returned. That was OK.

One hot summer day the boys invited Fred to go swimming with them in the river. Bill wanted to go along too, and he asked so many times that finally Fred said he would take him, but he'd better stay away from the edge so he wouldn't get hurt or drown.

The water was nice and cool. The boys played water ball and splashed for a while, then sat on the bank and just talked.

Fred thought he would take one more swim. He jumped in and started swimming. But all at once he had a real bad pain in his stomach. When he yelled for someone to help him, nobody came. Then he heard a ringing in his ears as he went under and he felt sure he was going to drown. Everything seemed black around him, and there was that terrible ringing sound.

The next thing Fred knew, he woke up in a hospital bed. His mother was crying and saying something about his friend who had jumped in and saved his life.

"Who?" Fred whispered.

"Bill Jonas," his dad replied. "The other kids panicked and ran around yelling. Finally, somebody went to call an ambulance. But Bill jumped in and saved your life."

Fred opened his eyes wider. He saw Bill standing by his bed too. "Thanks, pal," he said. "You're a *real* friend."

Why did Bill help his friend Fred? Because Fred had been kind to him.

(Adapted from a story by Fred Markham in *Our Little Friend.*)

TODAY I FEEL LIKE HELPING

The Bible says, "I lie awake at night thinking of you—of how much you have helped me." Psalm 63:6.

DAVY went shopping with his mother. He liked to pretend that he was the owner of the store.

"May I have two cans of tomato soup, please?" his mother said. She pointed to the soup, and Davy picked up two cans and put them in her cart.

"Now, how about six cans of mushroom soup?"

"OK. Mushroom soup coming up," Davy sang out. He put the cans in the cart as carefully as he could. "Will there be anything else, Madam?" he asked.

"Yes, let's go over to the milk department," Mother said. "I need some milk today, too."

Davy lifted two heavy jugs of milk and put them on the bottom section of his mother's shopping cart. Then she showed him how to open a carton of eggs to check for broken ones. They chose one carton that looked perfect.

When they got home Mother went into the house with a large sack of groceries. Davy didn't run right in. Do you know what he did? He met her at the door with one of the jugs of milk in his hands. He was helping. And nobody had asked him to!

"Oh, thank you!" she said as she helped him put it on the kitchen counter. "My, what a big helper you are! I'm fortunate to have you as my little boy!"

Davy grinned and went back to the car for the other milk jug. It made him feel good to help.

Davy's brother Marc liked to help, too. After each meal Marc put his silverware on his plate and carried his dirty dishes into the kitchen to help clean up. Often he liked to set the table, too.

Have you ever tried to surprise your mother by setting the table? When I was a little girl my sister Jeanne, my brother Peter, and I liked to get up before anyone else, early in the morning. We tiptoed down the hall to the kitchen and got out the plates and silverware as quietly as we could. Then we carefully set the table and sneaked back to bed. But we wouldn't go to sleep. It was too exciting! We listened for our mother's happy "Oh, look! Some little elves must have come in and set the table! What a nice surprise!" We knew that she had no doubt it was us, because there are no such things as elves. But it was such a fun game that we did it again and again.

It feels good to help. Maybe you can help your brother and sister pick up their toys today; or make up your bed in the morning without being asked; or bring Daddy his newspaper when he comes home from work. Just see how good it feels to have someone smile at you and say Thank you, then hug you or pat you on the back. God likes to see us help others. He likes us to feel good, too!

TODAY I FEEL HONEST

The Bible says, "The Lord hates cheating and delights in honesty." Proverbs 11:1.

VIRGINIA Roberts will never forget the day she told the truth. It was both the saddest and happiest day of her life.

She was in a contest. A spelling bee. Children from all over had come to see who was the best speller in the state. They had won contests in their own schools, and then in their own cities, and their counties, and now only the ten best spellers competed in this final contest. Virginia hoped she would win. She would get a gold trophy to keep in her room, and her name and picture would appear in the papers and everything. And then she would get to be in a contest to see who was the best speller in America.

One by one, the children stood behind a microphone as the judges gave them one word after another to spell. Many of the words were easy for Virginia. She sounded them out carefully and spelled them slowly. Her hands were wet with nervousness as the first set of words ended.

On the second set, two children had to leave the stage. They couldn't spell their words. Now eight children remained in the contest.

On the third set, one child missed a word.

By the time they got to the ninth set, only two children remained: Virginia and one other little girl.

The judges said the word, "gregarious." The other little girl stood nervously behind the microphone and began spelling the word. She hesitated at one point, but finished the word correctly. Everybody clapped and clapped.

Now it was Virginia's turn. She started to spell her word. When she finished, everybody clapped and clapped and the judges started choosing another word for her to spell.

But Virginia knew something the judges didn't. She had spelled the word wrong. The judges thought they heard her right, but when she turned around and saw the word written on the sign behind her, she knew she had spelled it wrong.

Although Virginia knew what she should do, it was very hard. She wanted that trophy badly, and if she told the judges that she had missed the word, the other little girl would win it, and Virginia wouldn't have a chance. But she knew she had spelled the word wrong. And she knew that every time she looked at her trophy she would remember that it really shouldn't be hers. She knew she wouldn't be happy if she was dishonest.

Virginia walked down to the judges' desk and told them she had missed the word. "I spelled it wrong," she said, "even though it sounded right to you. I was wrong. I'm out of the contest." Then she turned and ran to the bathroom to cry. The other little girl won the trophy.

Virginia Roberts lost the contest, but she got her name in the paper anyway—not for being the best speller, but for being honest. She was happy, and everyone was proud of what she had done.

WHEN ALLISON PRAYED

The Bible says, "Pray for us." Hebrews 13:18.

ALLISON'S daddy was out of a job. He used to have a good job in a car factory. But one day his boss said that very few people were buying the cars they made, so they didn't have to make as many. They didn't need him anymore.

It was fun, at first, to have Daddy around the house all day. He fixed her wagon that had been broken for a while. Now he had time to read more stories to her while Mother was busy with the baby.

But after a while Daddy didn't fix as many things or read her as many stories as he used to. He just sat in his chair and looked through the paper to see if he could find a job. Daddy seemed sad a lot of the time now. He said he was worried.

Allison was worried, too. Daddy told her they couldn't buy her any new clothes or toys right now, and they couldn't drink milk at every meal because they didn't have much money since he didn't have a job. She became afraid that maybe her daddy would give her away since she was costing him money and was eating up the food he bought. So she tried not to eat, but got so hungry she ate anyway. Mother and Daddy told her to eat, but she worried that they were just saying that. Did they wish they had never had her? she wondered.

One day Daddy looked very, very sad. Allison walked by his bedroom door and saw him sitting on the edge of his bed, crying. It made her scared when her daddy cried.

Quickly Allison hurried to her own room. She wanted to do something to help, but she didn't know what to do. Then she thought of something. She could pray!

Dropping to her knees, she prayed, "Please, dear Jesus, please, please help my daddy find a job. Or please help him not to worry. I hate to see him cry! Please, please help daddy. Amen."

Then Allison got up off her knees. There stood her daddy in the doorway. And do you know what? He was smiling.

"Thank you, Allison," he said as he reached down and gave her a hug. "It makes me feel better to hear you praying for me."

"I was worried," Allison said. "I didn't want you to give me away, so I asked God to give you a job."

"We would never give you away, honey!" he told her. "We are a family. We belong together, and we will stay together. We need one another, and we love one another. Don't worry. I'll never give you away. But I sure feel happy to know you are praying for me!"

It's not easy to be a mother or a daddy. Your parents like to hear you pray for them. Tell God how much you love your parents, and ask God to help you show them how much. Ask God to help your parents not to worry. That is the biggest help you can give them.

FIRE!

The Bible says, "Overlook my youthful sins, O Lord! Look at me instead through eyes of mercy and forgiveness, through eyes of everlasting love and kindness." Psalm 25:6, 7.

"MOMMY! Mommy! Oh, Mommy!" Marc and David wailed as they streaked across the empty wheat field in back of our house and into the kitchen where I was working. "Mommy! Help! We started a fire, and we can't get it out. Oh, Mommy! Get the hose! Look!"

I glanced out the back door and saw a small black plume of smoke rising from the middle of the field. Orange tongues of fire licked into the air as it spread rapidly through the dry chaff. It was too far away for the hose to reach.

I called the fire department, grabbed a metal pan to smother the flames, and ran out to the fire. By the time I got there I saw the last of Marc's and David's coats melting in the center of the ring of fire. The little fingers of flame that crawled toward us I covered with the pan and smothered them. By the time the fire truck came bumping through the field toward us, most of the fire was out. But the firemen still sprayed the charred, black ground with their hoses so it wouldn't burst into flame again.

"We'll need the boys' names," one of the firemen told me. "Did they start the fire?"

"Yes," I nodded. "They've been good about not playing with matches. I don't know what made them do it."

"They probably won't do it again," the fireman said with a knowing nod. "I did this once when I was a kid, too. It frightened me so badly that I never wanted to play with matches again."

The man carefully wrote down Marc's and David's names and their address, and said that the fire chief would be over in the next day or two to talk with the boys about what they had done.

How would you feel if the fire chief was going to talk to you?

Marc and David were nervous. They weren't sure what he would do to them. When he came he was very kind, but serious. He told the boys how dangerous it is to play with matches, because fire can kill.

"Everyone has done something wrong sometime," the fire chief said. "Mothers, fathers, doctors, policemen, grandparents — all of us have done something wrong sometime. We understand. The most important thing is not that you never do something wrong, but that you learn a lesson from it and don't do it again. You did the right thing by telling your mother at once when you couldn't put out the fire."

Maybe you have never started a fire or played with matches. That's good! You don't have to do something wrong to learn a lesson. But maybe you have done something else wrong. Maybe you have broken something and then hidden it. Maybe you once took something from Daddy's dresser or Mother's purse. That is wrong if you haven't asked first. It didn't make you feel very good either, did it? The only way to feel good again is to make it right. Tell your parents what you did and say you're sorry. They know you're learning, and they love you. You can't do anything to make your parents stop loving you. And you can't be so bad that *God* will ever stop loving you, either.

TODAY I NEED PROTECTION

The Bible says, "If God is on our side, who can ever be against us?" Romans 8:31.

MANDY's sister, Judy, was at school.

"Now's my chance to play with her little stove set," Mandy thought. "I'll just sneak into her room and play with it so quietly that nobody will know."

Softly she crept into Judy's bedroom. There in the corner sat the stove with its pots and pans and kitchen spoons and things.

She set all the dolls in a circle.

"Now, children," she said, "we'll have breakfast in a minute. You just sit quietly and wait while the cereal finishes cooking." Mandy reached up to get some bowls off the shelf above the stove. The shelf was just a little bit too high, so the bowls slipped and crashed onto the stove.

"Oh!" Mandy gasped. She stared at the stove. One of the falling bowls had broken off a small black knob on the front. Now what'll I do? she thought, near tears. Judy will be mad!

All at once she got an idea. She would get Daddy's special glue from the garage and put the knob back on.

Mandy hurried back to her sister's room with the glue. She smeared some on the stove and the little black knob. Then she pressed the knob onto the place where it went on the stove. It didn't stay—it just slid down the side. Trying again, she put more glue on it. But the knob just wouldn't stick. At last she took the knob to Mother and told her what she had done.

"Can you fix it, Mother?"

Mother tried to glue the piece on, but she couldn't get it to stay either. "I think Daddy is going to have to screw it on," Mother said. "It just won't work to glue it."

Mandy thought about what Judy would say when she came back from school. She would see the broken stove and would be mad. "I just know she won't listen to me when I say I'm sorry," Mandy said. "She'll hit me!"

Mother put her arms around her. "We'll tell her together," Mother said. "As soon as she puts her schoolbooks away I'll go in with you, and we'll tell her what happened. She won't hit

160

you with me there, and I'll explain that Daddy can fix it when he comes home. OK?"

That afternoon Judy listened quietly as Mother told her what had happened and how the glue wouldn't hold. "But Daddy will fix it for you with a screw when he gets home," Mother explained.

"I'm really sorry, Judy," Mandy told her. "I promise not to play with your things again, without asking."

Mandy was glad her mother had been with her when she talked to Judy. With Mother there, her sister didn't hit her and get all mad. God is on our side, too, against the devil. When God is with us, the devil can't do anything to us against God's will.

YOU ARE SMART!

The Bible says, "Teach a wise man, and he will be wiser; teach a good man, and he will learn more." Proverbs 9:9.

TREES and bright-colored cars flashed by the window as we drove on our vacation.

"Isn't there something we can do?" Marc pleaded from the back seat where he sat scrunched in his little corner. Baby Holly's car seat took up the middle of the seat, and Marc's little brother, David, curled up at the other window. There wasn't much extra room, and we had been driving all day long.

While I thought of a game we could play, Marc answered his own question by suggesting that we play a spelling game. He was almost ready for the second grade, and he enjoyed spelling words that I called out. So we did that for several minutes. It kept Marc busy, but still David was bored.

"Let *me* spell one now," David asked, and so I said the word "No." David spelled it perfectly and was pleased with himself.

"OK, spell *car*," Marc challenged him.

"K–R–R," David said with a grin.

"No!" Marc cried jubilantly. "David can't spell an easy word like *car*? I can't believe it!"

"I guess I'm just dumb," David mumbled.

"No, you're not dumb," I said. "You just don't know how to spell lots of words yet, because you haven't been to school. But that doesn't mean you're dumb."

Everyone is smart at something. Being smart means you understand. Do you have a baby brother or sister at your house? Does your baby talk? If he doesn't talk really well, does that mean he is dumb? No! It just means he hasn't learned that yet.

Let's talk about all the things you understand. Do you know how to turn on the radio? Or how to make the sound soft or loud? You must be smart!

Do you know how many wheels a wagon has? Or a motorcycle? You must be smart!

Do you know how to turn the pages in a book, and can you tell if somebody is holding it upside down? Well, then, you must be very smart! Just think about all the things you understand. It doesn't mean you are the smartest person in the world, but nobody expects you to be. Even your mom and dad don't know everything about everything. But they are smart! And the more you learn, the more you understand. As you grow up you will learn about lots more things that you do well.

You are smart! And you can use your mind to learn more about the things in the world, and more about God.

BEING DIFFERENT IS SPECIAL

The Bible says, "See how very much our heavenly Father loves us, for he allows us to be called his children." 1 John 3:1.

THE little white mouse in Stevie's first-grade room was missing. Just that morning one of the children had cleaned the mouse's cage, and while he had the door open the mouse had run out of the cage and now hid somewhere in the room.

Some of the children squealed and stood on their chairs.

"What if he runs up my legs?" one of the little boys giggled, a delighted shiver running up his back.

With everyone laughing or screaming or giggling, it was impossible to hear the mouse if he was scratching somewhere.

"Quiet! Quiet!" the teacher shouted above the noise, clapping her hands to get the children's attention. "We can't hear the mouse with all this racket. We need to have it quiet! Now, I want each of you to sit very still, and we'll see if the mouse will come out. He's probably just as scared of you and your noise as you are of him."

All the children sat as quietly as they could. One little girl swung her feet under her desk, and they hit the floor with a squeak.

"Shh!" the teacher said.

But even after five minutes, the mouse hadn't come out. Where could he be?

Teacher looked across the room at Stevie. He was sitting the quietest of all, his head tilted at a curious angle.

"Can you help us, Stevie?" teacher asked.

Stevie smiled. "Yes, I think I can. If you all can be really quiet for just a little bit, I might be able to find the mouse!"

Nobody moved. Still Stevie sat, his head cocked to one side. Then, all at once, his face broke into a wide, happy smile. "It's in the wastebasket!" he cried. "Look in the wastebasket!"

Teacher lifted some papers from the wastebasket. There in the bottom, crouching very still, was the little white mouse, just as Stevie had said.

How did Stevie know where the mouse was? Stevie Wonder was blind. And since he couldn't learn about the world with his eyes, he had learned to use his ears very well, and he could hear the mouse in the wastebasket when the other children couldn't. Stevie was different from the other kids.

Maybe you, too, are different in some way. Maybe you are blind like Stevie. Or maybe you can't hear soft sounds very well. Maybe you wear glasses. Maybe you have to sit in a wheelchair because your legs will not hold you. Maybe you have some fingers or toes missing.

There are many ways to be different. It's OK to be different. All of us are different in one way or another, and God knows how we are different. He still loves us enough to call us His children.

SILVER PUDDING

The Bible says, "Then Jesus took the loaves and gave thanks to God and passed them out to the people. . . . And everyone ate until full!" John 6:11.

IF somebody told you that you could have anything you wanted for supper tonight, what would you ask for? What would you have to drink? And for dessert?

My children love my spaghetti sauce. And it makes me feel good when they say that nobody can make it like I can. Have you ever taken a bite of spaghetti and had one piece hanging out of your mouth, and then slowly sucked it in? It sort of tickles, doesn't it? It's messy, too. The sauce kind of piles up at the corners of your mouth and maybe drips down if you have a lot on it. It's not very good manners, but sometimes it just happens.

Do you like mashed potatoes? My mother used to make a little well in the top of the potatoes and put a scoop of butter in it. The heat from the potatoes made it melt, and when the first person scooped up his serving, the yellow butter would run down like a little river. She did that with the gravy, too. Do you like to do it?

How do you eat an ice-cream cone? Do you lick all around the edges and then bite off little nibbles of the cone? Or do you bite off chunks of ice cream and cone together?

I like soft chocolate-chip cookies with a glass of cold milk. And I like pizza with so much chewy cheese on it that it pulls out like strings when I take my piece.

Some people like peanut butter on their pancakes. Some prefer just syrup and butter. Other people put applesauce on top of their stack. How do you like yours?

When I was a little girl in Ceylon I went with my parents to a fancy wedding feast. The hosts served dates stuffed with almond-flavored frosting, and little curry puffs and layered sandwiches. But the food I enjoyed eating most was custard with a very thin layer of melted silver on top. It was thinner than the aluminum foil your mother uses in cooking, and it was OK to eat! I remember that it did not have much taste and that it melted in my mouth, but it was fun to eat because it was so different.

God has given us lots of different foods to eat. Sometimes

we don't think we will like something that Mother has fixed, but unless we take a bite, we won't know whether or not we do. It's exciting to try new foods. It shows that you are growing up when you take a taste of something you have never tried before, instead of making a fuss.

Food is good for us. God wants it to taste good. He wants us to enjoy our food and to eat until we're not hungry anymore. Aren't you glad your parents know how to cook the good food that God made?

TODAY I FEEL DISTRUSTFUL

The Bible says, "Heaven and earth will pass away, but my words will never pass away." Matthew 24:35, N.I.V.

IT was Marty's first day at school, and he was very excited. He had a new backpack to carry his schoolbooks and pencils in, and new shoes and jeans—everything was new! And he couldn't wait to make some new friends.

When the teacher showed him to his seat, she placed him beside a boy named Joey.

Marty liked him at first. Whispering to Marty about recess, Joey said that Marty could play with his new yoyo then. Joey promised him lots of things that morning, and then recess came. Marty raced out the door after him, but Joey was too fast. He stayed off in a far corner of the playground with some other boys all during recess and didn't do any of the things with Marty that he had promised.

Finally the first day of school ended and Marty walked outside. Joey ran up to him.

"Wanna come over to my house to play?" Joey asked. "I have a neat racetrack and cars in my room!"

"I'd have to ask my mother first," Marty replied. He wondered if the other boy really did have a racetrack as he said he did.

"I don't live far from here," Joey continued, pulling on his backpack. "Why don't you ask your mom?"

"OK," said Marty. "Why don't you walk with me to my house, and I'll ask my mother if I can come over. Then I can walk with you to your house if she says I can, and I'll know where you live."

"Great! I'll wait for you outside!" Joey said.

Marty hurried inside to talk to his mother. He wasn't gone very long, but when he came back outside, Joey had gone. Marty called and called for him, but he didn't answer. Where could he be? He just wasn't anywhere around.

The next day at school Marty asked him where he had gone so quickly. Joey just shrugged his shoulders. "I got tired of waiting!"

Marty decided then that he couldn't trust Joey. Joey didn't keep his promises.

Do you know people you can't trust? How do you feel when you are with them?

God tells us in the Bible that we *can* trust *His* words. You can be sure that all the promises in the Bible will come true—because Jesus said so! Ask the person reading this book to you what some of his favorite promises are. Jesus made those promises to you, too.

THE SNAKE AND THE CHICKENS

The Bible says, "Call upon me in the day of trouble." Psalm 50:15, K.J.V.

SOMETHING was wrong in the chicken house. My great-grandma Hines realized it by the squawking and screeching of the hens out there. She knew that they had eggs they were trying to hatch, all snug and warm under their feathers. Usually things were quite peaceful in the chicken house. But not today.

Grandma dropped her broom. It clattered to the floor as she dashed outside, wiping her hands on her apron and holding up her skirts so she could run faster.

As soon as she looked in the door of the chicken house, Grandma screamed. For there on the floor was a big, black snake, its tongue darting quickly in and out, its head moving slowly from side to side. The chickens were standing on their nests, their feathers ruffled out, and their little eyes blinking frantically as they squawked. All twelve of the eggs that were supposed to be hatching were gone. The nests were completely empty.

Turning, Grandma ran for Grandpa. "Get your gun!" she hollered, waving her arms. "Get your gun and hurry!"

Grandpa couldn't imagine what was going on, but he grabbed his gun from the corner of the barn and hurried outside to her.

"Snake!" she managed to cry, as she sank to the ground. "There's a snake in the chicken house. And he's eaten the eggs!"

The snake hadn't moved very far by the time Grandpa got to the chicken house and banged the door open. He saw bulges and lumps in the snake's body—the eggs he had swallowed.

Taking careful aim, Grandpa pulled the trigger on his gun. With one shot he killed the snake. Then Grandpa pulled out his knife and quickly slit the snake open. The eggs, still warm, tumbled out softly, and Grandpa wiped them off and placed them gently back in the hens' nests.

The happy mother hens turned the eggs and rearranged them just so, and then at last, with soft clucking, they settled down onto the eggs to keep them warm.

Grandma wondered if the eggs would hatch after all that. Imagine her happy surprise one morning when she went out to the chicken house and saw twelve yellow little heads with bright black eyes peeking out from under the mother hens' wings. All the chickens had survived because their mothers had asked for help from someone bigger than themselves.

Your parents are bigger than you are. And God is bigger than they are. When you need help you can ask both of them for help. They love you very much.

TODAY I FEEL LIKE CHOOSING

**The Bible says, "Choose you this day whom ye will serve."
Joshua 24:15, K.J.V.**

HOLD up your right hand. Now hold up your left. Do you have any more hands? No, you have just two, don't you? A right one and a left one. Maybe you eat with your right hand, and maybe with your left. It really doesn't matter. But whichever hand you eat with or draw with or throw a ball with is the hand you do it with best, isn't it?

Burt had a problem. When he was on vacation he fell on his right hand and broke it. The doctors had to put a cast on it so he couldn't move it while it healed. All Burt's friends drew little pictures on the cast and signed their names. That made it pretty fancy. But still, it wasn't much fun to have that heavy cast on his arm. It was hot, and it made his arm itch. And he couldn't go swimming.

That was a problem. But the biggest difficulty was that he had broken his right hand, and he used that hand to eat with—before the accident. Now he had to learn to eat with his left hand for a while until his right hand had healed. That would take six weeks—that's six Sabbaths—until he could use his right hand again.

Have you ever tried to eat with your left hand? It's hard. Eating peas was especially difficult. They rolled off Burt's fork, and he wasn't much good at aiming his fork at them to poke them. He was very glad when the doctor said his cast could come off.

Some people can eat with either their right hand or their left hand equally well. But they are unusual. Mechanical robots can do things with either hand. But they have to do whatever someone tells them to do. Unless a person pokes the right buttons to make the robot do something, it can't.

I'm glad I'm not a robot, aren't you? God gave us good minds that we can choose things with. If it's a rainy day, what would you decide to wear outside? If you had only $2 and you could buy either some food or a cheap toy, which would you choose if you were hungry?

It's important to make good choices. Just as you have two hands, one that you eat with better than the other, we have two choices to make about whom we will worship. We can follow the devil's way or we can follow God's way. That's an easy choice to make, though, isn't it? Sometimes we follow the devil's way and fight and talk mean, or tell little lies, but it doesn't feel right, does it? Like Burt, we are glad when we do things right and say we are sorry and choose God's way again. What are some choices you have made today? What's the most important one?

THE LITTLE PRINCE

The Bible says, "Ye shall be my sons and daughters, saith the Lord Almighty." 2 Corinthians 6:18, K.J.V.

A LITTLE prince was born. The whole world waited to hear the news of his birth, and church bells rang for hours when he was born. People stood outside the palace and cheered. Some even cried tears of joy. Everyone was so excited about the little prince. They wanted to know his name, what he looked like, and everything about him.

He was named Prince William of Wales. Many people sent special presents to the tiny prince. His bedroom looked like a toy store. It had big stuffed animals, little cars, silver rattles, and everything else a little boy could ever want.

Of course, his father was a prince and his mother was a princess, and his grandma was a queen, so they could have bought him anything he wanted. But they didn't have to, because so many people were interested in him and wanted to buy him presents to show how happy they were that he was born.

But babies don't know as much as you do, do they? Prince William didn't really care about all those presents just then. He didn't even know what they were. He was just like any other baby, just wanting to drink his milk and have his diaper changed and sleep. The royal baby didn't care that his mother was a princess—he just wanted her close by. In fact, he didn't even know what a princess was.

I'm sure God was happy when Prince William was born. But Prince William is no more special to God than you are. God was just as happy when you were born, as He was at the birth of Prince William. In fact, in God's eyes you are a prince or a princess, too! How? Because you are God's child, and God is the king of heaven and of the whole world.

God has special presents in store for you. Like little Prince William, you don't know about all of them now, but when you get to your home in heaven God will show them to you.

Perhaps the best present of all will be to sit down with Jesus and listen to Him tell stories; or to take long walks with Him in the mountains and not get tired; or to play with the animals. I've always thought it will be fun to slide down a tall giraffe's neck! And I also want to hug a big daddy lion real tightly and bury my face in his mane.

I may never have a castle here on earth, and I will probably never have all the things that I think I want down here. But that's OK. God has promised neater things to me someday. I'm a princess. And when it's time, God will give me all the wonderful presents that He has promised. Won't that be a happy day?

STOLEN CHOCOLATE

The Bible says, "There is a way which seemeth right unto a man, but the end thereof are the ways of death." Proverbs 14:12, K.J.V.

WAY up high in Mother's cupboard was a little brown box with white letters on it that said Chocolate. I saw her get it down and use some of it when she made a chocolate cake. Oh, it smelled good! I loved chocolate. And I saw more squares of deep, dark chocolate inside the box, all wrapped up in crinkly white paper. Right then I decided that someday I would get the box down and eat a whole square by myself when Mother was busy.

All day I followed Mother around, hoping she would leave long enough for me to scoot a chair over to the cupboard, get the box down, and take the squares of chocolate to my room. But she worked in the kitchen most of the morning. Finally I got my chance.

"I'm going over to the neighbor's house for a few minutes, Nancy, but I'll be right back," she said.

"OK. Don't worry about me; I'll be all right!" I smiled, thinking about the chocolate.

Mother was going to visit my music teacher. I figured she would be there for a while. Better for me, I thought. That will give me more time.

As soon as I was sure Mother was gone and hadn't forgotten anything, I pulled a chair over to the cupboard and climbed up onto it. I had to stretch way up to reach the box of chocolate, almost knocking Mother's spice cans down, but finally I got hold of the box and grasped it tightly in my hand.

I breathed deeply. Oh, how delicious it smelled! All that yummy chocolate in there. And I planned to eat a whole square.

Quickly I opened the box and lifted out one of the carefully wrapped pieces. Then closing the box, I returned it to its spot on the shelf. After climbing down and putting the chair back in its place, I hurried to my room and shut the door.

"This is going to be good," I said to myself as I peeled back the paper. Then I popped the whole square of chocolate into my mouth and started chewing.

Ugh! It tasted awful! It was bitter—not sweet! It had smelled so good to me that I was sure it would taste that way, too. What was wrong with it? I wondered.

I couldn't get to the bathroom fast enough to spit out the chocolate and rinse out my mouth. It was the worst stuff I had tasted in a long time. Although I had thought it would be good, it turned out bad.

The Bible says that life is like that sometimes. It might seem like more fun to grumble and fight and pinch somebody just because we feel like it. Or it might seem like more fun to disobey Mother and Father or disobey God's commandments and take something that isn't ours, or tell lies. But in the end it doesn't make us very happy at all.

TODAY I FEEL COPIED

The Bible says, "But Jesus [said], 'Follow me.'" Matthew 8:22.

SUCH a shouting and commotion came from the top floor of the playhouse in the backyard that I heard it from inside the house and ran outside to see what was going on.

"David is following me everywhere I go!" Marc shouted in exasperation.

"What's wrong with that?"

"I just want to be alone!" he said with a determined shake of his head. "How come everything I do and everywhere I go, the little copycat has to follow? First I was playing in the sandbox, and David had to be there. Next I decided to play on the swing set, and he followed me there. Then Buster and I decided to play up here in the playhouse, and along comes the little brother."

"David doesn't want to play by himself, Marc," I told him. "You are his brother. He likes to be with you."

"But why does he have to copy me?"

"Because he thinks that what you do is nice," I said.

"I made some paper airplanes, and David had to make his the very same way. Then I colored mine silver, and David had to copy it. He couldn't make his red or blue or something. Oh, no. It had to be silver, too." Marc sighed heavily and leaned back against the wall.

"Marc," I said, waiting until he looked at me. "The nicest compliment anyone can give you is to copy you. When you see someone doing things the same way you do, it means he thinks you have good ideas. He wants to be like you."

Marc thought that over for a little bit and finally agreed to let David play with him in the playhouse, even if he did copy.

Does someone you know copy you? If you wear your hair in braids, does that someone soon start wearing braids, too? Or have you ever done a trick on your swing set and pretty soon one of your friends is trying to do it, too?

How does that make you feel? If it makes you angry, don't let yourself stay angry for long. Just remember it means that he is showing that he likes you.

Jesus asks us to copy Him. He wants us to be kind to

172

others and to go to church on Sabbath and make others happy, just as He did. Jesus is happy to see us copying Him.

JUDSON'S MISTAKE

The Bible says, " 'Rise in the presence of the aged, show respect for the elderly and revere your God.' " Leviticus 19:32, N.I.V.

JUDSON'S grandpa looked a lot like the pictures of Santa Claus. He had a soft, round tummy, a white beard, and blue eyes that twinkled when he laughed. And Judson just loved him!

One summer his parents allowed him to stay with his grandpa and grandma for a whole week. He helped Grandpa work on his car, and they made wooden toys together in his garage. Sometimes they even went for hikes in the woods together. It was a busy, fun week.

One evening after supper Judson ran over to where Grandpa was sitting on the couch and climbed up beside him. He liked to put his head on Grandpa's soft tummy, and this time he patted Grandpa's tummy before he put his head on it.

"Hi, fatso!" Judson smiled as he patted Grandpa's soft, round tummy.

Grandpa took him by the shoulders and looked seriously at him. His eyes no longer twinkled, and he now frowned. Judson was scared.

"Don't you ever talk like that to me again," Grandpa said sternly. "That's not the way to talk to anyone, but especially not a grown-up, or your Grandpa!"

Quickly Judson nodded. "I'm sorry," he said.

"Have you heard the story in the Bible of the young people who made fun of Elisha and called him a 'bald head'?" Grandpa asked.

The boy shook his head.

"Well, they had heard about how Elijah, God's prophet, had gone up to heaven in a chariot, leaving Elisha to carry on with the preaching. Elisha was bald. When he traveled through one town several young people saw him and began making fun of him. 'Go up, thou bald head!' they jeered, as they pointed at him and laughed.

"Just then, two bears came out of the woods and they attacked the children who had made fun of Elisha."

"Are bears going to attack me now?" Judson asked, afraid.

Grandpa shook his head. "No, God wasn't trying to tell us that when you call people names bears will attack you. He wanted to show that we must respect people who are older than we are. We don't make fun of the preacher, or our teachers, or our parents' friends. We don't call them bad names, or stick out our tongues at them, or laugh at the way they look. And we don't go jumping on them or hitting them, or doing anything mean. Adults can be your friends, but you treat them differently from the way you treat friends who are your own age."

Judson nodded again. "I'm sorry," he said. "I love your soft tummy. Is that OK to say?"

Grandpa nodded and hugged him tightly. His eyes twinkled again.

WHAT FREDDIE DID

The Bible says, "Whatever you do, do well." Ecclesiastes 9:10.

MANY years ago, before there were electric lights, a little boy we'll call Freddie was on a ship with his parents, traveling across the ocean. Just before he went to bed one night, he heard someone shouting, "Man overboard! Man overboard!" Then Freddie heard the thudding of many feet running on the deck above him.

His father hurried up to see if he could help. Freddie wondered if the man had jumped on purpose or had fallen in by accident. Whatever it was, he knew he wouldn't want *his* father out there in the ocean on such a dark night as this! He prayed that the men would be able to find and help the person. Then he went to the porthole and stuck his head out to see if he could see anything. Freddie heard lots of people talking excitedly, and one woman was sobbing, but it was too dark to see the water. Then a life ring splashed into the water, and someone yelled to "Grab onto the ring!" but the man in the water couldn't see the ring. It was just too dark.

All at once Freddie had an idea. A glass lantern with a candle burning inside hung from the ceiling of his cabin. Carefully Freddie climbed onto a chair and lifted the lantern from its hook. Then he held it out of the porthole as far as his little arm would reach.

"I see him!" someone shouted. "There's a light and I can see the man! Throw the ring farther!"

There was a splash again as the life ring hit the water. A few moments later Freddie heard the people cheer, "We have him! He's saved!"

Freddie's father came back down to the cabin a short time later.

"They found him, didn't they?" the boy asked with a smile.

"Yes! But how did you know?"

"I helped them." Freddie grinned. "I held the lantern."

The next day the captain invited him and his father to sit with him at his table. The captain made an announcement that it was Freddie's lantern that helped them see the man and rescue him. His daddy was proud of him.

Freddie wouldn't have been much help up on deck, trying to toss the life ring, would he? Some jobs are grown-up jobs. But Freddie did the best he could with what he had. What are some things you do to help?

(Adapted from *More Little Visits With God* by Allan Hart Jahsmann and Martin P. Simon.)

TODAY I DON'T FEEL SORRY

The Bible says, "I will be sorry for my sin." Psalm 38:18, K.J.V.

SYLVIA sat down on the couch.

"Hey! Get up!" Peter cried. "You're sitting on my papers!"

"Oh, don't get all mad," Sylvia said, as she stood up again. "Here are your old papers." She threw them on the floor.

"I think you have something to say to Peter," Daddy interrupted.

The girl heaved an angry sigh. "I'm sorry," she snapped.

"You don't sound as if you mean that," Daddy said. "Saying 'I'm sorry' isn't enough. You must really feel sorry, too."

"Well, I said I was sorry, and I can't help how I feel," Sylvia replied.

Her father looked disappointed. "It's not just the words that count," he said. "It's not even enough to put your arms around Peter while you say you're sorry. Once a man kissed Jesus, but that kiss was wrong. Do you remember who that was?"

"Yeah, Judas," she replied, still pouting.

"Do you know why Judas' kiss didn't mean anything?"

"Yeah. Because he didn't mean it," Sylvia answered.

"That's right. Judas kissed Jesus, but not because he loved Him. It makes a difference *why* you do or say things."

"But I don't feel sorry that I wrinkled Peter's papers," she explained. "You made me say 'I'm sorry' even though I didn't feel like it."

"Yes, I asked you to say you were sorry so you would learn how to be kind," Daddy said. "And there's a way to learn how really to feel sorry, too."

"What's that?"

"Imagine you are Peter," Daddy said slowly. "How would you feel if someone wrinkled up *your* papers?"

"I wouldn't like it one bit," she replied firmly.

"No, you wouldn't. One way really to feel sorry is to pretend that you are that other person. Imagine how he is feeling—how you would feel if you were he—and then you will probably feel sorry for him. You will mean it when you say, 'I'm sorry.' "

Sylvia sat quietly for several minutes, looking at her toes.

"I'm sorry, Peter," she said at last.

"Oh, that's OK," Peter told her. "I'm sorry I made a fuss about my wrinkled papers. They were just some yucky old pictures I didn't care about anyway."

She got up and gave him a big hug. "I love you, Peter," she said. "I really do!"

THINGS GOD HATES

**The Bible says, "The Lord detests the way of the wicked."
Proverbs 15:9, N.I.V.**

MOTHER had made spaghetti, Karena's favorite food, for supper. All afternoon the sauce had cooked on the stove, and its delicious aroma filled the whole house. By now Karena was so hungry for it that her mouth watered.

"Go ahead and sit down," Mother said. "I'm going to finish feeding the cat. She's been begging for some supper too."

Mother opened a can and spooned some cat food into the cat's dish. Then she laid the spoon on the counter as she hurried to wash her hands and take her place at the table. After the blessing, Mother lifted some spaghetti from the dish and onto Karena's plate. Then she reached for the sauce.

"Oh, dear," Mother said. "I forgot to get a spoon. Would you get one for me, honey?" she asked Karena.

"Sure!" Karena hurried from her chair to the silverware drawer. But then she saw the spoon on the counter. She didn't stop to see if the spoon was dirty or not; she just picked it up, hurried over to the table, and stuck it in the sauce.

Mother looked up just as the girl put the spoon in the sauce. "Wait!" she cried. "Not that spoon!"

But it was too late. The spoon was already in the sauce.

"What's the matter with that spoon?" Karena asked.

"That's the spoon I fed the cat with," Mother explained. "It has cat food on it."

Gasping, Karena put her hand to her mouth. "So now the spaghetti sauce has cat food in it?" she said with a shiver.

Mother nodded. "Maybe we can scoop out the sauce that the spoon touched," she said.

Karena wasn't sure. "I don't know," she said, wrinkling up her nose. "I would be afraid that I'd eat some cat food anyway. I'd rather eat a sandwich, I think." Karena was disappointed. She was hungry for spaghetti, but the thought of eating cat food made her feel sick. She just couldn't eat that spaghetti now, no matter how hungry she was!

The Bible tells us that sinful things make God sick, too. I don't mean sick like a stomachache or headache. God doesn't get sick like that. But He gets very sad to see lying and cheating, stealing, and being unkind, or anything else that is wrong. He loves the people who do these things, but He can't stand what they are doing. We don't want to make God sad. That's why we choose every day to be loving and honest and kind, isn't it?

HOW OLD IS GOD?

The Bible says, " 'O God, you live forever and forever!' " Psalm 102:24.

ONE day Charlie's mother took him to see the hospital where his grandma was born. Charlie could hardly believe that a building could be that old and still be used, but it was. And the nursery where his grandma had been a baby was filled with more new babies, as it had been since his grandma was born. It seemed as if that building must have been there forever.

A few years ago, some astronauts went to the moon and walked on it. They even brought back some moon rocks for scientists to study. Charlie couldn't believe that those rocks had been up there for so many years without any people having touched them.

Our earth is very old, too. In some places of the world trees are now alive that were tiny sprouts when only Indians lived here in America.

One tree in California was so big that a car could drive through the tunnel that was made in the trunk of the tree. Imagine a tree wider than a car! That tree grew in that spot for hundreds of years. It was a seed once, and then a sprout, and then a little tree, a bigger tree, and finally a huge tree. But one day somebody built a fire in it. The person burned it down. Now that giant tree is gone.

That's how things are here on our earth. Everything has a beginning and an end. Beginnings are exciting. I like the beginnings of vacations, but I'm sad when they are over. I like the beginning of a birthday party, because I can imagine all the fun it will be, but I'm sad when the party is over. When a baby is born and starts its life, it is exciting for everybody. But when that baby has grown up to be a grandpa or a grandpa and dies, we are sad.

A lady in our town will have her one-hundredth birthday tomorrow. Imagine living for one hundred years!

God is much older than that, but He is still alive, because in heaven there are no endings. And something else is special about God. He has always been alive. There never has been a time when He wasn't alive. Hard to understand, isn't it? It's like your wading pool. The edge of it just goes around and around and around. You can walk around it all day and never come to the end, can't you? That's how it is going to be for us some day in heaven. We will live happily with God and everyone else who loves Him—forever!

TODAY I FEEL SPECIAL

The Bible says, "For God has said, 'I will never, *never* fail you nor forsake you.'" Hebrews 13:5.

A LITTLE girl was lost in the woods. With her parents she had gone on a camping trip and had wandered away from their tent. She didn't come back for lunch, and she didn't return for supper. Now many people were worried about her. They wanted to help find her.

A long line of grown-ups and children searched the forest carefully, looking in hollow logs and under bushes. They checked everywhere. But they couldn't find her.

"What are we going to do now?" the little girl's mother cried. "We have to find her before it gets dark!"

The ranger stroked his chin. "I guess we'll have to bring in the police dogs," he said. "They can almost always find missing persons like this."

When the dogs arrived, the policeman asked for one of the little girl's dresses. "If you have one that she wore this morning, or maybe a pair of her pajamas, the dog can sniff them and get her special smell," he said.

So that's just what the little girl's mother did. She brought out her daughter's sleeping bag and her pajamas.

Carefully the dog sniffed inside the bag, and then sniffed

the little pink pajamas. Finally he began sniffing the ground, following the special scent he had smelled on the girl's things.

The policeman went with his dog through the forest. Around a rock, under a big tree, the dog kept sniffing carefully. Sniff, sniff, sniff. At last the dog stopped at a rock and began barking.

"She must be in there," the policeman said. He pulled away some fallen branches and discovered a small cave in the rocks. And there on the floor of the cave lay the little girl, sound asleep. She was safe!

God has given you a special set of footprints and fingerprints that no one else has or ever will have. You smell different from anybody else. That's how the search dogs are able to find missing people.

Now you aren't better than anyone else, and no one else is better than you. You are just special. God has promised that He will never leave you or stop watching over you. To Him you are very special.

TODAY I FEEL DUMB

The Bible says, "Give thanks to him and bless his name." Psalm 100:4.

DO you like to make things with your blocks?

One day Kyle was trying to construct a tall building with his blocks. Just when he thought he was finished, the blocks would come tumbling down, and he would have to start all over from the beginning. Has that ever happened to you?

Over on the other side of the room his big sister Karen was watching him. She saw that he was getting angry.

"Here. I'll help you make that," she offered. Carefully she laid the bottom blocks in a square. Then she added more and more on top of them, until the building was quite high, with fancy corners and balanced blocks in the middle. Then Karen added the very top block—the one that always made Kyle's buildings fall down. But her building didn't collapse.

"You can make better buildings than I can," Kyle said, a note of disappointment in his voice. "I guess I'm just dumb."

"Oh, no you're not!" she said. "Building blocks gets easier as you get older. You'll see."

"Not everyone can do the same things well," Mother said. She had heard them from the kitchen. "There will always be things that other people can do better than you can. *But*" —she stopped with her finger in the air—"there will always be things that you can do better than someone else. God gives each of us special gifts or talents. And just because Karen can build a fancier building than you can, Kyle, doesn't mean that she is a better person than you are. It just means that she built a fancier building than yours."

"You can run faster than I can," Karen told him.

"And you can sing better than I can," Kyle replied.

"Why, sure!" Mother agreed. "And there will always be some- body who can run faster or slower than you do, Kyle, and Karen will find that there will always be somebody who sings better or worse than she does. If you can't sing the loudest, or run the fastest, or paint the prettiest, that's OK, as long as you are doing the very best you can, that's what counts."

"I wish I could do everything well," Karen said.

"I know," Mother replied. "But don't worry about what you can't do. Be happy for what you are able to do well."

What are some things that you can do well?

THE MYSTERIOUS DOG

The Bible says, "A good man is concerned for the welfare of his animals." Proverbs 12:10.

ONE gray, rainy afternoon a large dog wandered the streets of Portland, Oregon. There was something strange about this dog. Although several cars honked at him, the animal didn't look at the cars or the people. He just plodded along beside the road with his head down, sniffing the cold pavement.

Pam Booth was driving home from work when she saw him. She loved dogs and could see that this one needed help. But she couldn't take him home, because her own dog had just had ten puppies, and she couldn't take care of another big one. So she decided to help the animal find its home.

By the time Pam decided to help the dog, she had passed him, so she had to find a place to turn around. When she got back he had crossed to the other side of the street. Pam turned around again, but the dog crossed the street again. Finally she just stopped her car across the street from the dog and got out in the rain.

"Here, doggy," she called softly, holding out her hand to him. The dog didn't even look at her. He just kept on sniffing the road. Pam talked softly and reached out to take his collar. As soon as she did so, the dog sat down. She pulled, but he didn't get up. Tugging harder, she tried to lift him by his tummy. Finally he got up a little bit and limped across the street with her to her car. When she opened the front door, the dog jumped in, put his head on his paws, and sighed.

"I wonder whom you belong to," Pam said to him as she felt along his collar for a tag. There was none. Pam decided to knock on all the doors in that neighborhood to find out if anyone knew whose dog this was. She knew he belonged to someone because he was wearing a collar.

Pam went from door to door along one side of the street and then the other, but nobody had lost a dog. Her clothes and hair were dripping wet, but she decided to go to one more house at the end of a long driveway. The woman there told her it looked like the dog that belonged to the people who lived on the street behind hers. So Pam got directions to the house and went back to her car.

She found the house easily enough. As soon as she asked the man at the door if he had lost a dog, he hurried toward her car. "Yes! I lost my dog several days ago!" he said quickly. "I've had signs posted everywhere and ads in the newspaper for him." When the man saw the dog, he threw his arms around its neck and the dog licked his face happily. "Oh, thank you," the man said over and over. "Thank you for being so kind to him."

"Something seems different about him," Pam started to say, and the man nodded.

"This dog is both deaf and blind," he said. "If you hadn't helped him, he would never have found his way home."

DON'T WAIT!

The Bible says, "Seek the Lord while you can find him. Call upon him now while he is near." Isaiah 55:6.

HOPPING out of the car, Janie ran next door to talk to her friend Karen.

"Guess what!" she called as she hurried to Karen's backyard. "Mr. Parker just took me for an airplane ride! He's my daddy's friend. And he said if any of my friends want to go, he'll take them for a ride, too. Would you like to go?"

"Well, yeah. But I want to finish this mud pie I'm making, first," Karen said.

Janie helped her with her pie. Then they set it out in the sun to dry. "You'd better ask your mother now if you can go for a plane ride," Janie said. "Mr. Parker said he's going to give airplane rides only this morning. After lunch he'll put away the plane."

Karen nodded. "OK," she said. "But I want to get my dolls all set up for their tea party first. You want to bring your dolls over, too?"

Janie ran home to get her dolls, though she could tell by how hungry she felt that it was almost time for lunch. "Don't you think you'd better get your airplane ride now?" she said when she returned with her dolls. "My tummy feels as if it's almost lunchtime. Do you even want to go for a ride?"

Again Karen nodded vigorously. "Oh, I do want a plane ride!" she said. "But I just want to get things ready here first, so I can play when I get back. I'll go ask my mother if she can take me now."

A few minutes later Karen walked slowly out the back door. Janie had gone home, but all the dolls were sitting as she had put them, waiting for their tea party.

"It's too late for an airplane ride," Karen told her dolls. "Mr. Parker has put his airplane away and gone home."

Why didn't Karen get an airplane ride?

Because she was so busy doing everything else that she didn't take time to ask for her airplane ride while Mr. Parker was there. When she finally stopped her playing to ask him, he had gone home.

Sometimes we do that with Jesus, too, don't we? God never goes away as Mr. Parker did, but sometimes we get so busy and eager to start our day that we don't take time for worship. We think that other things are more important than talking to Jesus. But when we don't begin our day by talking with Him, we miss out on something that could make our day go happier: remembering that we are special to Jesus and that He loves us. When we remember that, it makes our day much nicer.

SOMETIMES I FEEL EMBARRASSED

The Bible says, " 'Go easy on others; then they will do the same for you.' " Luke 6:37.

SHARI lifted her tray of food off the counter at the cafeteria and hurried to the table to eat with her friends. Just as she neared the table her foot caught on the leg of somebody's chair, and with a loud clatter both Shari and her food fell to the floor.

Everyone stopped talking for a moment and looked at her. She felt embarrassed to be sitting on the floor with spaghetti in her lap and her salad sticking out between her toes. She wished the floor would open up and swallow her.

Can you imagine how Shari felt? Have you ever felt that way?

Everyone gets embarrassed sometimes. Lots of people drop their food at cafeterias, and lots of people sometimes say things wrong, and others laugh at them.

Have you ever been embarrassed? When I get embarrassed, my face feels hot and turns red, and I wish I could hide from everybody. I wonder if they will always remember what I did. Sometimes they do, but if they're really my friends, they like me anyway. And after a while I can laugh about it, too.

One day I dropped my tray in the cafeteria, just as Shari did, only I didn't fall in it. But I had to pick it up and apologize to the janitor for making a mess for him to clean up. I was embarrassed.

A lady rushed over to help me pick up my plate and as

much of the food as we could. She told me that she had dropped a tray of food once, too, and she knew just how I felt, so she wanted to help me. She remembered what it felt like to be embarrassed.

If you have ever been embarrassed, you can remember what it feels like. You can help others feel better and not laugh at them when they're embarrassed. That's what Jesus would want you to do.

SMART CHICKENS

The Bible says, "Now I pray to God that ye do no evil." 2 Corinthians 13:7, K.J.V.

ROBBIE looked down at the flower in his hand. It was a perfect rose from his neighbor's flower garden.

"Why did you pick Mr. Boysen's rose?" Mother asked softly.

Her son shrugged. "I don't know. Cassie said to do it, so I did." He looked up at his mother as if he thought that was a good enough reason.

"Does Cassie tell you everything to do?" Mother asked.

"No."

"Well, then, why did you pick this rose? I have told you before that you are not to touch Mr. Boysen's flowers."

"Well, Cassie said she thought I was too scared to pick one. She said I was chicken, so I had to show her that I wasn't," Robbie explained.

Mother put her arm around his shoulder. "Tell me something," she said. "If Cassie told you to jump off a cliff, would you do it?"

"No! I might get hurt!" he replied in alarm.

"But what if she laughed and said you were probably too scared to jump off. Would you show her that you weren't scared after all?"

"No, I would tell her that it was dangerous to jump off cliffs, so I just wasn't going to do it!"

"Well, I know that picking someone else's flowers is not as dangerous as jumping off a cliff, but you are old enough to say No when someone tells you to do something wrong. And you knew that picking that rose was wrong, didn't you?"

Robbie nodded.

"Some children like to see others get into trouble, so they tell them to do things that are wrong, and then laugh at them when they get punished."

"That's not fair!" Robbie exclaimed.

"I know it's not fair," Mother agreed. "And it doesn't have to happen to you again. Next time someone suggests you do something that is wrong, just politely tell him that you won't do it. Then you'll stay out of trouble. And that will show that you're really growing up! Sometimes it's smart to be chicken!"

Has anyone ever called *you* "chicken" for not doing something? What would you say if someone did?

TODAY I FEEL LIKE LYING

The Bible says, "Stop lying to each other; tell the truth." Ephesians 4:25.

I ONCE heard the story of a boy who watched over his father's sheep. Every morning he took them far up into the hills to find green grass and cool air so they would be comfortable with their woolly coats.

One day someone saw a wolf in the hills, watching the sheep as though to kill one. It made the boy scared to go up alone.

"I'll tell you what," the boy's father said to him before the boy left with the sheep. "If you see the wolf trying to get our sheep, just blow this loud whistle, and all of us men from the village will run up and drive away the wolf."

So the boy hung the whistle around his neck and started up into the hills.

All day long he watched the sheep, and he never saw the wolf. How happy he was that evening when he returned home with the sheep, safe and sound.

The next day the boy took the sheep up into the hills again. He still watched for the wolf, but he didn't see it.

I wonder if the men from my village will really come if I need them, he thought after lunch, as he fingered the whistle around his neck. Perhaps I'll blow the whistle just for practice, to see if they can even hear it!

He blew hard on the whistle and waited to see what would happen.

Sure enough, in a few minutes all the men from his village raced up the hillside with sticks, ready to chase the wolf away.

The boy felt embarrassed. He explained it had been just for practice.

A few days later the boy playfully blew the whistle again, but just a few men arrived to help. "Where's the wolf?" they asked.

"Oh, I was just fooling," the boy said.

Eventually the boy really did see a wolf. He blew on his whistle. But nobody came. He blew again. And then he saw his father hurrying up the mountainside alone. His father raced after the wolf and scared it away.

"The other men thought you were fooling them again," the father said as he walked back to the boy. "You lied to them, son."

When the boy blew the whistle the first time, it was like lying to the men—like shouting "There's a wolf up here!" when there really wasn't one. After two times the men didn't believe the boy when he blew the whistle, and they didn't want to help him anymore.

That's how it is with lying. People can't trust you if you lie. And no one will come to help you when you *really* need help if you have fooled them before—no one, that is, except Jesus. He asks you to stop lying. Or if you have never lied, don't ever start, because when you lie, it doesn't make anyone happy.

DON'T FORGET
THE THANK-YOUS

**The Bible says, "It is good to say, 'Thank you' to the Lord."
Psalm 92:1.**

DAVID was a very fortunate boy. He had a big brother named Marc who helped him with the things he couldn't do by himself. If David couldn't reach a toy on a high shelf, Marc would get it for him. Or if David couldn't open his jar of paste, Marc could. And since David didn't know how to write his own name on the pictures he drew, his brother did it for him.

Yes, David was a very lucky boy. But Marc did so many kind things for him that pretty soon David seemed to think it was something that his brother should always do. He didn't think that Marc might want to be doing other things instead of helping him.

At first David said Thank you each time his brother helped him. But after a while he would just ask Marc to do something for him, and after Marc did it, David would forget to say Thanks.

One day Marc got tired of doing things and not being thanked for them. David had asked him to get down his bag of blocks, and Marc hesitated.

"If I get them for you, what will you do?" Marc asked.

"I'll play with them!" David replied.

"But before you play with them, what will you do?" Marc asked again.

"I'll ask you to get them for me," David said, puzzled. "What do you mean?"

Marc sighed. "You haven't been saying Thank you anymore, David, when I do nice things for you. If I get your blocks for you, will you thank me?"

"Well, sure, if you want me to. I just thought you liked doing things for me, so I didn't need to thank you."

He was wrong, wasn't he? Marc did enjoy helping his brother, but he also liked to hear his brother say Thank you.

God does lots of nice things for us, too. But unlike Marc, God doesn't stop doing nice things for us if we don't say Thank you. God will still give us food and flowers and love, no matter what we do. But I'm sure it makes Him smile when we tell Him Thank You.

Won't you remember to say Thank You when you see a gorgeous flower, or a tiny hummingbird, or when you bite into a crunchy apple today? You can say Thank You all day long and still not run out of things to thank God for. Why don't you start right now?

THE LITTLE ORPHAN LAMB

The Bible says, "John saw Jesus coming toward him and said, 'Look! There is the Lamb of God who takes away the world's sin!'" John 1:29.

ON a cold day in the spring a shepherd named William found a dead lamb in the field. Its mother was standing over it calling "Baa, baa," wondering why her baby wouldn't get up. William moved the mother sheep aside and picked up the dead lamb. He didn't know why it had died, but he had an idea that just might make the mother sheep happy again. You see, one of William's other sheep had twin babies, but for some reason she didn't want to feed the littlest lamb. Whenever it would come up to get some milk the mother sheep would run away or kick it. She only took care of the bigger lamb. The shepherd could have fed the little lamb with a baby bottle. But since he had a mother sheep who needed a baby and a baby lamb who needed a mother, he decided to make both of them happy. This is how he did it.

As soon as a lamb is born the mother sniffs it all over and remembers its special smell. No other lamb smells like hers. If any other lamb but hers comes up and tries to nurse, the mother sheep will kick at it or run away. The baby has to cry and run around until it finds its own mother. Only its own mother will let it have something to eat.

William knew that the mother sheep had smelled her lamb before it died. He had to put that special smell on the little orphan lamb so the mother would think her baby was alive again and would let it nurse.

So he cut the wool off the dead lamb, draped it like a coat

over the little orphan lamb, and carried the baby sheep to the mother.

She sniffed the wool and seemed unable to believe that her baby was alive again. The mother sheep touched noses with the lamb. Then the lamb tried to get some milk. At first the mother sheep moved away. Next she sniffed the lamb some more.

"Baa-aa," the little lamb cried as it tried again to eat. But the mother wasn't sure.

It took several more minutes of careful sniffing before she finally stood still and let the baby nurse.

Before long the mother sheep knew the smell of her new baby, and William didn't have to keep the wool coat on the lamb whenever it was time for it to eat.

And so a little lamb who needed a mother found one because another lamb died.

Jesus is called the Lamb of God. He died so we could go to heaven and live forever. Now we are a part of His family.

TODAY I FEEL LIKE TALKING TO JESUS

The Bible says, " 'You shall not misuse the name of the Lord your God.' " Exodus 20:7, N.I.V.

ANNA was saying the alphabet to herself. "A, B, C, D, E, F, G," she repeated, then stopped. "Mommy, how come Linda always says the letter G when she's surprised at something?"

Linda was the neighbor woman next door. She worked outside in her yard a lot, and Anna talked to her sometimes. But Anna had noticed that Linda said the letter G whenever she found something she didn't like. One time she said it when she found some molehills in the backyard, another time when she found her rake outside in the rain, and once when she couldn't dig up the ground easily. Anna wondered why she repeated G all the time.

Mother pulled Anna up onto the couch beside her. "Linda isn't just saying the letter G, Anna," Mother explained. "She

190

may not know it, but when people say G, it's as though they are starting to say 'Jesus,' but they don't finish His name. It's as if they are blaming Jesus for what makes them angry. They are misusing His name."

"Is it kind of like they're making fun of Him?" Anna asked.

"Yes, it is," Mother agreed. "How would you like it if whenever someone got mad he would say 'Oh, Anna!' in an angry voice?"

"I wouldn't like it at all," Anna replied soberly. "Especially if it wasn't my fault!"

"That's right. The Bible says that the names of Jesus and God are so very special that someday when God's name is said, everybody will kneel down."

"Is it OK to say Jesus' name when I'm praying?" Anna questioned.

Mother nodded. "It's very much OK," she said. "Because when you're praying, you're talking to Jesus—you're not making fun of Him. When I talk to you, I sometimes say your name, don't I, so you'll know that what I am saying is especially for you. When we're praying, what we're saying is especially for Jesus."

What are some special things you do when you talk to Jesus?

THE TROUBLE WITH TREASURES

The Bible says, " 'Don't store up treasures here on earth. . . . Store them in heaven where they will never lose their value.' " Matthew 6:19, 20.

WHEN I was a little girl we had a puppy named Duchess. Duchess loved cheese. Whenever she smelled it, she would run into the kitchen and stand on her back legs, jumping up and down with her front paws in the air—just like a circus dog. We would usually give her a piece of cheese. Then, grasping it firmly in her mouth, Duchess almost always ran out the door and down the steps to the backyard. What do you suppose she did with her cheese?

One day I followed her outside and stood far enough away so she didn't know I was watching.

As I watched, Duchess dug a shallow hole in the dirt with her front paws. The dirt fairly flew out behind her. Then she laid her treasured piece of cheese in the hole and covered it with more dirt, pushing it over the cheese with her nose.

"Duchess!" I called, and she came running over to play.

That evening I told my brother what I had seen her do with her cheese.

"Let's go see if she's eaten it yet," Peter said.

We went outside and scraped the dirt away. There was Duchess' cheese, all right, but it was dirty and had ants crawling all over it! We knew she would never eat it now.

That's what often happens to things we try to save here on earth. Have you ever saved a piece of gum, and then forgotten about it for several days? When you find it again, it's hard and dry.

Once two brothers grew up together in England. One brother became a businessman and made a lot of money. But when he died few people had ever heard of him, and all his money was given away. He couldn't use it when he was dead.

But his brother, David Livingstone, became a doctor and a missionary to Africa, and helped the people who lived there. When Dr. Livingstone died, he had hardly any money at all. But he did have a lot of friends. Those were *his* treasures.

When Jesus comes, Dr. Livingstone will probably have many of his treasures—his friends—up in heaven. But his brother will have none of his treasures, for we won't take any money with us to heaven. Our friends are the only treasures we'll have from this earth. Take good care of your friends!

TODAY I FEEL LIKE BEING ALONE

The Bible says, "And when he had sent the multitudes away, he went up into a mountain apart to pray: and when the evening was come, he was there alone." Matthew 14:23, K.J.V.

ONCE a tiny green caterpillar lived on a green leaf in the forest. Every day he nibbled and munched and nibbled away till he grew into a bigger and bigger caterpillar. Finally, after a few weeks, he was so big that he had to shed his skin because it was too small.

Autumn came, and the big green caterpillar had to be alone. Carefully he attached himself to the stem of a leaf and curled the leaf around himself in a special cocoon. The cocoon turned brown and looked dead and dry. Now it was called a chrysalis. Something special was happening inside.

After several weeks the chrysalis began to move. Very slowly, something inside the dried-up-looking chrysalis began to wriggle out of the end. It squirmed and twisted and finally crawled out onto the leaf. But it didn't look like a caterpillar at all. And it wasn't a caterpillar. Do you know what it was? It was a beautiful butterfly. For a moment the butterfly perched on the leaf and unfolded its wet, new wings. They dried quickly in the sun. And then with a soft flutter they lifted the butterfly up and away over the meadow. He had changed from a caterpillar into a butterfly while he was all alone.

Sometimes we like to be alone, don't we? I have a little boy who sometimes likes to just go to his room, and build things with his blocks or play pretend games with his little cars. He doesn't like to watch TV because it's so noisy, and he says he can't think very well while it's on. Instead, he likes to be alone so he can use his own mind to look at books or dream of things he would like to do.

Sometimes mothers and fathers send their children to their rooms to be alone when they get cranky and fight with their brothers or sisters. They know that all children need time alone to think about things without anyone else bothering them. If your parents have you go to your room sometimes, it's because they love you and know what is best for you. After you are there a while, you are ready to play nicely with others, aren't you? You have turned into a beautiful person, just as the caterpillar turned into a beautiful butterfly while he was alone. People like to be with butterflies more than they like to be with caterpillars, but every butterfly was once a caterpillar, wasn't it?

Jesus liked to be alone sometimes, too. It feels good to think quietly.

CAVES AND PATHWAYS

The Bible says, "Make me to go in the path of thy commandments." Psalm 119:35, K.J.V.

SHAWN and Tony were visiting the Ape Caves in Washington State. The Ape Caves are long tunnels made by hot lava from a volcano many hundreds of years ago. The hot lava, or melted rock, poured out of the volcano and down the mountainside. When it cooled, it left many tunnels like tubes of rock that people now walk through and explore.

It was dark in the caves. But Shawn and Tony were with their parents and some friends, and each had a flashlight, so they were all right. They followed the tube cave as it turned corners and went downhill and uphill. Sometimes they saw other openings that led off from the main tunnel they were walking in. They wanted to explore those smaller tunnels.

"No, you boys had better stay with us," Daddy told them. "You might get lost in one of those other tunnels, and we would have no way of knowing where you were!"

Soon everyone was tired.

"Let's go back," Mother suggested. "We have a long walk before we get to the opening."

Everyone agreed. But Tony and Shawn waited until their parents had started back down the tunnel. They walked slowly together.

"I want to see where one of those side tunnels goes," Tony said. "I know we'll be all right if we just go down it for a little way and then turn around and come back to this one."

Shawn wasn't sure. "I don't want to get lost," he said.

"Aw, come on! We'll just go in a little way, and then we'll return to this one!"

Reluctantly Shawn followed Tony into one of the side tunnels. It was lower than the main one, and they had to stoop over to walk.

"Let's go back," Shawn said. "I don't like this at all!"

Tony shrugged. "OK, scaredy cat!" he said, and started back to the main tunnel. They walked for a long time.

"Are you sure this is the way we came in?" Shawn asked slowly. He felt they had walked far too long.

"Of course it is! We didn't go off on any other tunnels!" Tony said. But he was getting nervous, too.

Finally, their trail opened up into the large, main tunnel. At last they were safe.

If Shawn and Tony had followed the path their parents said to take, they wouldn't have been afraid.

God wants us to go in the path of His commandments, too. Have you learned the Ten Commandments? If we follow them, we won't be unhappy with ourselves, because God's way is always the best way.

HOW TO BE KIND TO JESUS

The Bible says, " 'Anything you did for one of my brothers here . . . you did for me.' " Matthew 25:40, N.E.B.

JOSHUA looked out the kitchen window at a bright-red cardinal hopping about in his yard. The sun shone warmly on the grass, and bright flowers that he had planted all by himself bloomed in the flower bed. Joshua smiled. And then a frown crossed his face.

"Mommy," he said, "look at all the gifts Jesus has given to us. I want to do something for Jesus as He does for me!"

"Just seeing you enjoy His gifts and taking care of them makes Jesus happy," his mother said.

"I know, but I want to show Jesus how much I love Him. Is there some way I can do that—besides praying?"

Mother smiled. "Yes, there is a way," she said.

"Oh, boy! How can I give a present to Jesus?"

Mother reached into a cupboard and took out a large, blue glass. She filled it with cold water, as cold as she could get, and handed it to him.

"Here, Josh, why don't you take this to Daddy? He's out in the front yard mowing the grass. He could probably use a cool drink."

"OK," Joshua said. "And then you tell me how I can give a present to Jesus!"

When Joshua came back in with the empty glass, he found Mother in his bedroom sorting through his clothes.

"Let's take out the clothes that don't fit you anymore," she said. "You can help me."

So they both looked through his clothes, folding the shirts and jeans that were too small and laying them neatly in a paper sack.

All day long Joshua worked with his mother. They cut a bouquet of fresh flowers and took them to their neighbor who had been sick. Then they delivered the sacks of clothes to the church welfare center. When they returned home, Joshua set the table for supper.

As he ate, Joshua was thinking of all he had done that day.

"We were really busy today, Daddy!" he said happily. "But Mommy! You never told me how I could give a present to Jesus."

Mother smiled at him. "Well, let me see," she said slowly. "You gave Jesus a drink of cold water; you gave Him a bouquet of flowers; you gave Him some clothes; and you set the table for Him ... "

"But I didn't do that for Jesus—!"

"Oh, yes you did!" Mother said. "Jesus said that whenever we are kind to others, it is as though we are being kind to Him. So you gave Jesus lots of gifts today!"

TODAY I FEEL LIKE GRUMBLING

**The Bible says, "Always give thanks for everything to ... God."
Ephesians 5:20.**

SUSAN frowned at her face in the mirror. "Why do I always have to make up my bed in the morning?" she grumbled to her mother as she combed her hair. "And how come I have to help clear the table, too? That's your job—not mine!"

Mother took a deep breath and sighed deeply. "When you've finished combing your hair, Susan, come out to the living room, please. I want to read something to you," she said.

"Uh-huh. OK," Susan muttered. "I have to put this barrette in first."

When she sat down beside her mother on the couch, she noticed that Mother had her Bible open.

"We already had worship," Susan said. "Do we have to have it again?"

"Reading the Bible is not just for morning and evening worship," Mother answered. "We can find help in it all day long. Here! I want to read something in the Bible that we need to think about right now."

Susan settled back on the couch as Mother began to read Ephesians 5:19, 20: " 'Talk with each other much about the Lord, quoting psalms and hymns and singing sacred songs, making music in your hearts to the Lord. Always give thanks for everything to our God and Father' [T.L.B.]. What do you suppose that means?" Mother asked.

"I guess it means I should sing more," Susan said.

"Yes, I guess it does. And it says we should make music in our hearts, always thanking God! Do you think grumbling makes music in your heart, Susan?"

"Probably not. But how can I be thankful for everything? How can I be thankful for dirty dishes and making up my bed in the morning?"

"Well," her mother said, "whenever you see our dirty plates, you can be thankful that we had some food to put on them that made them dirty. And whenever you make up your bed, you can be thankful that you have such a nice cozy bed and so many warm covers at night. Lots of people can only dream about such things."

"Do they really?" Susan asked.

"Yes," Mother said sadly. "Many children would feel rich if they had only one real toy. All they have to play with are sticks and cans."

Susan looked at the toys scattered around the room. "I'm thankful for this mess," she said. "At least I'm thankful I have the toys that make a mess. But I wish they *weren't* messy!"

"We can fix that," Mother replied. "We'll count your blessings while we put them away."

ONE FROZEN TONGUE

The Bible says, "The wise in heart accept commands." Proverbs 10:8, N.I.V.

IT was a cold winter night in Tennessee. The next morning everything was frozen: roads, trees, streams, fields. Since I had lived most of my life in the mission field, where it always feels like summer, I couldn't remember much about how winter felt. I was excited about sledding and making snowmen and all the other things you can do with snow. But I didn't know how winter can hurt you.

My school had a drinking fountain just outside the door of the first-grade room, on the porch. When we lined up to go back to class after recess, we all stopped at the fountain to get a drink first. With winter here, even the drinking fountain was frozen, and icicles hung down from the pipes underneath like a long, white beard.

"Make sure you don't put your tongue on the metal part," my friend Elizabeth Ann warned me. "It can burn you."

"Really? But it's not hot—it's cold!"

"I know, but it still burns. My daddy says that some of your tongue will stick to the metal if you try to pull away."

It sounded pretty scary to me, but it made me curious. How could something frozen burn me? I had to see for myself!

During recess the next day, I wandered over to look at the drinking fountain. I thought I might snap off an icicle to suck on. Or I could eat some of the frost that covered the metal parts at the top. Maybe the frost was thick enough that I could just lick some of it off. Surely something cold couldn't burn me! I leaned over and nibbled on one of the icicles. Then I stuck my tongue out and touched the ice with my tongue. Nothing happened. But when I began licking the frost on the metal parts—Wham! Just like that, my tongue stuck to the metal—and it *burned!*

It's hard to yell for help when your tongue is hanging out of your mouth, but you can sure cry! Big tears started rolling down my cheeks. I was afraid to pull away in case half of my tongue would remain on the drinking fountain, so I just stayed there, hoping somebody would find me and help me out. I didn't know what else to do.

Soon I heard someone laugh. "What are you doing?" It was Elizabeth Ann. "Stay right there!" she said, as though I could do anything else. She ran quickly for a glass of warm water and poured it over my tongue and the metal. At last I was free.

My tongue was sore and burned for several days. Oh, how I wished I had just trusted what Elizabeth Ann had said about frozen metal and tongues, instead of trying it out for myself.

Sometimes we do the same thing with God. He tells us not to do things, but we do them anyway. By the time we're sorry, we have been hurt and know we shouldn't have done them. God will forgive us, but we injure ourselves by disobeying Him.

TODAY I FEEL HAPPY

The Bible says, "You saw me before I was born and scheduled each day of my life before I began to breathe." Psalm 139:16.

ANDY and Ryan Hayton were expecting a baby brother or sister very soon now. They had watched their mommy's tummy grow bigger and bigger, and they had felt the baby kicking and even saw their mommy's tummy moving as the baby stretched its arms and legs from inside. It was exciting— almost like Christmas—because while they could look and listen and pat from the outside, they couldn't know what was inside that special package.

At last the day came when Mommy went to the hospital. Then their daddy called to tell them that their baby was a girl. Now they had a little sister in their family.

Oh, how proud those two big brothers were! They named their baby Louisa and helped their mother take good care of her once she was home from the hospital.

Ryan wanted to do something very special for the baby. In his bedroom he had a big picture of Jesus on the wall. He liked looking at that picture when he got up in the morning and before he went to sleep at night. It reminded him that Jesus was with him all the time. And now that Louisa was here, Ryan wanted to give his special picture of Jesus to her, for her bedroom wall.

"Mother," Ryan said, as she was dressing the baby. "You can take my picture of Jesus and hang it in Louisa's room, now. Jesus knows *me* pretty well, but He doesn't know Louisa very well yet—she's so new."

Ryan's mommy smiled at him. She gave him a big hug, and then she explained that Jesus had known Louisa all the time she was growing inside her tummy. He knew Louisa first, before anyone else did.

Jesus watched over you, too, while He made you. He has a special plan for your life and has given you talents with it in mind. Have you discovered them?

Maybe you can sing all the songs in Sabbath school. That means Jesus has given you a talent for music. Or maybe you can color your pictures neatly and well. Jesus has given you a talent for art. Perhaps you have many friends. Sometimes that is a talent too.

Some people have lots of talents, and other people don't have as many. But whatever your talent, Jesus gave it to you for a special reason. And if you use your talents well, He has promised to give you more.

Jesus has been watching you for a long time. It makes Him happy to see you using your talents to make others happy.

WHO DID IT?

The Bible says, "I thought about the wrong direction in which I was headed, and turned around and came running back to [God]." Psalm 119:59, 60.

"I THOUGHT I told you to shut the back door last night," Daddy said to Carly when she came into the kitchen for breakfast one morning.

"I did," Carly replied.

"Well, it was wide open this morning. It would be no trouble at all for burglars to get in and take all our things when the door is open like that."

"I know I closed it," Carly insisted. "Honest I did!"

"Well, maybe you didn't close it tight enough, and the wind blew the door open. Just make sure you do a good job of closing it tonight after you come in," Daddy said sternly.

A few days later Daddy came in for supper after talking to the neighbor. "Who fed the rabbit last night?" he asked, looking around the table at Carly and her little brother Robbie.

"I fed him," Carly said, "and I know I closed his cage tightly and latched it. I made sure I did, after that night the back door was open!"

"Well, I don't know how he got out, but Mr. Vanderwing said when he drove in at midnight last night, he saw the rabbit hopping about in our front yard. You know that dogs could have gotten him, or he could have gotten lost. I don't know why we can't trust you with anything anymore," Daddy said sadly.

Carly didn't know what was going on, either. She knew she had closed the back door, and she knew she had locked the rabbit hutch. How could she prove she was still responsible?

The next day at lunch Mother seemed surprised that Carly was hungry. "I found a half-eaten cookie and some raisins under your pillow this morning," Mother said. "You know I don't want you eating between meals!"

"I didn't!" Carly exclaimed. "I don't know how that food got there!"

"Well, somebody must know," Mother said. "And it certainly isn't me. You've got to stop this, Carly, or else we'll start spanking again."

The next night Mother was sewing in the kitchen when

she heard footsteps in the hall. Holding her breath, she watched as Carly walked through the kitchen and out the back door to the rabbit hutch. Carly petted the rabbit and then returned to the house, leaving the back door open as she went back down the hall to her room. Mother realized then that Carly was walking in her sleep. Of *course* she didn't know what she was doing. She was sound asleep! When we're asleep we don't think about what we're doing. Mother hurried to tell Daddy what she had seen, and then he wasn't angry anymore.

It's normal not to know what we're doing when we're sleeping, but when we're awake we can get in trouble if we don't think about our actions. Before you do something you're not sure of, ask yourself, "Is it safe?" "Is it going to hurt somebody?" "Would I be proud to tell Mother about it?" If you think you'd be afraid to tell your parents about it, it's probably wrong. Don't do it.

SARA'S DOG

The Bible says, "But when I am afraid, I will put my confidence in you. Yes, I will trust the promises of God." Psalm 56:3, 4.

SARA had been blind since she was born, so she didn't know what her mommy and daddy and brother looked like, but she knew their voices very well. And she had learned to trust them.

One day Sara was given a friend who would stay with her day and night. Can you guess who that friend was? Her own guide dog! Specially trained to take care of blind people, Bruno had learned about traffic signals and doorbells and knew Sara's neighborhood very well. Sara would learn to trust him as much as she did her parents to keep her safe.

"Now I can go for walks all by myself!" she said. "And I don't have to wait for someone to go with me—except Bruno, of course."

Sara had to get used to Bruno at first. Holding on to the special handle, she told Bruno to walk. He walked carefully and slowly enough so she could keep up with him. It was kind of scary at first to trust a dog to take care of her. But in time Sara learned that she was safe with him.

One day Sara was playing down the street at the neighborhood park. All at once she heard someone start to cry.

"Oo-oh, Mommy," a little girl moaned. "Mommy!"

Following Bruno, Sara went over to the little girl. "Are you hurt?" she asked.

"Yes! Can't you see my knee?" the little girl cried angrily.

Sara shook her head. "No, I can't see," she said, "I'm blind. But I can get help for you!"

"Please. Get my Mommy!"

"I don't know where you live," Sara said. "But I'll get *my* Mommy, and maybe she can help you."

Bruno started quickly for Sara's home with the girl holding tightly to the handle of his halter. They had one street to cross. Sara never liked crossing streets, but she had learned to trust Bruno. She talked quietly to him as he stood at the curb, waiting for the cars to pass so it would be safe.

Then Sara felt Bruno step down into the street. Trusting him, she stepped into the street also. He led her across it, up onto the opposite curb, and safely home.

"I was scared," Sara told her mother later. "I never like crossing streets very much, but I just hung on to Bruno's halter, and he took good care of me!"

Sara trusted her dog. We have Someone we can trust, too. Someone much stronger and safer than a dog, for we can trust Jesus. Whenever you are afraid, it always feels better to tell someone about it. But if no one is around to talk to, you can always talk to Jesus. He is your very best friend.

TODAY I FEEL LIKE
A GROWN-UP

The Bible says, "Follow God's example in everything you do." Ephesians 5:1.

DO you like to dress up in grown-up clothes and play "let's pretend"? Barbie did. Mother had given her a suitcase with some old hats and shoes and dresses in it, and Barbie often dressed up like a mommy and played "let's pretend."

One day Randy came over. Mother found him some of Daddy's old clothes so he could pretend being the daddy while Barbie pretended she was the mommy of their family.

"Let's go to the store," Barbie said. "We can put some chairs together for a car and then use my doll buggy as a shopping cart."

"OK!" Randy agreed. "That'll be fun!"

So they put two chairs side by side. Barbie wrapped one of her dolls in a blanket, put on her hat, and sat down in her chair. "Here," she said, handing Randy a paper plate. "That can be the steering wheel!"

"Varoom!" Randy roared, pretending to start the car. "Fasten your seat belts!" He sounded just like his daddy.

After they had "driven" to the store, they got out of their chairs and walked slowly around the kitchen, pushing Barbie's doll buggy. Mother put some canned corn into their shopping cart, along with some apples and macaroni, and they used play money to pay her for them.

"Do you think people would think we were real grown-ups if we went to a real store?" Barbie asked seriously as she put the money back into her purse.

"No, I think people in the stores would know that you were children just dressed up. You can't be real grown-ups yet because you are still children, and no matter what kind of clothes you put on, you'll still look like children. But it's fun to pretend, isn't it?"

Barbie nodded.

"Do you know something that both grown-ups *and* children can be?" Mother asked.

"What is it?" Randy questioned.

"This is something you don't have to wait to be," said

Mother. "You don't have to wait until you're a grown-up to be a Christian. And just as you learn how to be a grown-up by copying grown-ups, you can learn to be a Christian by copying Jesus. By being kind and saying you're sorry when a friend of yours gets hurt, or by letting someone else have a turn on the swings, even though you yourself would rather swing. You can always tell the truth, and attend church every Sabbath. Those are all things that Jesus did when He was here!"

"That sounds like something I could do," Randy told her.

And *you* can, too.

TODAY I FEEL UNLUCKY

The Bible says, "Always be joyful." 1 Thessalonians 5:16.

RACHEL was angry. "Why did we have to come to *this* crummy old park?" she grumbled as she kicked at the grass. "All this park has are swings and slides. I wanted to go to a park that has a merry-go-round!"

"Do you want to go home, then?" Mother asked pleasantly. "You know the park with a merry-go-round is clear across town, and we don't have time to go that far and play before your sister gets home from school."

"Naw, I guess I'll just swing today," Rachel said as she sat down hard on a swing and began to push her toes into the dirt.

Just then another little girl ran from her car to the swings.

"Hi!" she said. "Doesn't this park have the neatest swings?"

"I guess. But I wish it had a merry-go-round, too!" Rachel replied.

"Oh, yeah. That would be nice. But some parks don't even have swings. And this one has swings *and* slides. That's enough to keep me busy!"

Rachel nodded. "I guess so," she said.

After a while, the other little girl and her mother spread out a blanket on the grass and opened up their picnic lunch. Rachel watched and listened quietly from her swing.

"Did you bring any punch, Mom?" the little girl asked. "I'm thirsty!"

"No, I'm sorry, honey. I didn't think to bring any!"

"Well, that's OK! At least there's water here!"

Rachel thought a moment. "I would be mad if *my* mother didn't bring any punch to a picnic. But that little girl didn't even get mad! She's going to drink water instead."

As Mother tucked Rachel into bed that evening Rachel was still thinking about the little girl at the park.

"She likes merry-go-rounds too, Mom, but she said she was just as happy with swings and slides. And she wanted punch at their picnic, but when there wasn't any, she drank just water."

Mother nodded. "She has learned to be happy always. We may not always get everything we *want*, but we can be happy with what we have."

"I want to be like that little girl," Rachel said.

And I'm sure you do too!

FAITHFUL DOG, URSA

The Bible says, "Yea, the darkness hideth not from thee; but the night shineth as the day: the darkness and the light are both alike to thee." Psalm 139:12, K.J.V.

URSA was a large, black Newfoundland dog. She seemed to be more trouble than she was worth to her owner, Mrs. Elizabeth Wiederhold, until one special summer.

That summer Mrs. Wiederhold was vacationing on an island off the coast of Maine with Ursa and two little poodles. Whenever Mrs. Wiederhold would sit down, along would come Ursa, bounding into her lap and nearly knocking her over. Ursa left dog hairs on the carpet, on the couch, and in the plates. Mrs. Wiederhold thought about giving her away to somebody else when the summer was over. Until one night.

The day before her vacation came to an end Mrs. Wiederhold took her little motorboat across the inlet to the mainland to pick up her husband and daughter. They had promised to come help her pack her things. Before she left, Mrs. Wiederhold lighted a kerosene lamp and left it in the window so her house would look cheery and she could see it when she came home. The dogs, she left romping about in the yard.

All afternoon Mrs. Wiederhold waited for her husband and daughter. When evening came and they hadn't arrived yet, she decided not to wait any longer. She couldn't leave the lamp burning in her house all night without anyone to watch it.

A heavy fog had come in, but Mrs. Wiederhold started for home in her little motorboat anyway, even though she could barely see through the fog past the end of the boat. Her little island was one mile from shore.

The trip home seemed to be taking forever. Finally Mrs. Wiederhold realized that she had gone past her island and was headed toward the open sea. She didn't know where she was or even which direction she should turn to get to her island. Then the motor on her boat stopped.

"Help!" Mrs. Wiederhold called, in case anyone could hear her. "Help! I need help!" But nobody seemed to be around. She was lost in that thick, gray fog. It was dark and cold, and big waves tossed the little motorboat this way and that. After a while, she stopped shouting for help. Instead, she just hung on to her seat.

While it was quiet, she heard a faint bark in the distance. Then she heard splashing. Ursa? Could it be her dog? It sure sounded like her bark.

"Ursa!" Mrs. Wiederhold called. "Over here, girl!" She heard a reassuring bark, closer now, and pretty soon, by the light of her flashlight, she saw Ursa's black head bobbing in the water beside her.

"Ursa!" Mrs. Wiederhold cried as she rubbed the dog's head. "How ever did you find me? Take me home!" Mrs. Wiederhold threw a rope, and Ursa caught it in her mouth. The dog started swimming through the waves toward home.

Mrs. Wiederhold tried to start the motorboat one more time. It sputtered and then puttered along as Ursa paddled home, towing the boat behind her. With an unbelievable sense of direction, Ursa brought her owner right to the dock at her home. Ursa had saved her life! The dog must have heard the familiar sound of the motor as Mrs. Wiederhold passed the island in the fog and jumped into the water and followed it to bring her home.

If a dog could find her owner in the darkness, I know God can find me, too, even in the darkest night.

TODAY I FEEL GROUCHY

The Bible says, "Do that which is good." Romans 13:3, K.J.V.

WHEN Mother walked into Janice's room one evening, she just about tripped over a doll and the other toys scattered about. "Janice, I want you to pick up your toys before you go to bed," Mother said seriously. "Do it now, please."

"Oh, Mother!" her daughter whined, flopping down on her bed. "Why do I have to do it now? Why can't it wait till the morning?"

"Because you might fall over something if you get up in the night. And it just helps you sleep better if you're in a neat and clean room."

The girl sighed loudly. "But I'm too tired to pick up all this mess right now! I don't want to do it. Besides, Molly made most of the mess. She should pick it up for me!"

"Molly doesn't live here," Mother said firmly. "It's your room. You pick it up. Now."

Just then the phone rang, and Mother went to answer it. It was Janice's grandmother.

"Yes, she's in her room picking up her toys," the girl heard her mother say. "Sure, I'll go get her."

Janice ran to the phone. Grandmother wanted to speak to her?

"Hi, Grandma!" she said sweetly, sounding like somebody other than the whiny little person she had been a few moments before. "Oh, I'm just picking up my toys before I go to bed so I don't trip over them in the night," she explained. Mother smiled to herself. Funny how different Janice's voice sounded when she wanted it to.

Everyone has two sides—like a pillow or a coin or a pancake. One side of us is nice and friendly and likes to talk kindly and share. The other side is grouchy and selfish and sometimes likes to fight.

Which side do you like being the most? Most of the time you keep your good side up, don't you? You like to play nicely with your friends and say Please and Thank you and smile a lot. When your good side is up you make your parents happy because you are fun to be around and you like to obey and keep out of trouble. But sometimes you put your bad side up.

You pout and whine and make life miserable for everyone around you. It makes you miserable, too.

Do you want to have a good day today? You can decide which side you want to put up. Nobody else can do that for you. If you want to have a good day, put your good side up. People will enjoy being with you. Everyone will then have a good day.

LO CHING

The Bible says, "And, lo, I am with you alway, even unto the end of the world." Matthew 28:20, K.J.V.

LO Ching was just a little boy when he learned about Jesus. He heard a missionary tell his parents about how much God and Jesus loved them and how Jesus was always with them.

"I wonder if Jesus really loves me," Lo said to himself as he went outside to play. Did God really know all the people in his country of China? Did God really know his name?

One day Lo was talking to his grandpa. "Tell me the story of the bird that you rescued," Lo pleaded, "the one that knew your name."

Grandpa tugged on his thin beard and chuckled. "Ah, yes. I will never forget little Shin-su. And neither will you, I see," he said. "Ah, yes. I was walking outside one day when I heard a tiny chirping on the ground under a low bush. I stooped over to look closely. There I saw a small mynah bird with a broken wing."

"Was his mother nearby?" Lo asked, though he knew the story by heart.

"Yes. The mother mynah began to fly toward me and tried to peck at me. She thought I was going to hurt her baby. She did not know that I was a friend. The small bird would have died had I not lifted it up and taken it to my home." Grandpa chuckled as he closed his eyes and leaned his head back in thought. He smiled. "Mama San treated that bird like a real baby. She mixed up a little bread, a little water, and a little rice, and I filled the little bird with food any time he opened his mouth. Soon he wasn't a little bird anymore. He was a fat, healthy bird. But his wing was too misshapen to fly. So he just hopped around the house and talked to us."

"Real words?" Lo questioned, his eyes open wide at the thought.

"Yes, real words. His first words were 'eat food!'" Grandpa chuckled. Then he chuckled again. "That made me happy. But I was *really* happy when one day he called my name. Then I knew I made him happy, too, and that I was special to him."

"He knew your name," Lo said reverently.

Grandpa nodded and smiled.

As Lo walked home, he wondered again if *Jesus* knew *his* name. He decided to ask the missionary when he saw him next. If Jesus knew his name, then Lo would know Jesus loved him.

The next day, Lo asked shyly, "Does Jesus really know my name?"

The missionary smiled broadly and opened his Bible. "Yes. God has a special verse for you," he said as he began to read in English. "In the Bible God says, 'And, lo, I am with you alway, even unto the end of the world.'"

Lo grinned happily.

Maybe your name is in the Bible, and maybe it isn't. Whether it is or not, that promise is for *you*, too. God says, "I am with *you* always." God loves you. You are special. You make many people very, very happy.

WHO KNOCKS?

The Bible says, "'I stand at the door and knock. If anyone hears my voice and opens the door, I will go in and eat with him, and he with me.'" Revelation 3:20, N.I.V.

BENJI was lying on the floor of the living room coloring in his favorite coloring book. Music played on the radio, and in the kitchen his mother was making supper.

Suddenly Benji heard the door squeak. He watched it

carefully, and as he watched, the door slowly swung open. A burst of cool air made him shiver.

"Who's there?" he asked, trying to sound brave.

Nobody answered as the door banged against the wall.

Benji got up and walked to the door. He looked outside, but nobody was there.

Mother had heard the door open, too. "Who is it?" she called from the kitchen.

"I don't know," Benji answered. "Nobody's there."

"Oh, it was probably just the wind, then," Mother replied. "It sometimes opens doors. Just close the door more tightly. Make sure it's latched."

Benji did as she said.

A short time later his mother was making lots of noise with her electric beater. It made the radio hum, too. There was so much noise in the house that Benji covered his ears with his hands.

Finally Mother stopped working. Benji still had his hands over his ears, so he didn't hear a soft knock at the door.

"Benji," Mother called. "Benji?"

"What, Mother? I couldn't hear you."

"I know you couldn't," she said. "Somebody is knocking at the door. Would you get it, please?"

The boy listened. Again someone knocked softly at the door.

When he opened the door, he happily saw his friend Carmen wanting to play.

How was she different from the wind? She didn't just open the door and come right in, did she? Carmen just knocked and waited for someone from inside to open it.

That's just the way Jesus is. He doesn't ever *make* us love Him and be Christians. He just waits for us to choose Him. Sometimes we say that Jesus knocks at our heart's door. How does He do that? Well, when you're playing you might be tempted to keep the best toys for yourself and let your friend have the others. But deep down inside you know that that really is not kind. That feeling is Jesus knocking at your heart's door. He doesn't make you share some of the best toys with your friend. Jesus lets you decide if you will or not. And when you decide to share, that's when you open the door and let Him in. Whenever you are kind, or tell the truth, or are a helper—whenever you choose to do the right thing—you are letting Jesus into your heart. Why not see how many times you can invite Him in today?

SOMETIMES I FEEL LIKE CRYING

The Bible says, "There is ... a time to cry." Ecclesiastes 3:1–4.

RODNEY walked from the car into the house. Sitting on the edge of his bed, he bit his lip. His throat felt stiff. Then his lips began to shake, and big tears rolled down his cheeks.

"What's the matter, honey?" Mother asked as she entered the room. She sat down beside Rodney and put her arm around him. "Why are you crying?"

He sniffed and wiped his nose with the back of his hand. "Daddy and I saw a dead cat on the road on the way back from the store," he said. "And it looked just like our kitty!"

Rodney didn't like to see hurt animals. It made him sad to see those that had been hit by cars. He was a big boy, but his mother didn't tell him to stop crying. It is OK for big boys and girls to feel sad and to cry.

The Bible tells us that Jesus cried. Jesus was big, and strong, and brave. But He cried when He saw people hurt and when He heard that one of His friends had died.

Sometimes people cry when they're happy, too. I cried happy tears when my babies were born and the doctor told me that they were healthy and strong. Maybe your mommy and daddy shed happy tears when you were born, too. Crying when we are happy or sad is much different from pretend crying.

One day in the store, I saw a little boy and his mother shopping for groceries. The little boy saw some gum that he wanted.

"Can I have some gum, Mommy?" he asked.

His mother shook her head.

"Puh-lease?" he persisted, wrinkling up his eyebrows in a frown.

Again his mother shook her head.

All at once do you know what that little boy did? He opened his mouth and let out a long, loud wail.

"Aa-aa-aa," he cried as he sat down hard on the floor. "I want some gum." Then he began to kick his legs and squirm about on the floor.

Have you ever seen someone do that? Sometimes children

212

do pretend crying like that when they want something or when they want someone's attention. They don't have to cry—they just make themselves sound like it. We call that "crying crocodile tears." Crocodiles are said to have tears running down their faces, but they're not sad and they're not hurt. They're just washing the sand from their eyes.

Most of us stop doing pretend crying as we grow up. It shows you are getting bigger when you don't whine if somebody tells you No.

There are better ways to get attention than pretend crying. You can tell someone you like their shoes, or their clothes, or something about them, and they'll give you some good attention.

When you *have* to cry, it's all right. God made us so we can cry. But make sure you don't cry "crocodile tears." What are some things that make you cry?

ABOUT BEING BEAUTIFUL

The Bible says, "Create in me a new, clean heart, O God, filled with clean thoughts and right desires." Psalm 51:10.

HAVE you ever wanted to be beautiful? Well, I have a secret for you. I know a way you can be.

Everyone said that Rachel was beautiful. "She's the nicest little girl to be around," they said. "I haven't ever seen a more beautiful child than Rachel!"

It made Tara really eager to see her. She could hardly wait to meet Rachel.

Finally she got her chance. Rachel and her mother were visiting friends in Tara's neighborhood, and Tara was invited to come over.

"What does a girl as beautiful as Rachel look like?" she wondered. "Does she have long hair tied up with ribbons? I'll bet she doesn't wear glasses like I do. And she probably will be wearing fancy, expensive clothes."

Tara looked down at her dress. It wasn't new. And it certainly wasn't expensive. It didn't even have any bows on it—just a few buttons on the front—and pockets—with rickrack around them. But it was one of her favorite dresses. She hoped Rachel wouldn't laugh at it. "I really wonder how beautiful she is," Tara said to herself.

When she and her mother walked into the neighbor's house, Tara looked all around for the beautiful little girl she had imagined. But all she saw were other little girls who looked just as average as she did.

Then the lady told them everybody's name.

"And this is Rachel," she said. "She used to live here, and she's back for a visit today!"

Rachel was smiling. She didn't look anything like Tara had imagined she would. Why, she had glasses on, too, and braces on her teeth. And her dress looked as ordinary as Tara's. But before too long Tara understood why everyone thought she was beautiful. Rachel was kind. When Tara fell down and scraped her knee during one of the games, Rachel was the one who helped her up and made sure she was all right. When Tara dropped her cupcake on the floor, Rachel shared hers. And when one of the kids started calling a little boy ugly names, she told him she didn't think that was very nice and that she liked the little boy.

"Is Rachel this way all the time?" Tara's mother asked the neighbor.

"Well, she's just like anybody else," the woman said. "She has some days when she's grouchy. But I've noticed she doesn't stay that way very long. She makes herself smile and be friendly most of the time. By now, it seems to be just the way she is. She doesn't have to try as hard to be happy—it comes naturally."

Rachel was beautiful, but not really beautiful on the outside. She was beautiful inside, where it counts. You, too, can be beautiful.

DIVING FOR PEARLS

The Bible says, "The price of wisdom is above pearls." Job 28:18, R.S.V.

THE sea was fairly calm as two men set out in their small boat for a special spot they had in mind. They had collected several basketfuls of oyster shells the day before and had seen many more that they would collect today. With any luck today's harvest could make them very rich.

The motorboat idled to a stop, and one of the men strapped a basket to his wrist and clutched a large rock to his chest. His friend would stay in the boat to hold onto a rope tied to the rock. With the go-ahead signal the diver jumped over the side of the boat and let the weight of the stone swiftly carry him down to the bottom of the Persian Gulf. He didn't have a scuba tank on, but just held his breath for one minute while he quickly collected all the oyster shells he could find and put them in the basket. His lungs felt as though they would burst before he tugged on the rope as a signal to his friend to pull the basket up. Then the man kicked his legs and swam up to the boat as swiftly as possible.

As soon as the diver's head splashed out of the water, he began gulping great mouthfuls of air. But he was smiling. Many more shells still covered the sea floor. The next time his friend would go down while he waited in the boat.

When both of the men were too tired to dive anymore, they sat in the boat and cracked the shells open. Some of the shells had pearls in them.

Have you ever seen a pearl? Pearls are beautiful white or pink stones that look as though they have rainbows in them. People pay lots of money for real pearls because they are so hard to find and they are so hard to collect.

Pearls are made when the oyster gets a little speck of sand inside its shell. The sand hurts the oyster, much as sand hurts our eyes. But the oyster can't blink. Instead it just starts to cover the sand until the hurt goes away. Layer after layer of coating goes on the speck until finally it is a beautiful pearl, the size of a pea. It takes quite a while for an oyster to make a pearl. And it's hard for the divers to collect the pearls. Anything worth having usually takes a lot of hard work.

The Bible says that learning about things is worth more

than pearls. Sometimes learning is hard, too, and it takes time. But if we do the same thing over and over and over again, finally we'll learn it. If we say our memory verse over and over and over again, pretty soon we'll remember it.

No one can buy knowledge. You have to get it for yourself by asking questions and remembering. But once you really learn something, nobody can take it away from you. It's yours to keep. You are smart! What are two new things you have learned about today?

(Adapted from *Listen to the Animals* by William Coleman.)

TODAY I FEEL USELESS

The Bible says, "And they brought young children to him, that he should touch them" Mark 10:13, K.J.V.

THE sun beat down on Harvey's back as he helped his father build a wall around the front of their property. There were many rocks around that he had to pick up. Some of them were too small to use but too big to leave lying on the ground. Father had said that he was to dump all of them in the rock pile.

"I wish there weren't so many little rocks," Harvey said with a sigh as he brought another armload to the pile. "They don't do us any good!"

"I wouldn't say that," Father huffed as he dropped a large stone into place. "Some of the smaller stones I can wedge into place between the large ones. Everything in our world has a purpose, no matter how small or worthless it seems sometimes."

"I guess so," Harvey agreed reluctantly. "But it takes so many trips to move these little rocks!"

"Anything worth doing takes a while," Father said. "We'll be glad we cleared the rocks away when we have a nice, soft lawn in front of the house with no rocks to cut our feet."

Harvey understood that. But his back ached. And he still kept thinking that if there weren't so many small rocks, he would have finished the job sooner.

Before too long it was time for lunch. Quickly Harvey ate

and then went outside to rest in the shade for a few minutes before getting back to work. As he leaned against a tree he heard a strange rattling sound, as though the rock pile were tumbling down. But he couldn't see any movement.

Curious, he wondered what could be going on. He walked slowly toward the rock pile, and the rattling got louder and louder.

Suddenly he stopped. The sound wasn't made by rocks falling down—it was the noise of a rattlesnake!

"Dad!" Harvey called as he reached to gather a handful of the small stones that had seemed useless before. "Dad! There's a rattler!"

As his father came running to help, Harvey started throwing the rocks toward the snake to scare him away. By the time his dad got there the snake had slithered across the road and was gone.

"You did it, son!" Dad said as he put his arm around Harvey's shoulders.

"Yeah. I used those small rocks."

"Everything has a purpose," Dad said again. "Little stones, little children … "

"Little children?" Harvey asked.

Dad nodded. "Even little children are important to Jesus. Little children can show big people how to love Jesus. And little children make big people happy."

(Adapted from a story in *Primary Treasure.*)

GEORGE'S HANDS

The Bible says, " 'For a man's heart determines his speech.' " Matthew 12:34.

GEORGE stared at the kitchen clock, wondering what made the little red hand go round and round so fast, while the larger black one went around more slowly. He liked seeing how things worked, and he wanted to find out what was inside that clock. But his mother had said he was not to take it apart. In fact, he wasn't even supposed to touch it.

One afternoon Mother had some errands to run downtown,

and George asked to stay home. He was old enough, and besides, his big brother Henry was going to be home, too. So Mother left them at home.

George's first mistake was to sit in the kitchen and stare at the clock. He was tempting himself to touch it. Before long he did just that. Then he did more than that. He stood up on the counter and took the clock off the wall. As he bent over to lay the clock on the counter, he lost his balance, and both he and the clock fell to the floor with a crash.

His head hurt, but he wasn't cut anywhere. He was worried about the clock, though. Was it broken? The clear, plastic cover had come off, and both the black hands and the little red hand no longer moved. Also, the clock wasn't humming anymore.

Instantly George knew he was in trouble. But he thought that maybe if he had the clock fixed by the time Mother got home, she wouldn't know anything, and he wouldn't get a spanking after all. So he pulled the hands off the clock and ran with them to find Henry.

"Please. You've got to fix these hands," George pleaded. "They don't work anymore."

"Where's the rest of the clock?" Henry asked. "There's nothing wrong with these hands; it's the *inside* of the clock that needs fixing!"

"But the hands aren't going right," George said.

"I know," his brother replied. "That's because there's something wrong *inside* the clock."

When Mother got home and saw the broken clock, she was upset. And after George got his punishment, she talked to him about *his* hands.

"When your hands do wrong, that's because there's trouble inside of you," Mother said. "If your hands pull hair or pinch or steal someone's things, putting medicine on them won't make them better. We have to fix what's inside you—your thoughts—before your hands will do right. First we think wrong, and then we do wrong. But if we think right, then we do right."

(Adapted from *Little Visits With God* by Allan Hart Jahsmann and Martin P. Simon.)

TODAY I FEEL LIKE POUTING

The Bible says, "When a man is gloomy, everything seems to go wrong; when he is cheerful, everything seems right!" Proverbs 15:15.

I like to watch faces. There are so many interesting ones around! Everyone has two eyes, one nose, and one mouth, but everyone looks a little bit different.

Have you ever watched your face in the mirror to see all the interesting expressions you can make? How does your face look when you're frightened? When you are confused? Or when you are angry? How about when you're acting silly? Can you pout? I'm told it takes more muscles to pout than it takes to smile.

Sometimes my children like to dress up and pretend they're somebody else. They put on different hats and some of their daddy's shirts and shoes and clump around the house as kings or pirates or angels. But it's interesting that just dressing up in funny clothes isn't enough. There's always a special look on their faces when they're pretending. How do you pretend to be a king or a pirate? What do you do with your face if you are pretending to be an angel? Do you smile?

Your face does whatever you tell it to, doesn't it? If you tell it to look mean at somebody, it will. And then what happens to that person? That person probably cries or looks mean himself. If you tell your face to pout at a friend, what does he do? He might go home and play with somebody else. Sometimes that's a good thing for him to do, because if you're feeling pouty, it might mean that you need to be by yourself to take a rest, anyway. But if you don't want your friend to go away, then pouting doesn't do you any good, does it?

People like to be around those who smile a lot and are friendly.

Here's something to try: Put on the meanest face you have and say, "Get out of here!" Now smile as big as you can and say it again with a smile. "Get out of here!" Does it make you laugh? It's hard to be mean when you're smiling, isn't it? A smile is really nice. Not only does it make you feel better; it helps your friends feel better too. A smile is the nicest gift you can give to the people you care about. Smile a lot!

ABOUT HEAVEN

The Bible says, "No mere man has ever seen, heard or even imagined what wonderful things God has ready for those who love the Lord." 1 Corinthians 2:9.

"MOMMY, will my puppy go to heaven when Jesus comes?" Paul asked one day. "And if he dies, will he be made alive like all the good people will?"

Mother thought a moment. "When you think of heaven, what do you think of?"

"Well," Paul said, closing his eyes. "I see pretty green grass, and blue rivers, and lots of pretty colored flowers everywhere. And I see lots of animals, too."

"Are there any people?"

"Yes."

"What are they wearing?"

"They're wearing long, white robes like we wear sometimes in Sabbath school. And everyone has a crown on."

"What are they doing?" Mother questioned.

"They are just standing around, talking to each other and petting the animals," Paul said.

"Does that sound like fun to you?"

"Yeah."

"Do you know what I see people doing in heaven?" Mother asked.

Paul shook his head.

"I see people playing in the water with the whales and riding on their backs. Some people are learning about how flowers grow and are digging in the soft, brown dirt in their gardens. Children are sitting on the grass with Jesus, listening to stories. And over there is Daniel talking about what it was like in that lions' den!"

"But will my puppy be there?" Paul asked again.

Mother smiled. "I don't know, honey," she said. "We are not told whether our animals from this earth will go to heaven or not. But the Bible says that no one has ever seen, heard, or imagined what wonderful things God has ready up in heaven for us. You will be very happy there, even if your puppy isn't there. And if it isn't, Jesus will be able to explain why."

Heaven is a happy place. Mothers and daddies won't get

tired there and will be able to spend all day with us. They won't have to go to work and leave their children with a baby-sitter. We will never get tired, so we won't need to sleep. We can just do fun things with those we love all day long, forever.

What are some things you look forward to doing in heaven?

WHEN THE TRAIN DIDN'T STOP

The Bible says, " 'Don't . . . [worry] about tomorrow. God will take care of your tomorrow too. Live one day at a time.' " Matthew 6:34.

WHEN I was a little girl in India we rode the train quite often on vacations. One night our train was almost empty. The only people besides myself in our train car were my mother, my brother Peter, and an Indian woman who didn't know any English. Daddy had gotten off to fill our thermos with water.

It was a hot, dark night. One yellow light bulb in the ceiling cast long shadows in the corners and under the hanging bunk beds on the wall. Mother busied herself laying out our sleeping bags, and Peter and I played with our toys. Suddenly the train started to move. But Daddy wasn't back yet! Glancing out the window, we saw the lights of the train station move slowly past. We weren't supposed to be leaving yet! Where was Daddy?

Fearing that he would be left behind, Mother jumped up from her seat and reached for a padded chain above the window that said "Pull to stop train." She yanked it, but the train didn't stop. Then she jerked on the chain, sometimes nearly hanging on it with all her weight, but still the train kept on moving. The wheels continued to squeak slowly along the tracks, the cars groaning and bumping into each other.

When the Indian woman looked up at Mother, she started laughing and saying something in her own language that we couldn't understand, and waving her hands at Mother to stop pulling on the chain and sit down. But Mother wanted to stop the train. She didn't want Daddy to be left behind.

Then the Indian woman motioned out the window where beggars, standing on the steps of the train, reached inside for money. They were also laughing. Still, Mother kept on tugging hopelessly on the chain.

All at once the train stopped. The brakes squealed, and the cars bumped together with a boom. Then, very slowly, as before, the train started again, but this time it was going back the other way, toward the station.

Now the Indian lady really laughed as Mother returned to sit with Peter and me. Soon we stopped at the station. Daddy climbed up the steps and into the train.

"Where were you?" Mother cried in alarm.

"I was getting water," he said calmly. "Why?"

"We started going without you! I pulled and pulled on the chain, but it took a long time for them to stop."

"The train was just changing tracks," Daddy said. "I could see from the station. I don't think pulling the chain made any difference at all." Then he and Mother laughed, too.

Sometimes we ruin today by worrying about what's going to happen tomorrow. Will it rain the day of my party? Will I be able to find the right present for my friend? Worrying won't change anything, just as Mother's pulling on the chain wasn't what stopped the train. Tell God your worries, and then trust Him to help you. God knows what is really happening, even when you think everything is going wrong.

SOMETIMES I FEEL LIKE HIDING

The Bible says, "The Lord God called to Adam, 'Why are you hiding?'" Genesis 3:9.

JOEY listened from behind a big box as his mother called his name upstairs. The basement was dark and cool. He was sure Mother wouldn't find him there for a long time. His heart beat wildly as he thought about what Mother might do when she found the beans all over the kitchen floor. Would she understand that he was playing farmer and the beans accidentally spilled as he opened the bag? Too afraid to find out, Joey stayed crouched behind the box for a long time. Then he finally got up and walked upstairs to see Mother.

All of us sometimes feel like hiding. Usually, when we do, it is because we have done something wrong.

Adam and Eve were the first people to hide. After Eve picked the fruit from the one tree that God said they must not touch, she went running to him. The fruit was so good, she wanted him to try it, too.

"No. God said we mustn't!" Adam told her. He started to feel afraid. But then he went ahead and took a bite of the fruit anyway. Right away he felt bad. Adam didn't want to talk to God, so he took Eve's hand, and they ran behind some bushes to hide.

People want to hide when they feel guilty. And sometimes we want to hide when someone has hurt our feelings. But hiding doesn't always help. It just makes us feel bad longer. That's why it's better to make things right as soon as possible, rather than to hide and worry about it.

Even though Adam and Eve had done wrong, God still loved them. He wanted to be with them. But even though He loved them, they still had to be punished by leaving the beautiful Garden of Eden and making their home somewhere else.

Your parents would never make you leave home for *your* punishment, but sometimes they might spank you or make you stand in the corner or go to your room. Sometimes it hurts to be punished. But being afraid doesn't feel good, either, does it? As long as you're hiding you feel afraid: Will you get spanked? Will someone be angry with you? Will they like you anymore? Will everything be OK? You won't know until you stop hiding and make things right.

If you have done something wrong, it's best to say you're sorry right away. Then you'll feel better sooner.

If someone you love has accidentally hurt your feelings, and that's why you feel like hiding, tell him about it so he can explain. Then he'll hug you and you'll feel better again. Don't hide. Talk to someone. Jesus wants you to feel good.

GOD LOVES BAD PEOPLE

The Bible says, "When Jesus came by he looked up at Zacchaeus and called him by name. 'Zacchaeus!' he said. 'Quick! Come down! For I am going to be a guest in your home today!'" Luke 19:5.

ZACHARY itched all over. He reached back to scratch his back. Then he scratched each of his arms. His legs itched, his feet—even the spaces between his toes. Everything itched until he thought he couldn't stand it anymore. Finally he ran into the house.

"Mommy! Mommy! I itch all over! What's the matter with me?"

She looked at his arms. Red streaks from his scratching covered them. But underneath the streaks his mother saw some red spots.

"Looks as if you have hives," she said.

"What are hives?"

"Hives are these red spots on your body," Mother explained. "I'll bet they're from the strawberries you had last night and this morning. That happens to Daddy, too, when he eats them."

"What do we do about them?"

"We'll call your doctor and see if he wants you to have some medicine to stop the itching. And then you'll just have to stop eating strawberries."

"Not eat strawberries? But I love strawberries!" Zachary protested. "I don't want to stop eating strawberries. No!"

"Do you like what they do to you?" Mother asked.

"Well, no. I don't like itching like this. But I sure do love eating strawberries. I love how they taste!"

"You love strawberries, but you don't like what they do, do you?" Mother continued.

Zachary nodded. "I'll never hate strawberries," he said. "Never! Even if they do make me itch!"

You know the story of Zacchaeus, don't you? He was a cheater. Nobody in town liked him at all. But then Jesus came into town for a visit, and He even had lunch with Zacchaeus! We don't usually eat lunch with people we don't like, do we? But Jesus ate with Zacchaeus. And that's how I know that He loved Zacchaeus, even though He didn't like what Zacchaeus did. God loves you, too. Even though you pout sometimes, or feel mean and angry sometimes, and even though you punch your brother. God still loves you. Nothing you can do can make Him stop loving you. You are very special to Him.

ABOUT BEING DIFFERENT

The Bible says, "Christ has given each of us special abilities — whatever he wants us to have." Ephesians 4:7.

WHAT does your mother put into vegetable soup? Some carrots? And potatoes? Maybe some onions and lentils and tomatoes? Green beans? Do you like vegetable soup? Are there people in your family who do *not* like vegetable soup? What kind of soup do they like instead? If everybody in your family likes vegetable soup, then your mother probably makes it often.

Can you think of something you like to eat or do that nobody else in your family likes? What is something that everybody *else* likes to eat or do, but *you* don't?

Mandy and her sister were taking swimming lessons. Her sister, Misty, loved to go swimming. She could do anything the teacher asked her to do. Misty could jump off the diving board and swim to the side. Or she could dive off the side of the pool and swim across the pool without choking or anything. She was really good at swimming!

But Mandy hated it. She was scared of the water, scared to jump off the board, and scared to dive off the side. Mandy couldn't swim across the pool without choking. But she had to go to her lesson because Daddy had already paid for it, and he said that she should know how to swim for safety reasons, in case she ever fell into the river behind their house. So Mandy went to swimming lessons, but she didn't enjoy them. She was a little bit jealous of Misty, because her sister was so good at swimming. The teacher always told the students to watch Misty every time they tried something new.

"I guess I'm not any good," Mandy said to herself as she watched her sister and the other children having fun in the water. "I can't swim, and I don't like the water, so I'm just dumb."

Mandy's daddy didn't know she felt that way because she never told him. He was proud of her for trying, even if she didn't do as well as Misty. But he could see that Mandy didn't enjoy herself.

When the swimming lessons were over, Daddy asked her if she would like to take gymnastic lessons.

The next week when Misty went to her new swimming lesson, Mandy went to gymnastics. And she loved it! Before too long, Mandy was doing cartwheels in the backyard, and double somersaults, and flips on the trampoline. She couldn't swim as well as Misty could, but, then, Misty couldn't do gymnastics as well as she could, either.

All of us have some things we do better than others. Just because you can't swim better than your sister or brother doesn't mean you are dumb. And just because somebody else likes something you don't like doesn't mean *they* are dumb, either. God made us all different. Nobody else in the whole world is exactly like you! And never will anyone be! You are special. So if somebody else likes doing something that you don't find interesting at all, don't make fun of him. He is just being himself. That's neat! You can be yourself, too. What do you think some of your special abilities are? Maybe your parents can help you find out.

SOMETIMES I FEEL JEALOUS

The Bible says, " 'I now see how true it is that God has no favourites.' " Acts 10:34, N.E.B.

QUIETLY Reuben stood under a tree and watched his little brother playing with his pet lamb.

Little pest, he thought. Joseph always gets whatever he wants. Just because he's Daddy's favorite, he thinks he's so smart.

Reuben remembered all the special things his father had done for his brother. He always got the best piece of dessert. Whenever Joseph wanted a donkey ride, Reuben had to stop

226

what he was doing and go with him. And now his father was spending all his time weaving a brand-new coat for Joseph. He never had time for Reuben or any of the other big brothers anymore—all because of that brand-new coat.

Reuben and Dan and all the other older brothers were angry at Joseph. And it didn't make them any happier when the boy told them about his dreams. Such strange dreams he had! One day he told them that that night he had dreamed he was in a field with twelve bundles of grain. And in his dream those twelve bundles bowed down and worshiped his bundle.

"You think that just because Dad thinks you're so neat we will bow to you, too?" Dan laughed, giving Joseph a gentle shove. "Those dreams are ridiculous, Joseph. They're just dreams. Stop being so crazy!"

But Joseph could not forget them.

One day when Joseph's brothers were away from home with the sheep, Joseph's daddy sent him to find them, to make sure they were safe. Joseph's brothers saw him coming a long way off. They weren't happy to see him.

"Here comes that dreamer!" they said. "Here's our chance to get rid of him!" They wanted to kill him, but one of the older brothers knew that was wrong. Instead, he talked the rest into selling Joseph to the camel traders as a slave. Then he would be taken far away to another country, and perhaps they would never see him again. That wasn't nice either, was it?

But that's just what they did. You know the rest of the story. Many years passed before they ever saw Joseph again. Joseph's brothers hated him because they thought he was their daddy's favorite son. They were jealous.

Everyone feels jealous sometimes. We may think our parents love our brother (or sister) more than they love us because he gets something we don't get, or we hear them telling him about something he did well. But remember all the times they have done that for you, too! Parents love each of their children in a special way.

How would you feel if your parents said they weren't going to celebrate your birthday this year because you already had received presents at Christmas? You would miss that birthday celebration, wouldn't you, even though you had received presents at Christmas. That's how parents think of their children. Even though you and your brothers and sisters are alike in some ways, you are different, too. And your family would miss you if you weren't around. Just because you are excited about your birthday doesn't mean you won't be excited about Christmas, too, does it? You are special—even when brother or sister is getting attention. Next time it will be you.

ABOUT BROTHERS

The Bible says, "There are 'friends' who pretend to be friends, but there is a friend who sticks closer than a brother." Proverbs 18:24.

BRAD's puppy, Cindy Lou, was in trouble. She wouldn't go to the bathroom on the papers that Mother had spread in the laundry room, and the dog kept following her around wherever she went, tripping her and nipping at her heels.

"That dog has to sleep in the playhouse tonight, she does!" Mother said firmly one evening. She shook her foot to make the puppy let go of her jeans. "I'm sick and tired of her, and I'm sick and tired of her messes. The whole house smells of dog! That's it! I've had it! Out she goes!"

"But, Mother," Brad began, "she's just a little thing, and she might get cold and scared out in the playhouse all by herself!"

"We'll fix up a bed for her and she'll be just fine," Mother said, pushing aside the puppy with her leg.

"But Mother," he protested, "I'll feel sorry for her out there all alone, and I won't be able to sleep either. If Cindy Lou has to sleep in the playhouse, then I'll sleep out there with her!"

His big brother Tom looked at him in astonishment.

"You sleep out in the playhouse?" he said with a laugh. "Why, if I remember rightly, you won't even walk around outside at night, let alone sleep out there by yourself!"

"Never mind! Cindy Lou is just a baby, and she needs someone to take care of her. She needs *me* with her!"

Mother didn't say anything. She figured that Brad would change his mind before long. But he didn't. When Mother started toward the playhouse with old blankets and a basket, he picked up his pillow and a sleeping bag and followed after her, carrying Cindy Lou. The more Brad thought about sleeping alone in the playhouse, the more he decided that maybe Cindy Lou would be OK by herself. But he was afraid Tom would laugh at him, and he didn't want that to happen. Then he remembered that Cindy Lou needed him—she really did!

When Mother turned to go back to the house, Brad thought about asking her to stay, but decided against it. Just giving her a kiss, he turned on his flashlight as he curled up next to Cindy Lou. He didn't think he would sleep much that night.

When he was sure that Cindy Lou was settled for the night, Brad turned out his light and closed his eyes to say his prayers. He stopped when he heard footsteps. The playhouse door opened and there stood his brother, carrying his pillow and sleeping bag, too.

"I thought I'd sleep out here tonight too," Tom said. "We can pretend we're camping out. You don't mind, do you?"

"No, not at all!" Brad exclaimed. He scooted over to make room for him. "I always feel safe with you, big brother," he said. Then he turned over, closed his eyes, and went to sleep.

Big brothers are nice to have around, aren't they? Jesus wants to be our Big Brother. He cares for us more than any big brother we could ever have!

SOMETIMES I FEEL HOPELESS

The Bible says, "When I was a child I spoke and thought and reasoned as a child does. . . . And now I have put away the childish things." 1 Corinthians 13:11.

SOPHIE stood at the bottom of a high mountain with her daddy and stared up at the top. Are we going to climb all the way up there? she wondered. It seemed a long climb—probably straight up the mountainside. Sophie was sure she couldn't go up that steep a mountain.

Daddy smiled as he threw a water jug over his shoulder. "This is going to be fun!" he said.

Carefully he began parting the bushes in an effort to find a trail he had used before. Soon they were on it, and Sophie followed along behind, holding on to the bushes and sometimes pulling herself gently along with them. The mountain didn't seem very steep at all. At times it even seemed to Sophie that they were walking on flat ground, it was so easy.

Finally, Daddy stopped to look down to where they'd come from.

"We're almost at the top!" Sophie laughed. She was surprised that she wasn't more tired.

Daddy nodded. "Yes, we really are almost at the top," he said. "That wasn't so hard, was it?"

"No!" Sophie agreed. "How come it was so easy?"

"Look at our trail," Daddy said. He pointed down at the path that wound through the bushes toward the bottom of the mountain. Like a snake, the trail zigzagged back and forth along the side of the mountain. "It wasn't so hard, because instead of going straight up, we walked back and forth, going up a little bit at a time," he explained.

That's how children grow up. Sometimes you may worry that you'll never be able to be as good as you want to be. You may think that you'll always be selfish. Or maybe you wonder if you'll ever be able to write or to read.

Everyone who is now grown-up has felt that way before. We learn things slowly as we grow up.

Have you ever noticed that if there's just one cooky left in the cooky jar, and both you and your Mommy want it, she'll let *you* have it? Or maybe she'll take just a pinch, but you get the biggest piece. That's because your mommy is grown up. When you grow up it will be easier for you to share and do other grown-up things, too. So don't worry about it. Just keep trying. Every time you share something or help someone up and tell them you are sorry they got hurt, you are learning to be a grown-up. Growing up comes a little bit at a time.

JESUS KNOWS EVERYTHING

The Bible says, "[Peter] said, 'Lord, you know all things.' " John 21:17, N.I.V.

DADDY's hammer was missing. He looked all through the garage, where he usually kept his tools, but he couldn't find it anywhere. Finally, he asked Mother and Matthew if they had seen it.

Mother hadn't seen it anywhere.

Matthew said he might know where it was.

"Well, can you show me?" Daddy asked. "I really need that hammer today!"

His son nodded sheepishly. "I can get it for you," he said.

"Did you take it to your room?" Daddy asked.

But Matthew didn't say anything. He had been building a special surprise boat for his daddy and didn't want him to know about it. "I'll get your hammer for you," was all he would say.

But Daddy was getting angry. "I have no way of knowing what happened to that hammer unless you tell me. Now, tell me. Did you take my hammer to your room?"

At last Matthew nodded. "Yes," he said in a quiet voice. "I took your hammer yesterday when you were at work because I wanted to make a surprise for you. But it's not a surprise anymore, I guess!" and Matthew began to cry.

Matthew thought his daddy knew everything, that he had guessed because the hammer was missing that Matthew had been making a present for him. His Daddy did know a lot, but not everything. He had not guessed what his son had been doing with the hammer.

The only person who knows everything is Jesus. Isn't it nice to have a friend like that? It's nice, but some people think it's also scary.

If Jesus knows everything, then He knows what we do when we are all by ourselves. He knows what we're thinking and what we're planning to do. But because Jesus loves us, it isn't scary to me. Because nothing we can say, or do, or even think can make Jesus stop loving us!

And since Jesus knows everything, He knows we love Him, even when other people may not think we are showing it. Sometimes other people don't understand what we're trying to do—like Matthew's daddy and the hammer. But Jesus understands.

One day in Sabbath school a little girl sitting next to Jill dropped the animal picture that she was going to put up on the board.

Jill reached for the picture on the floor. Her teacher saw her start to pick up the other girl's picture. She thought Jill was going to keep it and put up two pictures.

"Jill, give that picture back to Lily," the teacher said. She didn't know Jill was trying to be helpful. But Jesus did. Jesus knows everything. And Jesus understands!

SAVED FROM THE TRAIN

The Bible says, "It is not [God's] will that even one of these little ones should perish." Matthew 18:14.

MANY years ago my husband's grandpa Jicha (pronounced Yeeka) was head brakeman on a logging train near McKinleyville, California. Every day that train would go *chug, chug, chug* along the beach and then into the forest to pick up huge redwood trees that loggers had cut down. A big crane loaded the logs onto the special cars one after another until the train was quite long and had a heavy load to take to the sawmill. There the saws would cut the trees into boards for houses and ships and furniture and other things.

One day as the train *clickety-clacked* along the beach, Grandpa Jicha looked ahead down the tracks that seemed to stretch endlessly beside the ocean. What he saw made his heart start beating wildly. He couldn't believe what was going to happen. For there, standing in the middle of the railroad tracks several hundred yards away, was a little 3-year-old girl.

"Blow the whistle!" Grandpa Jicha shouted. "There's a child on the tracks!"

But the little girl just stood there watching that big, heavy train racing toward her. Too afraid to run, she just stood there with her mouth open, watching.

Grandpa threw on the brakes, and they started a loud, earsplitting screech as the metal scraped along the rails. White steam hissed out from under the train, and sparks flashed from beneath the wheels. The whistle was blowing, metal was screeching, the steam was hissing, but the little girl just stood still in the middle of the tracks, watching the train rush toward her. The heavy logs made it impossible to stop the train quickly. Soon Grandpa Jicha could see that the little girl was not going to move. Unless someone pulled her out of the way, the locomotive would crush her. It could not stop in time.

Grandpa could not let that happen. He decided to try something very dangerous that he had never done before.

Quickly, yet carefully, he worked his way along the side of the black, greasy engine, through the steam, till he stood at the very front of the engine on the narrow platform above the cowcatcher. He got his balance, and not a moment too soon.

Just before the train would have run over the little girl, Grandpa reached down and scooped her up in his arms, and the train rumbled over the spot where she had stood only a moment before.

At last the train screeched to a stop and Grandpa jumped down with the little girl in his arms. He tousled her hair, and she ran crying to her mother.

Grandpa didn't mind that she didn't say Thank you. He didn't care if anybody knew what he had done. Nor did he consider himself a hero. It didn't make any difference who that little girl was, or whether she was pretty or nice or had a lot of toys. Grandpa Jicha was not willing to let her get run over by a train. He would have done it for anybody. And that's how Jesus feels about us, too.

HEARING AND ASKING

The Bible says, "They found [Jesus] in the temple courts, sitting among the teachers, listening to them and asking them questions." Luke 2:46, N.I.V.

CHERRY ran down the sidewalk and up the steps into her house. "Mommy. Mommy!" she called, hurrying through the living room to the back porch. "Mommy! Kara's moving away! To New York!"

"Moving? Are you sure?" Mother asked as she fingered the leaves of one of her plants and carefully poured some water onto its roots.

"Yes! Kara's moving. And I'll never see her again. She says New York is very far away and they're going to go by airplane and everything."

"Are you really sure?" Mother asked again. She set down her watering can and looked down at Cherry. "Seems like Kara's mother would have told me if they were moving."

"She said they just decided to. I'm the first person she's told. I'd better tell Shannon. She's going to be sad, I'll betcha!"

Before Mother could stop her, Cherry ran out the back door, down the steps, and around to Shannon's house.

The news surprised Shannon. "Kara can't leave!" she said

firmly. "She promised me a trip to her grandpa's farm, and she hasn't done that yet."

"Yeah. And she promised to show me her underground cellar, and she hasn't done that yet, either! What if some grouchy old people move into her house when she leaves? Then we'll *never* get to do the things she promised."

"She just can't leave!" Shannon repeated. "It wouldn't be fair."

"You're right. It would be very mean of her."

"You know," Shannon said, as an idea flashed into her head. "Since Kara's going to leave anyway, we don't need her for our friend. She's not going to take me to her grandpa's farm, and she's not going to show you her cellar, so we don't need to play with her anymore. Just let her go to New York and make some new friends!"

"You're right!" Cherry agreed. And they didn't play with Kara for two whole days.

Kara felt very sad and left out. She tried to talk to them, but they just stuck their noses in the air and wouldn't tell her why they were angry.

Finally Cherry's mother told her to talk to Kara. Cherry told the girl that she was angry because Kara was moving away.

"I'm not moving away," Kara exclaimed, "I'm just going to New York for a vacation. I'll just be gone two weeks, and then I'll be back, and you can go to my grandpa's farm, and I'll show you my cellar then. I'm not leaving."

Cherry's mouth dropped open in surprise. "Oh, Kara, I'm sorry!" she said. "I told Shannon and everybody that you were moving away. I'm really sorry!"

What should Cherry have done before she told everyone that Kara was leaving? Cherry should have asked more questions. She should have asked how long Kara would be gone.

When Jesus was a little boy He listened and He asked questions until He understood. If something worries you, ask somebody about it. It is better to ask questions than to go on being worried or angry because you don't know.

234

WHEN BARNEY FORGOT

The Bible says, "The Lord is full of compassion and mercy."
James 5:11, N.I.V.

MOTHER came in the front door holding out Barney's wet,
muddy coat by the tips of her fingers. "Dear me, Barney. I
knew you loved your dog, but to give him your brand-new
coat to sleep on is a bit too much!"

"Oh, I forgot!" Barney said. He reached for the coat and
smiled a guilty smile. "I guess I left it lying by the front door
last night when I went over to Jesse's. Sorry!"

"You'll really be sorry if it happens again," Mother warned
him. "Seems like you've been leaving your stuff lying around
a lot here, lately. Daddy found your jar of caterpillars on its
side behind the toilet last night."

"Were they OK?"

"Yes! But if he hadn't found them, I suspect they would
have stayed there until they turned into butterflies and started
flying around the room," she said playfully.

"I'm sorry, Mom. I'll be more careful about putting my
things away from now on."

"I expect you will. Starting today, anything I find lying
around that's yours, I will keep until Christmas."

"But that's months away!" Barney cried.

"It shouldn't matter if you keep your things picked up.
Now, run along."

For the rest of that week Barney was good about picking up
his things and putting them away, especially his baseball
uniform. He was the pitcher, and the last game of the season
was coming up in two weeks. The team wouldn't let him play
without a uniform.

One night, after Mother's new rule had been in effect for
several days, Barney remembered his baseball uniform lying
in a heap by the shower. But he was already in bed, and he
was so tired that he decided he would get up early and put it
in the dirty clothes hamper first thing in the morning. Mother
wouldn't know he hadn't done it that night.

The next morning it was not there. Mother had found the
uniform and was going to keep it till Christmas. That meant
Barney wouldn't be able to play baseball with the team next

Sunday. It was no use asking her for the suit. She wouldn't go back on her word.

The Sunday of the big game came. Barney had to call the coach and explain why he couldn't play. He picked at his breakfast and lay around on the couch until lunch. All morning he kept thinking about the game coming up that afternoon. His team would probably lose without him.

Just before lunch Mother sat down beside Barney with a wrapped box in her hands. "For you," she said mysteriously.

"Really?" He ripped the box open. There was his baseball suit, all clean and folded. Now he could play with the team after all. With questioning eyes he looked at his mother. "Thanks! But why, Mom?"

"Because I love you. God doesn't give us blessings and happiness because we deserve them, but just because He loves us. I figured I could do the same for you."

ABOUT NAMES

The Bible says, "God will [give] you a new name." Isaiah 62:2.

DO you have a nickname? Does your mother ever call you Sweetheart, or Honey? Or does your daddy call you Buddy? Names are fun. And your name is very special.

When you were born, probably one of the first things your doctor asked your Mommy and Daddy was, "What are you going to call this baby?" That's what people usually ask when a baby is born: "What's its name?" Maybe your parents had a special name all picked out for you before your birth. Sometimes they do, you know. And sometimes Mommies and Daddies just like to look at their special baby for a day or two so they can pick out a name that fits him or her just right. Maybe they will give their baby boy the same name as his daddy, or his grandpa or uncle. Baby girls may get one of their mommy's names, or the name of an aunty or grandma. That makes that person very proud to have a baby named after him.

Usually your last name is the same as your daddy's. All the

people in your family usually have the same last name, and that's how other people know that you belong to each other and are related.

Many times mommies and daddies choose names that mean something special to them. For example, I know a little boy whose name is Nathan. *Nathan* means "gift of God." His parents had been told that they would probably never be able to have children. Then they adopted Nathan. They were happy to have a baby to love! To them, Nathan was a gift from God.

Maybe your name is David. If so, it means "beloved one." *Holly* means "holy." *Linda* means "beautiful." *Peter* means "a rock." *Christian* means we are like Christ Jesus.

Names can make us feel very good. But sometimes they can make us feel bad, too, can't they? No one wants to be called "fatty," or "pig," or "carrot top," or "spider"! That isn't kind. People want others to refer to them by their real name, or a name that they like and that makes them feel good.

The Bible tells us that when we get to heaven, God will give us each a special name. We'll probably still keep the one our parents gave us, but the name God gives us will be another one. I can hardly wait to see what my new name will be! What do you think yours might be? Can you think of a word that describes you?

Ask your Mommy and Daddy what your name means, and why they chose it for you. I'm sure they have a very special reason for naming you what they did.

TODAY I FEEL LIKE PRAISING GOD

The Bible says, "I will praise you, O Lord." Psalm 108:3, N.I.V.

RYAN was singing quietly to himself as he played. "Heavenly Father, I love You. Holy Spirit, up in heaven . . ."

"Why do you have to sing so much?" Ryan's sister Gail asked with a bit of anger in her voice. "The songs you sing don't make any sense at all. They're not real songs anyway!"

"Ryan is praising God!" Mother answered when he looked up in surprise without an answer.

"But does he always have to sing those silly songs? Can't he praise God some other way?"

"Yes," Mother said. "We can praise God in other ways. But singing his own songs is Ryan's way. And I have an idea that it makes God smile to hear him sing such loving songs."

Gail thought about making God smile. She wanted to make Him happy too.

"What are some other ways to praise God?" she asked Mother.

"Oh, there are several ways. We praise God when we say the blessing before meals. And you can praise God to your friends when you're outside eating an apple or a carrot. All you have to do is say something like 'M-m-m, this apple is sure good! Aren't you glad that God made apples so crispy and sweet?' That shows that you know who made the apple and you want everyone else to know too."

"I guess it makes God feel good, just as I feel good when you tell Daddy how well I set the table," Gail said.

"That's exactly right," Mother said with a smile. "God does many kind, loving things for us and keeps Daddy healthy so he can go to work and earn money to buy the things we need. God sends the sun and rain so our fruits and vegetables grow. And He gave us each other."

"Let's praise God right now!" Ryan said.

Wouldn't you like to praise God too and thank Him for what He has given you?

DUSTIN'S DUTIES

The Bible says, "A man can do nothing better than to eat and drink and find satisfaction in his work." Ecclesiastes 2:24, N.I.V.

IT was summer. Dustin's mother was busy canning fruits and freezing vegetables and working in the garden most of the day. She had given him some extra jobs to do while she was busy: jobs such as setting the table and then clearing off the dishes, emptying the dishwasher, and straightening the bathroom and keeping it clean. Actually, those extra jobs didn't keep Dustin that busy, and they didn't take long if he did them right away, but after a while he got tired of doing them. He would grumble and pout for so long, instead of getting started, that the jobs seemed hard and long, and grumbling about them took most of his time. It seemed like all he did was work, work, work.

"Daddy and I aren't just playing all day," Mother reminded him as she lifted a heavy basket of tomatoes onto the table. "We all have to work together to get the jobs done in the summer. What would you do if nobody did anything for *you?*"

"I'd be just fine," Dustin mumbled. "I could take care of myself and have lots of free time to play and do anything I wanted."

Mother looked at him for a long moment. "OK," she said. "We'll try it and see. Finish your jobs today, and then, starting tomorrow, you can just take care of yourself and do what you like. I'll take over your jobs for you. But remember: You don't do anything for me, and I don't do anything for you."

Dustin nodded, unable to believe his good fortune. Imagine not having to help around the house anymore!

The next morning he awoke to the smell of frying potatoes coming from the kitchen. He hurried to dress and ran to the kitchen where Mother and Daddy sat finishing their breakfast.

"Did you save some for me?" Dustin asked eagerly.

"You wanted to take care of yourself," Mother reminded him as she stood up to clear the table. "Go ahead and fix whatever you like for yourself."

With a sigh he poured some milk into a bowl of cold cereal and ate it slowly.

At lunchtime his bowl was still sitting on the table where he had left it, and while Mother and Daddy had lasagna and salad, Dustin chewed on a peanut butter sandwich he had made himself.

That afternoon his bike broke, but he knew he couldn't ask Mother to fix it. He was supposed to take care of himself today. Going inside for a glass of juice, he found the pitcher empty, and he couldn't open another can by himself. Mother had always helped him before.

Dustin went back outside, sat down on the steps, and put his chin in his hands. Then he sighed a long, heavy sigh. It wasn't really much fun when people didn't help one another. He remembered that it was kind of fun to help Mother with her work and chat together while they did it. It made him feel as if he belonged, and it felt good to know Mother needed him.

Getting up, Dustin went inside to find his mother. "I'm tired of not helping," he said. "I want to be a part of the family again. Can I empty the dishwasher for you?"

Mother winked. "You most certainly can!" she said. "Welcome back!"

TODAY I FEEL ANGRY

The Bible says, "Don't let the sun go down with you still angry—get over it quickly." Ephesians 4:26.

RUDY was angry. He had been playing at the park with his little brother when a bigger boy—larger than either of them—came over and grabbed the chain on his brother's swing.

"Hey, get off, kid," the other boy said. "I want to swing."

Jonathan was afraid of him. Quietly he slid off the swing and ran over to the slide.

But before long the bully, tired of swinging, sauntered over to the slide and climbed the steps right behind Jonathan.

"Hurry up, kid!" he said, banging his head into Jonathan's back. "You're in the way!"

Jonathan hurried up the steps as quickly as he could without falling. When he reached the top of the slide he sat down and slid to the bottom with a delighted giggle.

"Teeheehee," the other boy said, mimicking Jonathan. He stuck his foot out, and Jonathan tripped on it, falling down to the ground.

"You stop that!" Rudy said, coming over and standing as tall as he could. "You stop that, or I'm telling!"

The bigger boy put up his fists. "You wanna fight, kid?" he asked. "Come on! Let's see what you can do!"

Rudy didn't want to fight. Hurting someone or breaking things when you're angry doesn't help anything. Sometimes it makes things worse. But he *was* angry. It always made him angry to see bigger kids picking on someone smaller than them. He called to Jonathan, and they went home. That was the safest thing to do.

Everyone gets angry sometimes. The Bible says that Jesus became angry when He saw people using God's house as a marketplace. But He never hurt anyone. And He never got angry when people hurt Him.

It's all right to be angry when you see someone stealing, or hurting someone else, or making fun of God. But sometimes we feel selfish. Sometimes we get angry because someone won't let us have our own way. This kind of anger we must get over with quickly. And it's not OK to hurt someone or break things just because we feel this way. Jesus can help us choose not to be selfish. If we talk about what makes us angry, we can get over it faster.

The Bible says we shouldn't stay angry for long. That makes us miserable. Instead, we can ask Jesus to help us choose to be happy.

HERMAN AND JESUS

The Bible says, "We are convinced that one died for all, and therefore all died." 2 Corinthians 5:14, N.I.V.

MR. Ackerman had the best yard in the neighborhood. He had tall trees in his backyard with a swing on one of them. And one tree had a tree house that he had built for his grandchildren when they came to visit. Herman and his friends liked to play in his backyard, and Mr. Ackerman liked to have them visit, too.

"But please stay out of my flower beds," he said as he shook his finger. "I don't want my flowers trampled on."

"Oh, we'll be careful!" Herman and his friends promised.

One day Ryan was practicing jumping out of the swing. Now, jumping out of a swing is a rather dangerous thing to do if you're not old enough, but he was about 9 years old, so he knew how to do it. He waited until the swing was low enough to do it safely. Then he jumped and flew out of the swing, landing on the ground with a thud.

"Hey! That was fun!" Ryan said as he got up and ran back to the swing.

"It's my turn!" Jack said as he sat in the swing.

Ryan pulled on the ropes. "No it's not, it's my turn again. You were climbing the tree!"

"Was not!"

"Were too!"

"Nope!"

"Were!"

Suddenly Jack punched him in the chest. Ryan hit him back and pushed him out of the swing. They began fighting on the ground, rolling and rolling around the yard.

All at once Jack rolled into the flower bed and crushed several of Mr. Ackerman's flowers.

"Now you've done it!" Ryan said. He stopped to look at the flowers and knew Mr. Ackerman would be mad.

"I'm afraid you two boys can't come play here anymore," Mr. Ackerman said as he came out of the house. He had been watching from his window. "You'd better go home. Only Herman can play here."

It was a sad Ryan and Jack who walked home. Herman missed having his friends with him in Mr. Ackerman's backyard. For several days he wondered what to do. Then he had an idea. He told Mr. Ackerman he was sorry for what his friends had done and offered to take care of Mr. Ackerman's garden and buy him some new flowers if his friends could play there again with him.

Mr. Ackerman agreed. Now Herman was happy. Ryan and Jack were glad, too, for what Herman had done for them.

When Jesus died on the cross, in a way it was as if He did the same thing. He said, "Please forgive My friends, Father. I want them in heaven with Me." Even though Herman and Jesus had done nothing wrong, they took a punishment so their friends could be with them. And that's why Jesus is our very special friend. We get to go to heaven because of what Jesus did.

WHAT SUE DIDN'T HAVE

The Bible says, "For I have learned how to get along happily whether I have much or little." Philippians 4:11.

TERRY skipped home happily, whistling a happy tune. Her best friend, Sue, had invited her to spend a whole weekend at her house, and Mother had said she could go. She patted the invitation in her pocket to make sure it was still there. Now she would have to check the time they were coming for her.

Late that afternoon, when Sue and her mother came to pick Terry up, Terry could hardly sit still. The drive passed quickly as she and Sue discussed everything they were going to do, and soon the car pulled up in the driveway.

Terry lifted out her small suitcase and followed Sue inside. At the front door she let out a long "Oh-h-h." The house was enormous! It had a beautiful chandelier hanging over the entryway and polished wooden stairs that curved up to the bedrooms.

"Let me show you my room," Sue said, and Terry followed quietly. She had no idea her friend lived like this. Why, this was a mansion!

Sue's bedroom was as big as Terry's living room. She opened her closet to reveal hanger after hanger of dresses and skirts and blouses. It seemed like more clothes than both Mother and Daddy had in their closet. And it all belonged to one person. Terry hung up her things and then went outside with Sue to play.

That night the two girls had to eat in the kitchen because they were too dirty to eat in the dining room. They had to take showers downstairs before they could go up to Sue's room.

Sabbath morning dawned bright and clear, and they had fun telling all their friends at church about their weekend together. Terry told her mom she was having fun—and she was!

But that night Sue's daddy had to go to his office to do some work, and her mother worked downstairs on some "projects." Terry and Sue played a few new games that Sue's mother had bought just for that weekend, and then they went to bed.

Sunday morning Terry awoke to the smell of pancakes and

eggs. But when the girls got downstairs, they found that Sue's parents had already eaten and left. A note said that Sue's mother had gone shopping, and her father had gone to play golf. The pancake batter and eggs were in the refrigerator. They could make their own breakfast.

"Is it always this way around here?" Terry asked Sue as she stirred up the eggs.

"Yes, it is. Why? Don't you like it?"

"I'm having fun being with you," Terry said quickly, "but I think I would miss having my parents around if I were you."

"They're both very busy," Sue explained. "But they buy me a lot of stuff."

Terry nodded silently. When she got home that evening she hugged her parents. "It's good to be home!" she said.

"Didn't you have fun?" Mother asked.

"Oh, yeah! Sue has lots of stuff," Terry said, "but I don't think she is as lucky as I am. She seldom sees her family!"

"Everyone lives differently," Mother said. "I'm glad you're happy with us."

"I'd rather have *my* family than Sue's," Terry said.

And that's just the way it should be!

SOMETIMES I FEEL STUBBORN

The Bible says, "But be ye doers of the word, and not hearers only." James 1:22, K.J.V.

MY dad tells me that one day when I was a little girl, I came into the house with mud all over my face and tummy. "Go look at yourself in the mirror!" he said with a smile. "You're all muddy."

Running to the bathroom, I climbed on a stool and looked into the mirror. There I saw my muddy face and muddy tummy. But then I turned around and stared at the reflection of my back. It wasn't dirty.

"I'm clean!" I said as I hurried in to see Daddy again.

"You don't look clean to me," he said.

"Well, I looked at my back. And *it's* clean!"

It's sometimes hard to see ourselves dirty. It's hard to say that we have shoved someone down. It's hard to admit that we have taken someone else's toy or said naughty words. But we have to if we are going to get clean inside.

Daddy went with me back to the bathroom, where he washed my face and tummy and got all the mud off. Now I was really clean.

To get clean inside we have to ask forgiveness from God and from the person we were mean to. Then we will be clean inside.

Suppose your mother did this to you: If you asked her for some milk at breakfast, suppose she just smiled at you and said, "Yes, I hear you," but didn't give you any?

And if you needed some help with your socks and shoes, suppose she just smiled and said, "Sure, honey," but didn't help you?

How about if you said, "I'm hungry!" but Mother just sat in her chair and didn't fix you any food?

How do you feel when you tell a friend something important, and she doesn't seem to listen? It doesn't make you feel very good, does it?

God says we are to do more than just hear about what we should do. We are supposed to *do* the right things, too. When God asks us to be happy with what we have, then we are to choose to be happy. When He says we are to obey Mommy and Daddy, then we are supposed to do that and not just say we will. And when He tells us not to lie or steal, or that we should go to church on Sabbath, then that's what we must do. What are some other things that Jesus asks us to do? Do you do them? Only by doing them can we be really happy inside.

TODAY I FEEL WORRIED

The Bible says, "Anxious hearts are very heavy but a word of encouragement does wonders!" Proverbs 12:25.

ERIC was worried. His mother and father had told him that they were all flying to his grandmother's house for a vacation in two weeks. The thought of it frightened him.

"What's the matter?" his mother asked when she saw his solemn face.

"Nothin'," Eric said quickly.

"Aren't you excited about seeing Grandma?" she questioned. "She's looking forward to seeing you!"

"Oh, I'm excited about seeing Grandma," Eric said, "but I'm worried about getting there."

"What are you worried about?" Mother asked. "Maybe I can help you."

"Well, we're leaving for her house in two weeks, and Daddy said we're flying there . . . but"—Eric started crying—"I don't know how to fly!" He thought he had to fly like a bird. When his mother told him they were going to fly in an airplane, he felt better.

Shawna worried about going to preschool because she didn't know how to tie her shoes yet.

"What if my shoes come off?" she worried. "How will I get them back on?"

"Your teacher can help you," Mother explained. "She likes working with children. And she won't mind helping you at all."

Greg was afraid to go to preschool, too. He worried that he would have to go to the bathroom and wouldn't be able to get his pants snapped up again.

Mother had an idea. "Why don't we make sure you wear your belt on preschool day," she said. "You can zip your pants easily, but if you can't snap them, at least you can fasten your belt over the snap and nobody will know that your pants aren't snapped. They won't fall down, either, with your belt in place."

Greg was glad he had told his mother why he was afraid. Now he could enjoy preschool and not be scared.

Some children are afraid they'll go down the drain in the bathtub with the water. (They won't.) Probably other things bother you. You know what they are, even though nobody else does. But you don't want to say anything, because maybe you're afraid somebody will laugh at you.

Your parents would like to know what upsets you. If you tell them that you would like to talk about something that bothers you, they won't laugh at you. They will probably be able to help, and you won't need to worry about that thing anymore.

Tell your parents what you're concerned about. Because they love you, they want to help you not to worry.

SAVING SANDY

The Bible says, " 'This is our God, in whom we trust, for whom we waited. Now at last he is here.' " Isaiah 25:9.

ALTHOUGH she was supposed to be going to sleep, Gloria was listening to something her mother was saying in the next room.

"Gloria will be getting so many new toys for her birthday tomorrow that perhaps we should go through her toy box and take out the old, broken ones to make room."

"Good idea!" Daddy agreed. "I'll get a box for the worn-out ones."

The girl heard the sound of her old toys going thud, boom, into the box. She thought of her old broken drum, and the rusty plates and cups. Those things she wouldn't miss. And they were probably throwing away her old coloring books and dried-up Play-Doh, too.

All at once she heard something that made her lie very still and stare into the darkness so she could hear better.

"That old doll with the messy hair and broken arm can be tossed," Mother said. "Gloria will be glad to get a pretty, new one tomorrow, I'm sure."

Her heart started to pound. She started crying silently into her pillow. "They're talking about Sandy," she said to herself. "They can't throw Sandy away! Even if they think she's old and ugly, I love her!" Gloria couldn't go to sleep now while thinking about her favorite doll. Somehow she had to rescue her after Mother and Daddy went to bed.

Before long Mother and Daddy decided to stop sorting through Gloria's toys. The house became dark and quiet. When she was sure that Mother and Daddy were asleep, Gloria tiptoed out of her room and past her parents' bedroom. She stood at the top of the long, dark stairway. Sandy was down there somewhere in a box, and she had to rescue her before Daddy took her away in the morning.

Slowly, quietly, Gloria started down the stairs. She took a deep breath and held onto the railing as she started down. Once, when the stair creaked, she stopped and stood very still so she wouldn't wake up her parents. Finally she reached the bottom of the stairs and saw the big carton of her old toys waiting by the front door. The porch light shone in the front window enough so Gloria could see quite well as she started searching for Sandy. There in the bottom of the box was her favorite doll, squished by the other toys.

"Oh, Sandy, I'm sorry!" she whispered into the doll's messy hair as she hugged her close. Smiling, Gloria hurried up the stairs and back into bed with Sandy in her arms.

Jesus loves us even more than Gloria loved her doll. And just as Sandy couldn't get out of that deep box without help from above, we can't go to heaven without someone coming down and taking us there. Someday Jesus will come for us. We will be saved.

SOMETIMES I FEEL LEFT OUT

The Bible says, "For God treats everyone the same." Romans 2:11.

EVERYONE except Aaron was invited to Matthew's birthday party.

"Are you going to the party?" his friend Justin asked excitedly.

Aaron shook his head. "I wasn't invited," he said sadly.

Justin ran to ask another friend if he was going. That friend nodded, and the two boys began talking about how much fun it was going to be.

How would you feel if you were Aaron? Aaron wanted to cry as he thought that maybe he was a bad person and nobody liked him anymore. He felt left out.

Nobody likes feeling left out. We want to know that people like us and that they want to be with us.

The day of the party, Aaron thought about all his friends having fun together without him. He felt so bad, he didn't really want to play. But he went outside anyway and started kicking a ball around the yard.

Just then a new boy rode up on his bike. "Hey. May I play?" he asked with a smile.

Aaron smiled shyly. "Yeah, I guess," he said slowly.

The two boys kicked the ball back and forth to each other. Then the new boy suggested playing cars in Aaron's sandbox.

The new boy was so nice and they had so much fun together that Aaron forgot all about the party.

When it was time for him to go home, he gave Aaron a pat on the back. "Thanks for playing with me," he said. "All my other friends went to the park together and didn't invite me. So I was lonely."

"Really?" Aaron gasped. "Well, I'm lonely, too! All *my* friends went to a party and didn't invite *me!*"

Aaron and his new friend were both nice boys—they were just left out.

The next day Aaron's friends said they had fun at the party, but that they had missed him.

Just because you're left out sometimes doesn't mean your friends don't like you. Nobody can be included every time. Sometimes we do get left out. And when that happens we just put on a big smile and find something else to do or find another friend to play with. Tomorrow or the next day we'll be back together again with our other friends.

Sometimes we're accidentally left out, such as when someone is passing out gum to everybody and they forget us. When that happens, we just have to speak up and say, "I don't have any yet," and we'll get a piece. Then we feel better, don't we?

None of us is ever completely left out. We have a very special friend who always wants to be with us. That friend is God. He treats everyone the same, and He never goes away unless *we* tell Him to.

THE REAL SANTA CLAUS

The Bible says, "Whatever is good and perfect comes to us from God." James 1:17.

RIA giggled with excitement as she dusted off her wooden shoes and put them outside beside the front door. Tonight was Christmas Eve, the night Sinterklaas came to visit.

"I'm going to use Father's shoes," Ria's brother Hans said as he sat by the fire whittling on a piece of wood. "Father's shoes are bigger than mine. Sinterklaas can fit much more candy and goodies into them."

"Greedy boy!" Ria told him. "You should be happy with what you have!" Giving Hans a cheerful wink, she bounded up the stairs. She didn't have time to be angry. Tonight was Christmas Eve with the service at the church tonight and the lighting of the Christmas-tree candles. Now she had to start getting ready.

Oh, how she enjoyed Christmas!

Later that evening, after she and Hans were tucked in bed, Ria listened for the crunch of Sinterklaas' footsteps in the snow. There they were! Then the bumping of his sack as he filled her shoes with fruit and cookies. And there was usually a small gift in there, too.

Ria closed her eyes. She mustn't check her shoes tonight. Better to wait and dream about them and discover what was in them in the morning.

Is that what you do with your stocking at Christmas? Sometimes we like to pretend that Santa Claus comes to fill our stockings. Santa Claus is pretend, but Sinterklaas was a real man. He was a priest, called a "Bishop." And he liked to do things for the poor people in Holland, many years ago. But he never really came down their chimneys. The children just put their wooden shoes outside by the front door for him to fill. And Sinterklaas never rode on a flying sleigh pulled by reindeer. Someone made all of that up. But Bishop Klaas, also known as Saint Nicholas, was a real man. He liked to give presents to people.

God likes to give us presents, too. But the ones He gives us are better than Saint Nicholas'. God's presents are things like our families, and happy times, and good food and good minds. The Bible says that every good gift comes from God. Remember that this Christmas. Remember that, when you open your new toys and have fun with them. The toys may be from Mother and Daddy, or Grandma and Grandpa, but the happiness comes from God. Happiness is the very best gift of all.

SCRIPTURE INDEX

ACTS

10:34 226

ROMANS

2:11 248
7:19 90
8:28 115
8:31 160
12:20 139
13:3 208
13:4 108
13:9 151
15:13 113

1 CORINTHIANS

2:9 220
13:11 229
13:13 95

2 CORINTHIANS

5:14 241
6:18 169
10:1 15
13:7 185

EPHESIANS

4:7 38

4:7 225
4:25 186
4:26 240
4:28 102
4:29 123
4:32 44
4:32 79
5:1 204
5:20 197

PHILIPPIANS

4:11 243

COLOSSIANS

3:15 62
4:6 30

1 THESSALONIANS

4:16 131
5:16 205

1 TIMOTHY

1:19 91

2 TIMOTHY

1:3 43

HEBREWS

12:6 122
13:5 179
13:18 127
13:18 157

JAMES

1:17 249
1:22 244
3:15 105
4:7 81
5:11 235

1 PETER

1:8 46
5:8 55

1 JOHN

3:1 146
3:1 162
5:3 64

REVELATION

3:20 210
21:25 145
22:12 69

Quiet Thoughts for Busy Mothers

Time Out for Moms

Cheryl Woolsey Holloway's delightful devotional book for young mothers bubbles over with honesty, warmth, and sparkling humor.
She shares moments from her family life that have resulted in self-discovery, growth, adjustment, intense love, and turmoil. Mothers will find encouragement and strength to face the demands of their days and enjoy the rare luxury of being nurtured.
Paper, 94 pages. US$6.95, Cdn$8.70.

The Making of a Mother

Karen Spruill writes a surprisingly frank and personal book about motherhood. She shares her secret battles with frustration and feelings of inadequacy.

Then she tells what it took to set her free. She also gives tried-and-true advice on breast-feeding, toilet training, money matters, self-forgiveness, and child abuse. Fellow author and mother June Strong comments: "The chapter on discipline alone is worth the price of the book."

Don't miss this book that goes a long way toward healing the wear and tear of motherhood.
Paper, 128 pages. US$7.95, Cdn$9.95.

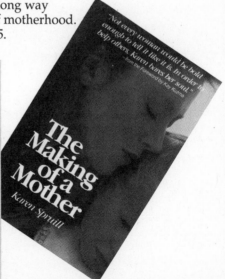

Especially for Preschoolers

Thank You, God, for My Body
Your body is fascinating when you haven't been in it for long. That's why toddlers love this book that introduces them to their bodies and their Creator. Bible verses, short rhyming prayers of thanks, and adorable color illustrations are combined in this big, easy-to-hold book with a sturdy, wipe-clean cover. Written by Edwina Grice Neely. Illustrated by Linda Grice McCall. Hardcover, 32 pages. US$6.95 each, Cdn$8.70.

Bible Promises for Tiny Tots
Volumes 1, 2, 3
George H. Taggart. Each two-page spread in these colorful books features a beautiful painting, a short Bible text, and a six-line rhyme. Printed on heavy tear-resistant paper. Paper, 30 pages. US$4.95, Cdn$6.20 each.

Bible Stories to Color
These four brand-new coloring books are filled with pictures adapted from The Bible Story. Look up the Bible text on each page to read to children about the event they are coloring. Blank-backed pages let your children use markers as well as crayons. Paper, 32 pages. US$1.49, Cdn$1.85 each.

To order, call
1-800-765-6955
or write to ABC Mailing Service, P.O. Box 1119, Hagerstown, MD 21741. Send check or money order. Enclose applicable sales tax and 15 percent (minimum US$2.50) for postage and handling. Prices and availability subject to change without notice. Add 7 percent GST in Canada.

Forever Stories
The Great Controversy for Kids

Take your children on a fantastic visual journey through the events of the great controversy, from the rebellion of Lucifer to the Second Coming. Written in simple terms and accompanied by brilliantly colored illustrations on every page spread, these stories by Carolyn Byers make the world of the Bible real and exciting. These delightful stories will quickly become your children's favorites, helping them develop a lifetime friendship with Jesus. Hardcover, five volumes. US$49.95 set, US$10.95 each. Cdn$62.45 set, Cdn$13.70 each.

To order, call
1-800-765-6955
or write to ABC Mailing Service, P. O. Box 1119, Hagerstown, MD 21741. Send check or money order. Enclose applicable sales tax and 15 percent (minimum US$2.50) for postage and handling. Prices and availability subject to change without notice. Add 7 percent GST in Canada.

My Bible Friends Videos

These popular stories, told by Uncle Dan and Aunt Sue, combined with video treatment of the beautiful scenes from the books, result in five exciting videocassettes that will hold the interest of preschoolers for hours. Each video contains four stories and is approximately 25 minutes in length. VHS or Beta. US$19.95, Cdn$24.95 each. US$89.95, Cdn$112.45 set.

To order, call
1-800-765-6955
or write to ABC Mailing Service, P.O. Box 1119, Hagerstown, MD 21741. Send check or money order. Enclose applicable sales tax and 15 percent (minimum US$2.50) for postage and handling. Prices and availability subject to change without notice. Add 7 percent GST in Canada.